Cross-National Crime

Cross-National Crime

A Research Review and Sourcebook

Jerome L. Neapolitan

Frank Schmalleger, Advisory Editor

GREENWOOD PRESS
Westport, Connecticut • London

Library of Congress Cataloging-in-Publication Data

Neapolitan, Jerome L., 1943–
    Cross-national crime : a research review and sourcebook / Jerome
L. Neapolitan.
      p.   cm.
    Includes bibliographical references and index.
    ISBN 0–313–29914–5 (alk. paper)
    1. Crime—Cross-cultural studies.   2. Criminology—Cross-cultural
studies. I. Title.
HV6251.N43   1997
364—dc21   97–8780

British Library Cataloguing in Publication Data is available.

Library of Congress Catalog Card Number: 97–8780
ISBN: 0–313–29914–5

First published in 1997

Greenwood Press, 88 Post Road West, Westport, CT 06881
An imprint of Greenwood Publishing Group, Inc.

Printed in the United States of America

The paper used in this book complies with the
Permanent Paper Standard issued by the National
Information Standards Organization (Z39.48–1984).

10 9 8 7 6 5 4 3 2 1

This book is dedicated to my research assistant, consultant, first editor, secretary, and typist—my wife, Cella

Contents

Acknowledgments

I would like to thank everyone who helped make this book possible—Tennessee Technological University President Angelo Volpe, Liberal Arts and Sciences Dean Jack Armistead, Sociology Chair Donna Darden, and Secretary Carol Gibbons for allowing me the time to write; Reference Librarian Linda Mulder for finding the hard-to-find; Mildred Vasan for her patient assistance; Nita Romer, Deborah Whitford, and Nancy Lucas for their editing talents; Frank Schmalleger for suggesting the original idea; Anna Alvazzi del Frate, Adam Bouloukos, Odile Frank, Roberto Gonzalez-Carames, Cynthia Harris, Matti Joutsen, Carol Kalish, Max Kommer, Gary LaFree, James Lynch, Edward Maguire, Pat Mayhew, Steven Messner, Phyllis Schultze, Miles Simpson, Gert-Jan Terlouw, Jan van Dijk, John van Kesteren, Wolfgang Rau, and Ugljesa Zvekic for their ideas and help in acquiring information and data; and Barry Stein, Ada Haynes, my son Matt, and the Buddies for their support.

Introduction

The purpose of this book is to stimulate and facilitate cross-national research on crime. Such research is necessary to avoid the insular and ethnocentric focus which dominates most crime research and public discourse. To elucidate the causes of crime, we cannot be constrained and biased by a particular situation. In the absence of a comparative frame of reference, it is not possible to distinguish speculative from actual causes of crime. Trying to explain a nation's crime problem by studying only that nation is like trying to explain crime at the individual level by studying just one person.

Without a comparative perspective with which to determine the causes of—and policies to combat—crime, we are often guided by intuition, political opportunism, and ethnocentrism. Cross-national crime research is necessary to determine the socioeconomic and cultural contexts that contribute to crime. Quality research on what is associated with crime across nations makes it much more difficult for opportunists to exploit a particular situation within a nation. By helping us distinguish specific from general and mediated causes, cross-national research complements rather than replaces intranational research. Given the very large differences in amounts and types of crimes across nations, research among nations on national attributes associated with crime variations should contribute greatly to our understanding of the causes of crime.

Cross-national crime research should be of interest to investigators and policy makers in virtually all nations. Indications are that crime has been increasing globally in the recent past and is likely to continue to do so in the future (Stephens, 1994; U.N., 1992, 1993b, 1995a). Several United Nations conferences have concluded that crime is a major concern in all its member nations (e.g., U.N., 1993a, 1996). Also, the apparent increase in transnational crime has contributed to greater interest among nations in crime situations in other nations (U.N., 1995b).

As many nations contain numerous societies or cultures, cross-national research is not truly cross-cultural. In some cases, cultures may be more similar across national borders than within a nation. However, crime and explanatory data are mostly available on a national basis, and crime policies are determined by nations. Thus, while some good anthropological and microlevel research can be done across cultures, research covering large numbers of nations and cultures must be done using national units. Certainly, as further addressed in this book, disaggregating crime data to blend micro- and macrolevel explanations is an important area for future cross-national crime research.

Until the 1970s there was virtually no such research; and while it has increased in the 1980s and 1990s, the amount relative to other crime research remains quite small. In addition to ethnocentrism on the part of investigators, the lack of quality data has not allowed for good cross-national crime research. Thus, results of this research have been neither consistent nor strong enough to have any influence on national crime policies or even help frame the discussion of crime problems. While there is still need for progress, the quality, quantity, and variety of cross-national crime and other types of data have improved greatly and continue to do so.

This book should save future analysts substantial time and effort in developing concepts and hypotheses concerning cross-national crime, in determining how to test these, and in acquiring data to conduct research. It should help them avoid the pitfalls and problems they might encounter if they had to begin research without the background and information provided here. Each new analyst does not have to go through the process of reviewing all the past literature, identifying data sources, and so on. I have tried to keep the book reasonably brief while still covering all important aspects of what an analyst needs to know prior to starting the research process. When an analyst encounters conceptual or methodological issues that need more complete discussion than is provided, this book points the reader to where it can be found.

This book is not intended to shape or direct cross-national crime research. Still, I have perspectives—and I believe insights—resulting from my own cross-national crime research and the writing of this book. Even if some readers disagree with some or all of these perspectives, the information provided here will still greatly facilitate their research efforts.

I use the term *nation* rather than *country* throughout this book, as it is the term used in cross-national crime research. I also use the terms *developing* and *developed* to distinguish between less- and more-developed nations. I recognize this is rather simplistic, and there is substantial variation within these categories. However, most research that distinguishes at all has used these two categories, and so they facilitate discussion. Other categorizations by level of development are discussed in Chapter 7.

Chapter 1 identifies and describes the different types of cross-national crime data available as well as the sources from which the data can be obtained. Chapter 2 discusses the issues surrounding the quality of official crime data in terms of making cross-national comparisons and doing cross-national research. Some recommendations are made regarding the use of data. Chapter 3 discusses unofficial crime data—victimization and self-report—in the same manner as Chapter 2 discusses official data. Chapter 4 provides a critical review of the major theories advanced to explain variation in crimes across nations and over time.

Chapter 5 reviews the literature on past cross-national research on violent crime—mostly homicides—noting consistent and inconsistent results. Chapter 6 does the same for property and other crimes. Chapter 7 discusses various methodological approaches and issues in analyzing cross-national crime data and makes some recommendations. Chapter 8 describes and discusses data for indicating explanatory variables, including those used in past research and many that have not yet been addressed. And the Conclusion looks to the promising future of cross-national crime research.

Extensive appendices are included to help locate data, information, and contacts relevant to cross-national crime research. I hope readers of this book obtain a better understanding of the state of cross-national crime data and research and then make their own contributions to the field.

REFERENCES

Stephens, G. (1994). The global crime wave. *The Futurist*, 28 (4), 22–27.

U.N. (1992). *Trends in crime and criminal justice, 1970–1985*. Vienna, Austria: Author.

U.N. (1993a). *Crime prevention and criminal justice newsletter, Nos. 20,21*. Vienna, Austria: Author.

U.N. (1993b). *Crime trends and criminal justice operations at the regional and interregional levels*. New York: Author.

U.N. (1995a). *Ninth United Nations Congress on the prevention of crime and the treatment of offenders, Dec. 1994*. Cairo, Egypt: Author.

U.N. (1995b). *Ninth United Nations Congress on the prevention of crime and the treatment of offenders, Apr. 1995*. Cairo, Egypt: Author.

U.N. (1996). *Fifth session of the United Nations Commission on crime prevention and criminal justice*. Vienna, Austria: Author.

Abbreviations

AIC	Australian Institute of Criminology
BJS	Bureau of Justice Statistics
CATI	Computer-Assisted Telephone Interview
CCDF	Comparative Crime Data Files
CIA	Central Intelligence Agency
CIESIN	Consortium for International Earth Science Information Network
COC	Correlates of Crime data file
DIC-ASC	Division of International Criminology — American Society of Criminology
ECOSOC	Economic and Social Council of the United Nations
FTP	File Transfer Protocol
GDI	Gender-related Development Index
GDP	Gross Domestic Product
GEM	Gender Empowerment Measure
GNP	Gross National Product
HDI	Human Development Index
HDR	Human Development Report
HEUNI	Helsinki Institute for Crime Prevention and Control
HRAF	Human Relations Area Files
ICPSR	Interuniversity Consortium for Political and Social Research
ICS	International Crime Statistics (INTERPOL)
ILANUD	Latin American Institute for the Prevention of Crime and Treatment of Offenders
INTERPOL	International Criminal Police Organization
ISRD	International Self-Report Delinquency study

IVS	International Victimization Survey (a/k/a International Crime Survey)
NACJD	National Archive of Criminal Justice Data
NATO	North Atlantic Treaty Organization
NCJRS	National Criminal Justice Reference Service
NCS	National Crime Survey
ODC	Overseas Development Council
OICJ	Office of International Criminal Justice
PPP	Purchasing Power Parity
PQLI	Physical Quality of Life Index
SID	Social Indicators of Development
SPSS	Statistical Package for Social Sciences
TIDES	Trends in Developing Economies
UCR	Uniform Crime Reports
U.N.	United Nations
UNAFEI	United Nations Asian and Far East Institute for the Prevention of Crime and Treatment of Offenders
UNAFRI	United Nations African Institute for the Prevention of Crime and Treatment of Offenders
UNCJIN	United Nations Crime and Justice Information Network
UNCS	United Nations Crime Survey
UNDP	United Nations Development Program
UNDY	*United Nations Demographic Yearbook*
UNESCO	United Nations Educational, Scientific, and Cultural Organization
UNICRI	United Nations Interregional Crime and Justice Research Institute
UNOJUST	United Nations Online Justice Information System
USSR	Union of Soviet Socialist Republics
WB	World Bank
WCJLN	World Criminal Justice Library Network
WDR	World Development Report
WHO	World Health Organization
WISTAT	Women's Indicators and Statistics database
WWW	World Wide Web

I

Cross-National Crime Data

1

Sources and Types of Data

Obviously, the first thing necessary in cross-national crime research is obtaining crime data for a number of nations. Just as in the case of intranational crime research, there are several types of data from which to choose.[1] The best type of data depends on the research question involved as well as the types of data problems one is willing to tolerate.

OFFICIAL DATA SOURCES

The data used most often in past cross-national crime research are the *International Crime Statistics* collected and issued by the International Criminal Police Organization (INTERPOL). INTERPOL data are available for more nations than any other source, have been collected annually since 1950, and cover many types of conventional crimes. In the past INTERPOL has collected annual data but issued reports biennially of two years' data; in 1993 and 1994 annual reports were issued. I do not presently know whether reports will be issued annually or biennially in the future. There is generally a large time gap between data collection and availability. For example, the 1991–1992 report was not available until 1995, and the 1994 report not until late 1996.

INTERPOL sends a standard form to all member nations, with data used to complete the forms collected by police in these nations. The reports are multilingual, including Arabic, English, French, and Spanish. Not all nations return the form, and membership in INTERPOL has varied over time. Therefore, which nations and the number of nations represented in the reports vary substantially. Also, many nations report data for only some crimes on the form.

The first report of *International Crime Statistics* was issued in 1954 and included data for only 36 nations. Over time the number of nations has generally increased, although some reports have data for fewer nations than the previous report. Some nations will appear in one report, be absent from the next, and reappear in a later volume. The 1991–1992 report included data on 112 nations, more than any previous report; but the 1993 and 1994 reports included fewer than 100 nations. Over 150 nations have appeared in at least one report.

The form was changed in 1977. Prior to 1977, INTERPOL used the crime categories of murder, sex offenses, larceny—subdivided into major and minor—fraud, counterfeit currency offenses, drug offenses, and total offenses. In 1977, serious assault and rape categories were added, and thefts were disaggregated into more precise categories. An "all kinds of thefts" category was created and subdivided into the categories of aggravated thefts, thefts of motor cars, and other thefts. Aggravated theft is further subdivided into two categories: robbery and violent thefts, and breaking and entering.

On the form used by INTERPOL, nations report the actual number of offenses as well as the rate per 100,000 population. They are also asked to report the percent of each offense which are attempts. Some nations report the percent attempts, while others do not. This creates problems in doing cross-national comparisons and analysis, which are addressed in Chapter 2.

Nations are also asked to report the percent of each offense committed by females, juveniles, and aliens. Each nation uses its own age limit for determining juvenile status, so data on juveniles are not directly comparable for many nations. This also is addressed in Chapter 2.

The INTERPOL form further requests information on the percent of cases for each offense that was solved by police. In INTERPOL's general instructions, one way in which a crime is considered solved is "police investigations reveal no penal offense was in fact committed." Therefore, the rates reported are inflated by cases which were not actually offenses. This problem, too, is addressed in Chapter 2.

INTERPOL's *International Crime Statistics* reports can be ordered from the main INTERPOL office in Lyon, France and through the INTERPOL office in Washington, D.C. (see Appendix A). The cost varies by the recency of the report requested and the current exchange rate, as the prices are in French francs. Some reports, usually the most recent, can be found in the libraries of larger universities. The University of Michigan Library, for example, has all reports from 1974 through the present.

The *World Atlas on CD-ROM*, published annually since 1991, includes INTERPOL rates per 100,000 for each offense. However, none of the other data—such as percent attempts and percent female—are listed (World Atlas, 1991–). The *Correlates of Crime: A Study of 52 Nations, 1960–1984* data set (COC), compiled by Richard Bennett (1990), includes INTERPOL rates per 100,000 for each offense, using pre-1977 categories and definitions, and breakdowns by sex and juvenile status. However, it fails to include such other data as percent attempts and cases solved. This data set is available in tape or diskette format from the Interuniversity Consortium for Political and Social Research (ICPSR).

Another source of international crime data based on police records is the United Nations Crime Survey (UNCS). Four surveys have been completed, and the fifth is in progress at this writing and should be available some time in 1997. The four surveys cover the time periods 1970–1975, 1975–1980, 1980–1986, and 1986–1990. The fifth survey will cover 1990–1994. The United Nations (U.N.) hopes to conduct future surveys on a biennial basis.

UNCS data is more official than INTERPOL data in that they are approved public statements by governments, whereas INTERPOL data are collected through police chiefs. Both, however, are based on crime reported to, and recorded by, the police. The U.N. also takes more care in trying to validate data, requesting verification and explanation when data points are more than 30 percent different from surrounding years. The U.N. also analyzes each past survey and questionnaire in order to improve the next effort, whereas INTERPOL continues with the same form and approach every year.

The U.N. distributes the survey to all member nations, but many do not respond and most who do fail to answer all questions. The first survey received responses from sixty-four nations for 1970 through 1975 and covered the crime categories of total adult offenses, total juvenile offenses, intentional homicides, assaults, sex crimes, robberies, thefts, frauds, drug trafficking, drug abuse, and kidnappings. Data for 1973 specifically were collected on number of law enforcement officers, judges, prosecutors, institutional personnel, non-institutional personnel, and volunteer personnel. Missing data ranged from 23.4 percent of nations for thefts to 81.3 percent for volunteer personnel.

Eighty nations responded to the second survey, and seventy-eight to the third. Both surveys covered the same crime categories: total crimes, intentional homicides, nonintentional homicides, assaults, rapes, robberies, thefts, frauds, drug crimes, kidnappings, briberies, and other serious crimes for 1975 to 1980. Both surveys also requested data on apprehensions, prosecutions, convictions, sentences, prison populations, prosecutors, judges, police, and so on. Some of these data were disaggregated by age and gender. There are also limited social and economic data in the data files for the second and third surveys. Response rates in both surveys to specific questions ranged from 9 percent to 80 percent, with responses to crime category questions being over 60 percent for most offenses.

One hundred nations replied to the fourth UNCS survey, which included the crime categories of total homicides, total intended homicides, attempted intended homicides, nonintentional homicides, total assaults, major assaults, total thefts, major thefts, burglary, robbery, rape, fraud, embezzlement, total drug offenses, drug trafficking, drug possession, bribery, and other serious crimes. For the first time, the survey was also given to major cities of the world, with sixty-seven responding.

Data were also collected on suspects, prosecutions, convictions, persons imprisoned, length of sentences, prison populations, and various criminal justice personnel. Many categories were broken down by age and gender. Limited social and economic data are included in this data set, with nations being divided into low, medium, and high on the Human Development Index (HDI) for the first time.[2] Response rates to specific questions ranged from 6 to 80 percent, with response rates to all crime categories being greater than 50 percent.

The fourth survey also included a supplement on transnational crime, that which transcends national jurisdictions. This supplement focused on nineteen categories of crime generally assumed to be of a cross-national nature. The transnational survey was sent to all nations and eighty-eight nongovernmental organizations, with substantive information being received on fifty-six nations.

Only limited trend or longitudinal analysis can be done with the first four U.N. surveys. First, for any specific crime category, the number of nations represented in two or more surveys is not large. The largest overlap is for robbery in the third and fourth surveys, with data for forty-two nations in both surveys. Looking at long-term change in crime rates from the first to the fourth survey results in generally small samples—in the twenties or low thirties.

Another problem is lack of consistency of data between surveys. There is a one-year overlap between surveys, and for some nations the crime rate reported for that year in the first survey differs drastically from that reported in the next. For example, the 1986 robbery rate for Kuwait in the third survey was 66 and in the fourth was 2,604. This renders any change over time meaningless and calls into question the accuracy of both rates. This is further addressed in Chapter 2.

The fourth UNCS survey is probably the first one to be of sufficient quality to do meaningful research. Much greater care was taken in survey construction and data collection. Developing nations—with the help of the U.N.—began keeping better records, the number of nations reporting increased substantially, and data were collected for cities as well as nations. The fifth survey should provide even better data, and along with the fourth survey should allow for analysis of change over time.

The U.N. data are available within several years of completion of the survey. Data from the fourth survey (1986–1990) became generally available in 1994, and data from the fifth survey (1990–1994) are expected to be available in 1997. Data can be obtained on diskettes from the United Nations Crime Prevention and Criminal Justice Branch (see Appendix A). Data from the survey are also available at the United Nations Crime and Justice

Information Network (UNCJIN) World Wide Web (WWW) address (see Appendix B). Data from earlier surveys can also be obtained from the National Archive of Criminal Justice Data (NACJD) branch of the ICPSR.

The World Health Organization (WHO) does not collect data on crime per se, but it does collect data annually on causes of death and reports these in the *World Health Statistics Annual* (WHO, 1948–). One of the cause categories is homicide, defined as "any act performed with the purpose of taking human life, in whatever circumstances" (WHO, 1995). The data are collected from public health agencies and are based on actual death certificates. Thus, WHO data do not include attempts and are not dependent on police practices or record keeping. So, they are likely to be more accurate than INTERPOL or UNCS data. This is further addressed in Chapter 2. WHO also has a category of deaths caused by "other violence," although it is unclear to what this refers.

While WHO has issued these annual reports since 1948, only those since the early 1960s appear to be readily available. WHO periodically revises its definitions and causal categories. An earlier definition of death by homicide, for example, included deaths that were due to "operations of war" and "legal intervention." The former was dropped in the mid-1960s and the latter in the mid-1970s. The possible biasing effects of this for cross-sectional and trend analysis and comparisons are addressed in Chapter 2.

The number of nations for which homicide data are available from WHO has been in the lower seventies in recent years. However, it was in the lower forties in older editions of the *World Health Statistics Annual*. Relatively few developing nations are included in the WHO reports, although efforts to include more such nations are underway. African and Asian nations have been particularly underrepresented. And the year represented in any one annual varies among nations. For example, in the 1992 annual, the year represented varied from 1984 to 1992, with data for most nations being from 1988 to 1992.

An advantage of WHO homicide data over those of INTERPOL and UNCS is that they are broken down into more specific gender and age categories, with male and female rates reported for ages: 0, 1–4, 5–14, 15–24, 25–34, 35–44, 45–54, 55–64, 65–74, and 75 and older. It is important to remember that INTERPOL and UNCS distinctions by gender and age are for offenders and WHO distinctions are for victims.

Also issued annually is the *United Nations Demographic Yearbook* (UNDY) (U.N., 1948–), reporting deaths caused by homicides using the same data as WHO. It does not, however, include breakdowns by age and gender. Fewer nations are represented in the UNDY than in the WHO annuals, and they are mostly the same nations. However, in any given year there are usually homicide data for several nations in the UNDY that are not represented in the WHO annual. Thus, using both sources can increase sample size.

World Health Statistics Annuals and *United Nations Demographic Yearbooks* can be found in most larger university libraries. They can also be purchased from WHO and the U.N. (see Appendices A and C). WHO data have just recently been made available via FTP and may soon be available through the WWW (see Appendix A).

There are several other sources of cross-national crime data based on official records that are not ongoing and do not contain recent data. The best of these is the Comparative Crime Data Files (CCDF) compiled by Archer and Gartner (1984). Data were collected for 110 nations and 44 major cities for the years 1900–1974 for murders, homicides, manslaughters, rapes, assaults, robberies, and thefts. In no single year were data acquired for all nations, and for the early years the numbers were quite small. For example, in the first years data were acquired for no more than 11 nations for any single crime category. By 1920 the maximum was 17, by 1940 it was 23, and by 1970 it was 71. Data were gathered through correspondence with national and metropolitan government sources, annual statistical reports and other official documents which published annual crime data, and secondary examination of records kept by various national and international agencies.

The indigenous classifications of nations were used to categorize crimes, rather than the forced choice approach of INTERPOL and the UNCS. Archer and Gartner (1984) believe this makes their data of better quality than that of INTERPOL or UNCS. While the enormous effort of this pioneering work is to be admired, the quality of any crime data—and particularly that of developing nations—from so far in the past is questionable. CCDF data are available on tape, diskette, or CD-ROM from the NACJD branch of the ICPSR.

Gurr (1977) created a cross-national crime data file for sixteen western nations, plus Israel and Japan. Data were gathered from national statistical sources for both offenses known to police and convictions for as many years as possible from 1945 to 1974. Crime categories covered were manslaughter/ murder, assault, robbery, burglary, larceny, white collar crime, sexual and moral offenses, and public order offenses. These data are also available in various electronic formats from the NACJD branch of the ICPSR.

A problem with data collected by individual investigators rather than organizations is that they quickly become dated. The CCDF and Gurr (1977) data, for example, are now more than twenty years old. Still, they have value for benchmark comparison in terms of whether nations which were relatively low or high in crime in the past remain so today.

The Council of Europe has recently released an early draft model of the first *European Sourcebook of Crime and Criminal Justice Statistics* (Council of Europe, 1995). This includes official reported crime as well as police, court, and corrections data for twelve Western European nations. Crime categories covered for 1990 are attempted intentional homicide, completed intentional homicide, assault, rape, robbery, all thefts, theft of motor vehicle, theft of bicycle, burglary, domestic burglary, drug offense, and drug trafficking.

Work is currently underway to expand the *Sourcebook* to include all Western European nations and to cover the years 1990–1994, with the final model issued in 1997. It is hoped the *Sourcebook* will become a publication issued every five years. It is also possible the data will be made available on the Internet. Crime and criminal justice data in the *Sourcebook* are almost certainly more valid and reliable than that of INTERPOL or the UNCS. See Appendix A for information on acquiring the *Sourcebook*.

The Asian Crime Prevention Foundation issued the *Asia Crime Report No. 1* in 1993, which included crime and corrections data for Hong Kong, India, Indonesia, Japan, Republic of Korea, Malaysia, Republic of the Philippines, Sri Lanka, and Thailand. There are no data explanations, and the contents and methods used to compile data vary across nations. Thus, use of these data for cross-national comparisons or research may not be valid.

Other researchers have collected more in-depth data from official sources for smaller numbers of nations or cities (e.g., Adler, 1983; Clinard & Abbott, 1973; Ellis, 1992; Gurr, Grabosky, & Hula, 1977; Wikström, 1991). These data may be available from the researchers and often include more detailed information on the offense, offender, and crime situation.

Crime and criminal justice data are available for some nations at the Internet site, *The World Factbook of Criminal Justice Systems* (see Appendix A). These data are also available by direct contact with official agencies within nations. This is, of course, quite time consuming, but generally the data will be of better quality and more complete. The United Nations annually publishes the *World Directory of Criminological Institutes*, with recent issues having information on over 400 institutes in over seventy nations (U.N., 1989–). The UNCJIN web site has addresses and telephone numbers for criminal justice agencies in over fifty nations under the International Document Exchange Program.

There are also several Internet sources which give general appraisals of the crime situations in nations, rather than specific rates for specific crimes. The Overseas Security Advisory Council (OSAC) is probably the best of these. Data on the general crime situation—as well as that which applies specifically to American visitors—is provided for about 130 nations. Similar, but generally less comprehensive, appraisals are provided for about 200 nations in U.S. State Department *Consular Information Sheets*. These are available from the U.S. State Department in hard copy or via its Internet site. The Foreign and Commonwealth Office of the United Kingdom provides similar, but briefer, appraisals for about 30 nations. In the extensive *Library of Congress Country Studies*—which have thus far been completed for 71 nations—information is often provided on the crime situation.

The Human Relations Area Files (HRAF) include crime data on some small, nonindustrial societies representative of the major world cultural regions. As this book is on cross-national—not cross-cultural—crime, these data will not be further discussed.

VICTIMIZATION DATA

It has long been acknowledged that many crimes do not come to the attention of police, and for this and other reasons official crime data often do not accurately indicate the amount of crime in a given area. Some nations, such as the United States, use household surveys in order to discover how many and which people have been victimized by various crimes. While these surveys are useful for intranational research, variations in samples and methodologies render them of little use in cross-national comparisons. To remedy this, the Ministry of Justice of the Netherlands in conjunction with the United Nations Interregional Crime and Justice Research Institute (UNICRI) organized the International Victim (Crime) Survey (IVS).

The IVS samples households in different nations, using a standard questionnaire asking the same questions in roughly the same manner. The first IVS in 1989 involved fifteen developed nations, one developing nation, and one Eastern-Central European nation in transition. The second survey in 1992 included fifteen developed nations, thirteen developing nations, and seven nations in transition. The third survey in 1996 included thirteen developed nations, twelve developing nations, and fifteen nations in transition. All together, fifty-four nations have participated, eighteen twice and nine three times.

The survey questions respondents who are sixteen and older on the following offenses: theft of cars, theft from cars, vandalism to cars, theft of motorcycles, theft of bicycles, burglary, attempted burglary, pickpocketing, robbery, noncontact personal theft, assaults with force, assaults without force, sexual assaults, and offensive sexual behavior. Respondents are also questioned on the location and circumstances of the offense, whether police were involved, satisfaction with police, and any victim assistance. Questions are also asked on fear of crime, crime prevention behavior, attitudes about criminal sentencing, and general satisfaction with police. Some basic socio-demographic and lifestyle data are also collected.

The samples used in developed nations were based on the whole nation; while in developing and transition nations, they were from a single major city. Computer-Assisted Telephone Interviews (CATIs) were used in the developed nations, while face-to-face interviews were used in the other nations. The importance of these differences in use of the data in cross-national research issues is addressed in Chapter 3.

IVS data can be obtained by contacting any of several people affiliated with the Ministry of Justice in the Netherlands (see Appendix A). The first two surveys are also available via the UNCJIN WWW site and from the NACJD branch of the ICPSR. The data come with a Statistical Package for

Social Sciences (SPSS) codebook. Several publications using and reporting the data have been issued, and more are forthcoming (Alvazzi del Frate, Zvekic, & van Dijk, 1993; van Dijk, Mayhew, & Killias, 1990; Zvekic & Alvazzi del Frate, 1995). The intent is to repeat the survey on a regular basis, expanding the number of nations involved and working to improve the methodology.

SELF-REPORT DATA

The major problems with victimization data are that they provide no information about offenders and do not address victimless crimes, such as drug use. In order to get individual-level information and avoid the problems of official data, some researchers have turned to self-report data. Once again, due to differences in samples and methodologies, self-report data from studies in different nations have not allowed for cross-national comparison or analysis.

In most cases, self-report research has limited itself to sampling juveniles, and this is the case with the first international self-report study, the International Self-Report Delinquency study (ISRD). Work on this project began in 1988 with a NATO advanced research workshop, resulting in a publication on self-report research in various nations and self-report methodology called *Cross-National Research in Self-Reported Crime and Delinquency* (Klein, 1989). Eventually, a common questionnaire was constructed and administered in thirteen developed nations. The first results of this research were reported in *Delinquent Behavior Among Young People in the Western World* (Junger-Tas, Terlouw, & Klein, 1994). A second report is in progress and should be available in the summer or fall of 1997.

Four of the self-report surveys—those of England, the Netherlands, Portugal, and Switzerland—were based on national random samples; one— Spain—was based on a stratified national urban sample; three were on city samples—Mannheim (Germany), Belfast (Northern Ireland), and Athens (Greece); four on school samples—Omaha, Nebraska (USA), Helsinki (Finland), Liege (Belgium), and several Italian cities; and a cohort study was done in New Zealand. Pilot studies were carried out in several other nations. The surveys were coordinated by NATO through the Ministry of Justice in the Hague, the Netherlands.

The questionnaire covered five areas: prevalence and frequency of delinquent behavior, circumstances of the act, social reactions to discovery of the act by others, social and demographic background variables, and such social control theory variables as family and school relations and attitudes. There are ongoing discussions as to whether to conduct future surveys, which would include more nations and use more standardized samples. It may even become a regular event or part of the IVS. Due to differing sample frames, use of data from the first ISRD for cross-national analysis is limited. This is further addressed in Chapter 3.

The ISRD data from the surveys are not yet available, but they will be made available after the second ISRD book is published. This should occur sometime in 1997. A second and improved ISRD is being seriously considered, but it is not yet definite. For more information, contact Gert-Jan Terlouw at the Hague, the Netherlands (see Appendix A).

CONCLUSION

The quality, quantity, and availability of cross-national crime data are increasing at a rapid pace. With the exception of very limited research involving only a few nations, it is only in the 1990s that use of victimization or self-report data in cross-national crime research has been possible. Various organizations are actively working to improve the quality and availability of data, such as, The United Nations Interregional Crime and Justice Research Institute (UNICRI), the World Criminal Justice Library Network (WCJLN), the Helsinki Institute for Crime Prevention and Control (HEUNI), and the Bureau of Justice Statistics (BJS). The data, sources, and contacts covered in this book are current at writing and provide information that will allow readers to keep pace with further developments.

NOTES

1. Gary LaFree reviews sources of cross-national homicide data in "Comparative cross-national studies of homicide," *Homicide studies: A sourcebook of social research*, M. Dwayne Smith and Margaret Zahn, Eds., Beverly Hills, CA: Sage, 1977.

2. The Human Development Index is defined and discussed in the *Human Development Report*, UNDP, New York: Oxford University Press, 1990–.

REFERENCES

Adler, F. (1983). *Nations not obsessed with crime, Vol. 50*. Littleton, CO: Fred B. Rothman and Company.

Alvazzi del Frate, A., Zvekic, U., & van Dijk, J. (Eds.). (1993). *Understanding crime:Experiences of crime and crime control*. Rome, Italy: UNICRI.

Archer, D. & Gartner, R. (1984). *Violence and crime in cross-national perspective*. New Haven, CT: Yale University Press.

Bennett, R. (1990). *Correlates of crime: A study of 52 nations, 1960–1984*. Ann Arbor, MI: Interuniversity Consortium for Political and Social Research.

Clinard, M. B. & Abbott, D. (1973). *Crime in developing countries: A comparative perspective*. New York: John Wiley & Sons.

Council of Europe. (1995). *European sourcebook of crime and criminal justice statistics: Draft model*. Strasbourg, France: Author.

Ellis, H. (1992). Crime and control in the English-speaking Caribbean: A comparative study of Jamaica, Trinidad, Tobago, and Barbados 1960–1980. In H. Heiland, L. Shelley, & H. Katoh (Eds.), *Crime and control in comparative perspectives* (pp. 131–162). New York: Walter de Gruyter.

Gurr, T. (1977). Crime trends in modern democracies since 1945. *International Annals of Criminology,* 16, 41–85.

Gurr, T., Grabosky, P., & Hula, R. (1977). *Politics of crime and conflict: A comparative history of four cities.* Beverly Hills, CA: Sage.

Junger-Tas, J., Terlouw, G. J., & Klein, M. W. (Eds.). (1994). *Delinquent behavior among young people in the western world: First results of the International Self-Report Delinquency study.* New York: Kluger Publications.

Klein, M. W. (1989). Epilogue: Workshop discussion. In M. W. Klein (Ed.), *Cross-national research in self-reported crime and delinquency* (pp. 425–438). Norwell, MA: Kluwer.

U.N. (1948–). *Demographic yearbook.* New York: Author.

U.N. (1989–). *World directory of criminological institutes.* New York: Author.

van Dijk, J., Mayhew, P., & Killias, M. (1990). *Experiences of crime across the world: Key findings of the 1989 International Crime Survey.* Deventer, Netherlands: Kluwer.

WHO. (1948–, annual). *World health statistics annual.* Geneva, Switzerland: Author.

WHO. (1995). *World health statistics annual.* Geneva, Switzerland: Author.

Wikström, P-O. (1991). Cross-national comparisons and context-specific trends in criminal homicide. *Journal of Crime and Justice,* 14, 1–25.

World atlas on CD-ROM. (1991–). Novato, CA: Mindscapes (Software Toolworks).

Zvekic, U., & Alvazzi del Frate, A. (Eds.). (1995). *Criminal victimization in the developing world.* Rome, Italy: UNICRI.

2

Evaluation of Official Crime Data

Most cross-national crime research has used official crime data. The most important sources of these data are the International Criminal Police Organization (INTERPOL), the United Nations Crime Survey (UNCS), and the World Health Organization (WHO). INTERPOL and the UNCS collect data based on crimes which come to the attention of police and are subsequently recorded as crimes. WHO collects data on causes of death from public health agencies and then records those in which homicide is the cause of death. Because of certain advantages and disadvantages of official crime data, they must be used carefully in research.

Official crime data are fairly inexpensive—in some cases free—and generally easy to obtain. They are available for a larger sample of nations than other crime data, are issued on a regular basis, and have been issued for a number of years. Thus, they allow for both cross-sectional and trend analyses for large samples and varied subsamples of nations. The properties of nations—both stable and changing—that cannot be reduced to the individual or small-group level can be studied as to their effects on crime. Since the seminal work of Durkheim (1966, 1973), it has been generally accepted that macrolevel structural and cultural factors influence individual behaviors and explain variations in frequency of human behavior across nations and time.

Thus, official data can contribute to our understanding of the national characteristics that contribute to crime, its control, and the processes over time that influence it. However, official crime data—particularly those based on police records—have flaws which might adversely affect cross-national research and comparisons. These flaws must be considered and, wherever possible, adjusted for in comparative analysis. This chapter examines the more important flaws and makes some recommendations regarding the use of official crime data.

DEFINITIONAL PROBLEMS

Nations differ in defining what constitutes criminal behavior and in using these definitions to categorize and classify criminal behavior. Past research indicates that definitional problems may not be severe for traditional crimes, as there is substantial consistency across nations for such crimes as murder and theft (Hindelang, 1974; Kick & LaFree, 1985; Mulvihill & Tumin, 1969; Newman, 1976). Still, there is likely to be some variation in cross-national definitions and classifications, particularly for minor and sexual offenses. Official police data reflect the legal codes and practices of a nation, and these might vary considerably among nations. INTERPOL and the UNCS try to adjust for this by having nations place crimes in broad categories that subsume many of the definitional differences among nations. Each nation is allowed some latitude in interpretation of the categories provided, and in some cases legal codes are too different for the categories to be used in a similar manner. Thus, many nations cannot or do not place the same crimes in the same categories. For example, in contrast to all other Western nations, the Netherlands has no crime category for robbery, and Japan classifies assaults resulting in death in the assault, not the homicide, category (Kalish, 1988). Also, when crimes are forced into broad categories, important variations within the category may be concealed. Two nations may report the same number of thefts; but in one nation 90 percent may involve forcible entry, while in another only 20 percent (Lynch, 1995a).

Many conventional crimes, such as murder and theft, have ancient origins and thus are quite similarly defined across nations (Clifford, 1983; Hoebel, 1954; Kick & LaFree, 1985; Scott & Al-Thokeb, 1980; Wilkins, 1980). In support of this, research on the perceived seriousness of different crimes has found that what is considered and defined as serious is quite similar across nations (Akman & Normandeau, 1968; Evans & Scott, 1984; Hsu, 1969; Newman, 1976; Scott & Al-Thokeb, 1977; Valez-Diaz & Megargee, 1971). The apparent existence of legal universals and consistent cross-national seriousness perspectives suggest some crimes may be cross-nationally comparable.

Still, it is possible that variations in legal systems and definitions might bias cross-national comparisons and research using official crime data. For example, He and Marshall (1995) found that INTERPOL crime data from China paint a very misleading picture of the extent and nature of crime in that nation. They argue this is due to unique Chinese legal philosophy and the resultant ways in which crimes are defined and recorded. Souryal (1990) has noted that Islamic nations which are dominated by traditional Shariah law differ greatly from other nations in legal definitions and the manner in which crimes are recorded.

INTERPOL and the UNCS sometimes include explanatory footnotes that illuminate discrepancies among nations as to how they completed the surveys. For example, some nations do not report a "theft of motor cars" rate to INTERPOL but include these in the "other thefts" category. When a nation does this, INTERPOL includes a footnote. Such explanations are not provided for many discrepancies, however, and when they are their meaning is not always clear (Kalish, 1988). In general, INTERPOL and UNCS data are largely unannotated, so many discrepancies go unidentified.

INTERPOL also instructs nations that if offenses are directly related, only the most serious offenses should be counted. Since this is clearly a matter of judgment, it is another possible source of bias—possibly systematic—as nations may implement this differently. *International Crime Statistics* also includes cases where "police investigations reveal no penal offense was in fact committed" (INTERPOL, 1992). This not only inflates the amount of crime in some nations but may do so variably among nations, introducing another possible source of bias. It is not clear how the UNCS handles these issues, but these surveys likely have similar problems to those of INTERPOL.

Definitional and categorizing problems not only make cross-national analysis problematic but also may adversely affect time-series and/or trend analysis. For example, even when there has been little actual change in the amount or pattern of crime, a change in the legal codes of a nation or in the way a nation classifies crimes might greatly influence the crime rate over time. A dramatic shift in a crime rate in adjacent years—particularly if the shift continues in future years—probably indicates a change in definition or classification rather than a change in the amount of crime.

It is generally agreed that homicide is the most similarly defined and classified crime across nations (Ali, 1986; Gartner, 1995; Hindelang, 1974; Huang & Wellford, 1989; Lynch, 1995a; Wilkins, 1980). There is little subjective interpretation as to whether a life has been taken, and murder is universally regarded as a serious, criminal offense. Rape and/or sexual offenses are probably least similarly defined and classified cross-nationally, as there is great variation in cultural and legal interpretations of these offenses (Ali, 1986; Kalish, 1988; Wilkins, 1980).

Even homicide suffers from definitional differences among nations. Nations appear to differ as to how they distinguish homicides from other casualties. As noted, Japan, unlike most nations, does not define an assault which results in death as a homicide. Nations also differ as to whether people who kill in duels or survive suicide pacts have committed homicides (Wilkins, 1980).

Classification of casualties as homicides is particularly problematic in nations experiencing war, rebellion, or severe political and civil conflicts. For example, in the 1994 INTERPOL report Rwanda claims exactly 1,000,000 homicides which translates to a rate 12,500 per 100,000. Clearly, this overly exact and absurdly high figure is an estimate which includes deaths resulting from war and civil conflict. It is not appropriate to use these data in cross-national homicide research and comparisons.

Nations may also vary in their distinguishing between intentional and unintentional homicides. Both sources explicitly ask for information on intentional homicides, but it is not clear whether nations use the same criteria in making the distinction between intentional and unintentional homicides. INTERPOL reports only intentional homicides. WHO data, which are based on death certificates, do not distinguish between intentional and unintentional homicides.

The UNCS requests information on total, intentional, and unintentional homicides. The extreme differences in the proportion of total homicides classified as intentional—the range is from 10 percent to inexplicably over 100 percent—indicate the use of varied criteria across nations. Furthermore, the combined intentional and unintentional figures do not always equal the total figure. Kalish (1988) found that some nations reporting to INTERPOL and the UNCS routinely combined intentional and unintentional, while others did not.

As to negative influence on past research, the most important definitional problem is that regarding attempted versus successful homicide. INTERPOL defines murder as "any act performed with the purpose of taking human life in whatever circumstance" (INTERPOL, 1992). This definition includes both successful and attempted homicides. Some nations include attempts in their reports, while other nations do not. Most of those that include attempts also include the percent of the reported rate that is attempts, but some nations in some years include attempts without information on the percent.

In the first three UNCS studies, some nations included attempts in the rates reported, while other nations did not. And yet the nations that included attempts in their reported rates gave no information as to what proportion of the rates were attempts. The fourth and fifth UNCS surveys include a category of "intentional completed homicide," which is the equivalent of INTERPOL homicides adjusted for attempts. In the UNCS surveys the total of intentional homicides does not always equal the combined attempted and completed figures.

The great majority of past research which has used INTERPOL homicide data has not adjusted rates for percent of attempts (e.g., Bennett, 1991; Krahn, Hartnagel, & Gartrell, 1986; Messner, 1982). This includes all research using the Correlates of Crime (COC) data set, as the percent of homicides which are attempts is not included. Prior to 1977, INTERPOL did not even include information on attempts in its biennial reports. Neapolitan (1996) found that the associations of unadjusted and adjusted INTERPOL homicide rates to relevant independent variables differ significantly. The use of unadjusted INTERPOL and/or UNCS homicide rates casts substantial doubt on the validity of much past research on cross-national variation in homicides.

Nations that include attempts have artificially higher homicide rates than nations that do not. Also, there is likely to be a great deal of cross-national variation in what constitutes an attempted murder. The Netherlands provides a good example of the problems inherent in the use of unadjusted homicide rates. In the Netherlands, many nonserious offenses are first recorded by police as attempted murders, for example, a driver of a car almost hitting a pedestrian (M. Kommer, e-mail message, July 16, 1995). The charge is later reduced and the penalty is usually a fine, but official police reports still include the offense as an attempted murder. Thus, the Netherlands' homicide rates that include attempts are very high, whereas the actual homicide rate is quite low. In 1990, for example, the Netherlands reported a homicide rate of 14.8 to INTERPOL, indicating that 90 percent were attempts. Data from the Netherlands Ministry of Justice indicate that a homicide rate of 1.5 is accurate for 1990. So, research and comparisons using unadjusted rates, such as 14.8 for the Netherlands, are severely flawed.

Police homicide data, therefore, must be adjusted for attempts. As this is not possible with the first three UNCS surveys, the COC data set, and INTERPOL data prior to 1977, these data should not be used in cross-national research. And although most INTERPOL rates can be adjusted for attempts, others will remain artificially high, as some nations include attempts without noting the percent. The fourth and fifth UNCS surveys have the category "intentional completed homicides." However, it is not clear whether all nations define this in the same manner.

WHO homicide rates are based on actual death certificates and thus do not include attempts. Therefore, they do not suffer from the same definitional problems as UNCS and INTERPOL rates. Furthermore, they are not directly comparable to even the adjusted INTERPOL and UNCS rates, as they are based on a count of bodies not incidents.

While WHO rates for recent years are probably valid homicide indicators, they are of questionable value in the years prior to 1975 (WHO, 1962–1981). WHO periodically revises the definition of what constitutes a homicide. Prior to 1975, "deaths resulting from injury by intervention of police and legal execution" and/or "deaths resulting from operations of war" were included in homicide rates (WHO, 1992).

As neither war deaths nor legal intervention deaths are generally considered homicides and both are likely to vary among nations, inclusion of these might bias research using WHO homicide rates prior to 1975. However, Gartner, Baker, and Pampel (1990) did a comparison of WHO homicide data with casualty figures from nations involved in wars which suggested only France actually included war deaths in homicide figures. As deaths from legal intervention probably constitute only a very small proportion of homicides in a nation, WHO homicide rates from prior to 1975 are probably not severely biased by the broader definition then in use.

In addition to the "homicide as cause of death" category, WHO has a "death by other violence" category (WHO, 1962–1981, 1979–1982). As it is unclear what constitutes a "death by other violence," some deaths placed in this category may legally be homicides. Thus, researchers should consider analyzing WHO homicide rates with and without "deaths by other violence." They should then compare the two to see whether inclusion of these rates alters research results.

Examination of INTERPOL and UNCS theft rates also indicates definitional and classifying problems that might compromise cross-national research on property crimes. INTERPOL's "all kinds of theft" rates and UNCS's "total theft" rates are not always equal to the sum of the rates of which they are supposed to be composed. For example, the INTERPOL "all kinds of thefts" rate is supposed to be equal to the "robbery," "breaking and entering," "motor car thefts," and "other thefts" rates combined; and for most nations this is the case. For some nations, however, the "all kinds of theft" rate is substantially smaller—and for some substantially larger—than the sum of the four individual rates. Similar differences can be found in the UNCS "total theft" rates and the rates of which it is composed.

Consider, for example, the INTERPOL theft rates for Norway and Finland in 1990. The "all kinds of theft" rate for Norway (4,147) is much greater than the sum of the four subrates (2,120). For Finland, the "all kinds of theft" rate (3,055) is much smaller than the combined four rates (4,317). So direct comparisons of theft rates in these nations cannot be done with any degree of assurance. And depending on how many nations exhibit such anomalies in a given year, explanatory analysis may be compromised.

Many nations include footnotes concerning some of the theft rates, which can be used to adjust rates prior to cross-national comparison or analysis. For example, many nations note that theft of motor cars is included in the "other thefts" rate reported. Thus, before comparing these nations with nations that report a separate "theft of motor car" rate, the "other" and "motor car" theft rates should be combined.

Clearly, direct inspection of the various theft rates of nations is important in identifying these anomalies. In cases where substantial anomalies are discovered, consideration should be given to dropping the nations from samples used in analytic research. Other types of deviant cases which indicate a definitional or classifying problem can also be identified through direct inspection of data. For example, Norway reports an INTERPOL "all kinds of theft" rate similar to other Western European nations. However, the "breaking and entering" rate reported by Norway is a small fraction of that reported by other Western European nations. Furthermore, the ratio of "all kinds of theft" rate to the "breaking and entering" rate for European nations in recent years is three-to-one or less. For Norway, the ratio in recent years is over thirty-to-one. So Norway apparently defines or classifies "breaking and entering" differently from other Western European nations.

INTERPOL theft data prior to 1977 are also of questionable validity. As noted earlier, INTERPOL disaggregated theft rates in 1977 from two categories—"major" and "minor" thefts—into four categories—"robbery," "breaking and entering," "other thefts," and "thefts of motor cars." Assuming that rates for most nations would not change greatly from 1976 to 1977, we can compare 1976 to 1977 rates to determine the 1977 equivalents of 1976 "major" and "minor" thefts. "Minor" thefts represented variably "breaking and entering," "other thefts," "all kinds of thefts," and for some nations none of these. As different nations apparently used different indicators of minor thefts, comparisons and analyses using minor thefts are meaningless.

Similarly, "major" theft rates varied greatly across nations as to what crimes it represented. In some nations, "major" thefts were "robbery" plus "breaking and entering," in others "breaking and entering," and in some "all kinds of thefts." Some research which has used theft rates prior to 1977 combined "major" and "minor" thefts into one total theft category. These total theft rates from 1976 also vary as to what their 1977 equivalents are.

Thus, INTERPOL theft rates prior to 1977 should not be used in cross-sectional analysis, and trend analysis should not be done using rates both before and after 1977. In both analyses, the rates for different nations and/or years would indicate distinctly different crime categories. This unfortunately includes the COC data set which has been used in much time-series cross-national research on thefts, as it includes INTERPOL theft data from 1966 to 1984.

The UNCS theft data also have discrepancies between different surveys which negate trend analysis between surveys and call into question the validity of cross-sectional analysis. For example, both the third and fourth surveys include the theft categories "total thefts" and "major thefts," and both also include the year 1986. When the rates for 1986 for these two categories are compared across the two surveys, they differ for more than half of the nations. The differences are often substantial and are sometimes due to the third survey rate being greater and sometimes the fourth survey rate being greater. This makes meaningful trend analysis impossible and casts doubt on whether nations are interpreting these categories similarly.

Some analysts have addressed the issue of the effect of definitional and classifying errors in cross-national crime data by comparing crime rates from different data sources. Vigderhous (1978)—comparing INTERPOL and WHO homicide rates—found a high correlation between the two sets cross-sectionally but not longitudinally. Huang and Wellford (1989)—comparing UNCS, INTERPOL, and WHO data—found homicides and robberies to be comparable across data sets; but thefts, assaults, and sexual offenses differed greatly. Bennett and Lynch (1990)—comparing INTERPOL, UNCS, WHO, and Comparative Crime Data File (CCDF) data—found that a nation-by-nation point comparison will often yield different results depending on the data set used. For analytic or cross-sectional analysis, however, they yield statistically and substantially similar results. They also concluded that comparisons of crime rates for individual nations will yield different findings, and rankings of crime rates within data sets will generate differences across data sets and therefore errors.

All three studies assume that if different crime rates in data sets are similar and/or yield similar research results, definitional and classifying differences among nations do not seriously bias cross-national crime data. This ignores the possibility that all the data sets might be inaccurate and biased in a similar manner. Only Huang and Wellford (1989) adjusted INTERPOL homicide rates for attempts, and thus the other two studies used many rates which were inflated by attempts. All three studies used data from 1980 or earlier, when data were available for a relatively small number of nations from INTERPOL or the UNCS. Also, most comparisons were done using nations for which data were available in both data sets being compared. Thus, comparisons were based on samples of only about thirty nations or fewer, most of which were Western developed nations. These comparisons tell us little about the comparability of data from developing nations to either developed or other developing nations.

Also, when using data from a single source, most researchers include all nations for which data are available. As the sample of nations is different for each data source, sample composition differences may influence research results. This possibility is not addressed in the above three studies.

Thus, these studies which have frequently been cited as indicating the validity and reliability of official cross-national crime data are based on data of questionable quality and small, biased samples of nations. With data now available for over 100 nations from INTERPOL, comparisons based on 30 or so nations are not very informative. At best, these studies indicate that crime data for the developed nations are likely to be valid and reliable. However, they tell us little about crime data for developing nations.

REPORTING AND DETECTION PROBLEMS

Crimes which become known to police do not include the "dark" figures of crime, that is, crimes which are not reported to or detected by police. If the proportion of crimes which become known to police systematically varies across nations, police crime data are systematically biased. As less serious crimes are probably reported and/or detected less often than more serious crimes, there is a greater likelihood of cross-national variation in the reporting or detecting of less serious crimes (Breen & Rottman, 1985; Lynch, 1993, 1995b; Skogan, 1974; Vigderhous, 1978; Wilkins, 1980). There is also variation among nations in the cultural stigma attached to being a victim of some types of crime, particularly sexual victimization (Ali, 1986; Arthur,

1991; Mushanga, 1992; U.N., 1995). Thus, there is likely substantial cross-national variation in the reporting of sexual crimes. The access people have to, and trust they have in, police vary across nations and thus can influence the proportion of crimes reported (Biderman & Lynch, 1991; Block, 1984; Mushanga, 1992; Putting Crime, 1995; Wolf, 1971).

Crimes come to the attention of police not only through being reported by victims but also through direct detection of police. Thus, the proportion of crimes committed that become known to police will also depend on the efficiency and discretionary practices of the police (Black, 1970; Groves, McCleary, & Newman, 1985; Marenin, 1993; Riedel, 1990; Schmalleger, 1994; Sparks, Glenn, & Dodd, 1977; Wilkins, 1980). These, in turn, will depend on the number of police, the quality of their training, and their cultural and political pressures (Arthur, 1991; Baxi, 1990; Teske & Arnold, 1982; Wolf, 1971). If these factors vary systematically across nations—that is, by level of development or cultural system—official police data will also be systematically biased. There is some evidence that police work in developing nations is less efficient and more biased toward the powerful than in developed nations (Arthur, 1991; Baxi, 1990; Black, 1970; Sparks, Glenn, & Dodd, 1977).

All analysts agree there are differences among nations in the proportion of crimes reported to and/or detected by police. Some researchers argue that there is sufficient evidence that these differences are essentially random and thus do not systematically bias research (Archer & Gartner, 1984; Bayley, 1969; Bennett & Wiegand, 1994; Sawyer, 1967; Tanner, 1970; Wolf, 1971). Some research has addressed the issue of reporting differences between developing and developed nations and has concluded that they are not significant (Bayley, 1969; Krohn, 1976, 1978; Krohn & Wellford, 1977; Sparks, 1976; Sparks, Glenn, & Dodd, 1977; Tanner, 1970; Wellford, 1974). There is also research indicating that the resources a nation devotes to police and the relative number of police in a nation have little association to crime rates, indicating that biases introduced by differences in access to police and the efficiency of police are not great (Bennett, 1976; Bennett & Wiegand, 1994). Even if reporting and detection variations among nations do not severely bias research using large samples of nations, research involving small samples must provide evidence that reporting and detection differences are not great among the nations.

The recently completed International Victimization Surveys (IVS)—the first of its type—questioned people not only as to their being victims of crime but also as to whether they reported the crime to police. This allows for an examination of which crimes tend to be well reported and which do not. Unfortunately, the great majority of nations in these surveys are developed. The IVS data indicate great variation among developed nations in the reporting of robberies, other thefts, assaults, sexual offenses, and vandalism (van Dijk & Mayhew, 1993). If there is great variation in the reporting of these crimes in developed nations, it is likely there is also great variation in developing nations and between developing and developed nations. The IVS data indicate the great majority of burglaries and motor vehicle thefts are reported, and thus reporting of these probably varies little, at least among the developed nations.

Homicide—being such a serious offense and difficult to conceal or ignore—probably comes to the attention of police in the great majority of cases (Clinard & Abbott, 1973; Mulvihill & Tumin, 1969; Riedel, 1990). In Islamic nations, however, the Koran sanctions punishment by the victim's family in certain killings, in line with traditional feuding values and religious ecology (Groves, Newman, & Corrado, 1987; Newman, 1979). This may somewhat reduce the number of homicides in these nations, as there may be some nonreporting and lack of official processing. This is probably becoming less frequent as Islamic nations modernize, however, and is not likely a major factor biasing homicide rates. Overall, reporting and detection variations probably do not greatly influence research on cross-national variation in homicides.

Sexual offenses, however, have such significant reporting variations as to make police data of little value in cross-national research. Since most burglaries are reported to police—according to IVS surveys—cross-national comparisons of burglaries are probably not greatly influenced by reporting variations. The IVS data also indicate motor vehicle thefts are reported to police at a high level. As they are probably greatly influenced by the relative number of motor vehicles in a nation, however, they are not appropriate for cross-national analysis.

Changes in the reporting of crime might adversely influence trend analysis of official data. For example, much of the apparent recent increase in assaults in Western nations is likely due to a higher sensitivity, and lesser tolerance, toward violence, resulting in a higher proportion of these offenses being reported (Eisner, 1995; Franke, 1994; Junger-Tas, 1996; Tonry, 1995).

RECORDING AND CLASSIFICATION PROBLEMS

Not all crimes reported to or detected by police become part of the official police records which are reported to INTERPOL, the UNCS, or other police data sets. There are likely to be both unintentional and intentional errors in the collection, recording, and classification of crimes (Bottomley & Coleman, 1981). Many police departments do a poor job of completely and uniformly gathering crime data from all sections of the country; and this is likely to be more true of developing nations (Biderman & Lynch, 1991; Clifford, 1983; Groves, McCleary, & Newman, 1985; Teske & Arnold, 1982). Thus, there may well be systematic bias in police data between developing and developed nations. Also, some nations use the 354-day Hijri year to calculate annual crime rates, resulting in proportionately lower crime rates for these nations.

Police may under- or overreport certain crimes due to the influence of political pressures or cultural values. Political instability and regime changes might influence legal definitions and the recording and classifying of some offenses, as well as the tendency of people to report offenses, all of which adversely affect trend analysis (Marenin, 1993). Furthermore, some crimes may be tolerated or even de facto decriminalized and thus not handled in an official manner (Arthur, 1991; Mushanga, 1992; Wolf, 1971). So when providing information to agencies such as INTERPOL, police may be under pressure to underreport in order to make the nation look good in the eyes of the world. Conversely, some police departments may overreport in order to justify greater resources for fighting crime. There is little hard evidence regarding any of the above, as such things are difficult to research. It is highly likely, however, that these factors influence police data in many nations. So the issues become (1) to what degree they influence police data, and (2) whether the influence is systematic across nations.

SAMPLES OF NATIONS PROBLEMS

The sample of nations for which crime data are available differs greatly in size and composition among the data sources as well as over time for each data source. It is generally acknowledged that the sample of nations included in analysis can have a substantial effect on the results of research (Kohn, 1989; Messner, 1989; Neuman & Berger, 1988; Williamson et al., 1977). Most common statistical methods used to analyze cross-national crime data assume nations are randomly sampled from the populations of all nations. Unfortunately, most past research on crime has used fairly small samples which have not nearly represented the population of the nations of the world. Analysts have defended this by noting that such samples include nations from all regions of the world and at all levels of development. Yet they ignore that many regions and levels of development are grossly underrepresented and that most samples are heavily weighted toward Western developed nations.

The relative proportion of developed nations in a sample may well have a great influence on research results, especially as level of development is often a key variable. The developed nations of the world—including the nations of Western Europe, Australia, New Zealand, Canada, and the United States—constitute about 40 percent of WHO and UNCS samples (now and in the past) and INTERPOL samples prior to the 1987–1988 report. These same nations represent less than fifteen percent of the nations of the world. Thus, most past research has probably been biased by the large proportion of developed Western nations in samples, as these nations have distinctly different crime patterns and historical and situational contexts from those of developing nations.

The developed Western nations all have high INTERPOL and UNCS theft rates compared to the great majority of developing nations; most have low homicide rates relative to many developing nations. The strengths of the positive association of development variables to thefts and the negative association to homicides will depend on the relative number of developed Western nations in a sample. Thus, these associations have probably been exaggerated in research using samples with a large proportion of developed Western nations.

Similarly, there is great geographic and thus likely cultural imbalance in UNCS, WHO, and INTERPOL (prior to the 1987–1988 report) samples of nations. UNCS samples have included few African and Latin American nations, while the WHO samples have included few African or Asian nations. UNCS, WHO, and earlier INTERPOL samples also include relatively few non-Christian nations. Recent INTERPOL reports have a much better geographic and religious balance of nations, and UNCS data sets are improving in sample size and composition.

Prior to the 1994 report, WHO included a large number of Latin American nations, however, recent issues have included only several. Efforts are currently underway to increase substantially the number of developing nations from all regions of the world in future WHO reports. All three sources have increased the number of nations in transition from Eastern-Central Europe and the former Soviet Union in their recent reports.

It may be that meaningful cross-national crime research is only now becoming possible for developing nations, other than research that is region specific. Fairly good quality data for a large number of developed nations have been available for a while, but this is not the case for developing nations. Thus, quality research including a large and representative sample of nations is only now becoming possible. Longitudinal research involving developing nations will become viable over the next few years, as only then will data be available for a representative sample of developing nations for a sufficient number of years.

Another sample problem is what to do with the formerly communist nations in transition of Eastern-Central Europe. The political, economic, and social situations of these nations have always made their inclusion in analysis with other nations questionable. The recent changes in these nations, including the creation of more nations, make it even more likely that, in analysis, they might unduly influence research, confounding and confusing results. INTERPOL and the UNCS include a good number of these nations in their samples. Analysts using these data sets must decide first whether they want these nations in analysis, and, if so, how to control for possible biasing effects.

Neapolitan (1996) looked at INTERPOL, UNCS, and WHO crime data, but, in contrast to other such comparisons, he took differences in sample size and composition into account as well as crime rate differences. He found both adjusted and unadjusted INTERPOL homicide rates differed in their association to relevant independent variables from both UNCS and WHO rates, which in turn differed in their association to these variables from each other. He also found that even for types of theft that are almost identically defined by INTERPOL and UNCS—for example, burglary and robbery—there are substantial differences in the associations of rates to relevant independent variables between the two sources. Thus, combined sample and rate differences between data sources will likely result in differing research results for both homicides and thefts.

Research focusing on the developed nations of the world can use any of the major data sources, as all include most of these nations and have for many years. Research focusing on specific geographic regions should probably use the data set which has a good representation of nations from that region, for instance, research on homicides in Latin American nations should use WHO data. Only the last few INTERPOL crime reports include a sufficient number of developing nations to be considered representative of the population of such nations.

AGGREGATION PROBLEMS

One of the major limitations of official cross-national crime data—even when valid and reliable—is that they indicate only macrolevel associations across space and time. And crime data are most useful in determining causal associations when collected in smaller units such as the incident, victim, or offender. Information collected at this level enables researchers to combine units into sensible aggregates, such as, neighborhoods, households, and so on (Lynch, 1995a, b; Messner, 1989). Macrolevel aggregate data also raise the possibility of the ecological fallacy (Gartner, 1995; Lynch, 1995a). As an example, police data may indicate a strong association between the degree of poverty in nations and a certain type of crime. It is impossible to know whether the crimes are disproportionately committed by the poor, upon the poor, or in poor areas within nations. Yet the conclusion may be drawn that the poor more often commit and/or are victimized by crime.

INTERPOL includes information on the percent of crimes in each category committed by juveniles, so juvenile and adult crime can be analyzed separately. INTERPOL also includes information on the age range used by each nation to determine juvenile status, and these vary greatly across nations. In the 1992 *International Crime Statistics*, the lower age for juveniles varies from zero to sixteen, and the upper age from fourteen to twenty. Obviously, meaningful comparisons of juvenile crime cannot be made across nations, since what constitutes being a juvenile varies so greatly. It may be that if the focus of research is some subset of nations—for example, only Western nations or only Latin American nations—variations in juvenile status are not so great. Researchers should carefully examine this before researching exclusively juvenile or adult crimes.

The proportion of crimes committed by juveniles will also be greatly influenced by the age structure of nations. To separate the factors which contribute to juvenile crime from the effects on crime of a high proportion of juveniles in a nation, controls for age structure must be included in analysis. It is also likely that the reporting and police handling of crimes committed by juveniles vary more cross-nationally than crimes committed by adults, further compromising the analysis of juvenile crime.

INTERPOL reports the percent of each type of crime committed by females, rather than separate rates of crime for males and females. Thus, in order to analyze male and female crime separately across nations, the proportion of the population that is female must be taken into account. WHO data include age- and gender-specific victimization rates for homicides. Thus, WHO homicide data can be disaggregated meaningfully by age, gender, or both in combination. It must be remembered, however, that these are victim, rather than offender, rates.

As both offending and the risk of victimization vary by age and sex, standardization for both is desirable. Deane (1987) suggests a method of indirect standardization that does not depend on knowing age- or sex-specific crime rates.

BOUNDARY PROBLEMS

Official crime data are available at the national level. On the one hand, this is advantageous as most readily available economic, demographic, and political data are also at the national level. On the other hand, the cultural boundaries that divide people subdivide and overlap political boundaries. Thus, cross-national comparisons cannot always be considered truly cross-cultural (Ember & Ember, 1995). And the manner in which cultural and structural factors interact and mediate each other may not be effectively analyzed when nations are the unit of analysis. As crime and other data are not available for a large number of cultural units worldwide other than at a national level, cross-national crime research will continue in the foreseeable future to be the best way to study crime cross-culturally.

NONTRADITIONAL CRIMES

Both INTERPOL and the UNCS collect data solely on traditional crime, which falls short of reflecting the entire crime problem in nations. The UNCS states in the summary of its fourth survey:

> The traditional measures of crime, such as the number of thefts, robberies and assaults, do not reflect the entire range of criminal acts that result in human suffering. Injuries stemming from white-collar crime, such as bad environmental management of factories or even

economics, or personal misery caused by financial speculation or the manipulation of international money transactions may be far greater than that of all recorded homicides. Such crime often remains unrecorded. (U.N., 1993:2)

It is important that methods for collecting and analyzing cross-national data on other types of crime be developed. As noted in Chapter 1, the UNCS in the fourth survey made an attempt to collect data on transnational crimes, but this early effort was not very successful. For the present, cross-national research on crime involving more than several nations will probably continue to focus on traditional crimes.

RECOMMENDATIONS FOR THE USE OF OFFICIAL CRIME DATA

Some analysts believe that the problems of official data are so severe as to make them virtually useless in meaningful cross-national crime research (Junger-Tas, 1994; Lynch, 1995b; van Dijk & Mayhew, 1993). However, these data have so many advantages over other types that we cannot afford to ignore them. These data are the only such available for a large, fairly representative sample of the nations of the world, particularly the developing ones. Official crime data are the only source of data on homicides, the crime of most concern to the majority of people. They are available from several sources, so research results can be compared and contrasted. And they are available across space and time. Furthermore, as discussed here, the quality of data has improved recently and should continue to do so as nations modernize.

Cross-national associations of crime to national indicators of structural, political, demographic, and cultural variables should make a substantial contribution to our understanding of crime patterns and the factors that contribute to their variation. Cross-national crime research which includes nations of differing levels of development, cultural configurations, and social problems can assist us in elucidating the causes of crime from a less insular and constrained perspective than is generally the case.

Thus, the issue is not whether to use official data but how best to use them, for many problems and errors can be controlled or reduced with careful use. What follows are recommendations based on the foregoing discussion. More recommendations are made in Chapters 5 and 7.

First, for reasons discussed earlier, INTERPOL data prior to 1977 and UNCS data prior to the fourth survey should not be used for comparisons across nations or over time. This is particularly true for INTERPOL and UNCS homicide rates, which contain attempted homicides for some nations and not others. CCDF data, while painstakingly collected, are probably of little value other than for very general comparisons. This is particularly true for developing nations, where data collection and record keeping were likely to be so erratic and inefficient in the past as to make their official crime data of little value (Clifford, 1983).

While the majority of past cross-national crime research has used INTERPOL data, UNCS data are generally considered to be of better quality (Kalish, telephone conversation, July 1996; Kangaspunta, 1995; Marshall, 1996). The UNCS attempts to verify and validate data collected, particularly when there appears to be some problem with reported data. INTERPOL simply reports data as they are supplied, regardless of how nonsensical they might be. The fifth UNCS survey, due in 1997, should be the best yet, as substantial effort has been made to improve over past surveys. INTERPOL data continue to have the advantage of being available for more nations over a longer period of time. If the focus of research is exclusively cross-sectional on European nations, the *European Sourcebook* appears to represent a considerably better source than INTERPOL or the UNCS (Council of Europe, 1995).

Even with the improved quality of official crime data in recent years, direct comparisons of any two nations must be made with caution and skepticism. This is particularly true if the nations being compared are at very different levels of development or from different geographic regions. When such comparisons are made, the crime rate for each nation should be examined as to whether it is anomalous in some manner, giving us reason to doubt the validity of either or both.

In comparing two nations, rates for adjacent years should be compared with the rate for the year used. If the latter is much higher or lower, it is probably not a good indicator of the level of that crime in a nation. Multiyear averages can be compared to account partially for deviant years. The rate under consideration can also be compared to rates for similar crimes in the same year in that data set as well as to identical or similar crimes for that year in another data set. If a rate is consistent—over time, with other similar crimes, and across data sets—it is likely to be valid, reliable, and useful for direct comparisons among nations.

Many analysts believe that given the flaws in official crime data, trend or time-series analysis is the best or even only appropriate use (Archer & Gartner, 1984; Gartner, 1995; Lynch, 1995b). Such analysis assumes that legal definitions and the reporting of crime remain relatively constant over time, which is more likely than that they are constant across nations. Thus, crime indicators need not accurately reflect the level of crime in a nation so long as the degree of inaccuracy remains constant over time. Most of the developed nations have reported crime data of reasonable quality for the past fifteen or twenty years. Thus, quality time-series and trend analysis can be done on these nations for this time period.

As previously noted, crime data from all these sources are of poor quality until recently, and thus time-series or trend analysis can only go back ten to twenty years, depending on the source used. As the number of developing nations for which data are available is not great in WHO data other than the Latin American nations, in UNCS data until recent surveys, and INTERPOL data until the 1987–1988 report, trend analysis in a large number of these nations is only now becoming possible.

Time-series analysis of the developing nations is also possibly biased due to the swiftness of modernization in some of these nations. As developing nations modernize, there may be fairly large changes in the reporting of crime and in the recording and collection of crime data. These can result in large changes in crime rates when there has been little change in criminal behaviors. The political situation in many developing nations is more volatile than in developed nations, and thus legal definitions and the reporting and recording of crimes probably change more often and drastically. Also, in developing nations medical care may improve greatly in a fairly short time, and thus the proportion of people who survive assaults might increase greatly, reducing homicide rates with no actual change in violent behavior.

Homicide is generally regarded as the most valid and reliable of official cross-national crime indicators. As noted, INTERPOL homicide rates must be adjusted for the proportion that are attempts, and only UNCS rates that do not include attempts should be used. As homicide rates are considered fairly valid and reliable, they can be used to check the quality of data for other violent crime across space and time. If rates of other violent crime—such as, rapes and assaults—are highly correlated with homicide across nations or show similar trends over time, we can have more confidence in the overall trends and variations in violent crime.

It would be interesting, for example, to compare the ratio of homicides to rapes in nations. If the ratio is particularly large in some nations, it may indicate underreporting of rapes in these nations. This would be particularly true if the ratio of homicides to other violent crimes in these nations was not particularly large. We would, in general, expect that nations high in one type of violence would also be high in other types.

In general, violent crimes other than homicides—such as, rapes, assaults, and robberies—should probably not be compared cross-nationally, unless there is substantial improvement in the quality of data. Indications are that definitional, reporting, and recording differences across nations are too great for the rates of these crimes to be suitable for analysis. This is particularly true for sexual offenses and rapes. Thus, cross-national comparisons of violent crime should probably be restricted to homicides.

Comparing homicide rates between developing and developed nations may also be somewhat confounded by the superior medical care available in developed nations. This may result in more people surviving assaults and homicide attempts, making homicide rates lower in developed nations given the same level and types of violent behavior.

Comparisons of the ratio of completed homicides to attempted homicides and/or assaults may be a way to test for the above possibilities. If these ratios are lower in developed nations or decrease over time, it could indicate that superior medical care is indeed a factor in lowering homicide rates.

Burglary seems to be the most valid and reliable measure of theft available from INTERPOL and the UNCS. The definitions of what constitutes a burglary or breaking and entering are similar across nations, time, and data sources. The IVS surveys indicate the great majority of burglaries are reported to police. Thus, definitional, reporting, and classifying errors are probably not very large. This is also true for motor vehicle thefts, but these rates are highly dependent on the relative number of motor vehicles in a nation and thus not of great value in cross-national comparisons.

Most previous research on thefts—particularly that using INTERPOL data—has used some type of total theft rate, combining burglaries, other thefts, robberies, and so on. The argument has been that these rates are more robust than other theft measures. However, we have seen that these rates are inconsistently defined across nations, time, and data sources. For many nations they also include motor vehicle thefts and robbery, which is more a violent than property crime.

In cross-national crime research, it is important to analyze multiple indicators and data sources whenever possible. Thus, while burglary may be the primary theft indicator under analysis, other theft indicators might also be examined. If the associations of relevant independent variables to several theft indicators are very similar, we can have more confidence in the findings. INTERPOL and UNCS burglary rates might be analyzed separately, as might INTERPOL, UNCS, and WHO homicide rates. This can be done both with samples of nations which are represented in two or more data sets and with the entire sample for which data are available. Consistent results across multiple indicators, sources, and samples would strongly suggest research findings are valid, whereas inconsistent results indicate that data or sample problems must be addressed.

While time consuming, direct inspection of crime data for each year and nation included in analysis is crucial. For example, Belgium in the 1994 INTERPOL report is indicated to have a homicide rate of 31.5, which is twenty-five times greater than previous years. First, this rate is based on 315 homicides, 195 of which were attempts. Second, a zero was left off the reported population, so the rate was calculated using a population of one million rather than ten million. In addition to looking for such obvious anomalies, the crime rate for a specific crime in a nation should not vary greatly from year to year. If such inspection indicates a sudden and permanent shift up or down, it is more likely due to a change in legal definition or the recording and classifying of the crime than in criminal behavior. In such a case, the periods before and after the shift should not both be included in analysis.

If just one or two years stand out as abnormally low or high in a series of years, it is likely due to a recording error in that year or years. Even if the deviant rate is accurate, it is likely due to some extraordinary and temporary upheaval in the nation and not indicative of the general rate of that crime in a nation. If a deviant rate is found, it can be dropped from analysis or modified through use of multiyear averages. Multiyear averages are useful in cross-national analysis in adjusting for random yearly fluctuations and deviant rates due to errors. They can also be used in trend analysis by comparing multiyear averages from two different time periods. As mentioned earlier, rates for crimes in a nation should also be inspected relative to rates for other similar nations and/or other similar crimes.

Direct inspection can also be made of rates for the same crime and year across data sets. If the rates for a crime are very similar or identical in two or more data sets, we can have greater confidence that the rate is accurate. If there is a large discrepancy between the rates from two data sets, at least one and possibly both are inaccurate. When such a discrepancy is detected, the methods already discussed can be used to identify which rate is most likely to be inaccurate. Each rate can be compared to rates for adjacent years, similar nations, and similar crimes. If one or both of the rates deviate greatly from the norm in these comparisons, then either or both are likely to be inaccurate.

An example of the foregoing is the 1990 burglary data for the Federal Republic of Germany. INTERPOL indicated the rate to be 1,749, while the UNCS rate was 319. As the INTERPOL rate is similar to burglary rates for other Western European nations and is similar to the relative size of other theft rates for Germany, it is probably a more accurate measure than the UNCS rates. In this case, if a researcher is analyzing UNCS burglary data, Germany should probably be dropped from analysis, or the INTERPOL rate might be substituted for the UNCS rate. The latter would be acceptable only if the burglary rates from INTERPOL and the UNCS were very similar for other nations included in analysis.

Another example is Sri Lanka and its INTERPOL and UNCS homicide rates in 1990. The INTERPOL rate adjusted for attempts was 11.2 while the UNCS rate was 2.2. In this case, there is no good way to check which might be more accurate. Thus, Sri Lanka should probably be dropped from both samples.

In analysis, there is always tension between maximizing both sample size and representativeness and including only nations for which quality data are available. I have noted several instances in which nations should probably not be included in samples studied. Most past research—with the exception of possibly removing nations with outlier rates—has simply included all nations in analysis for which data were available. There are several conceptual and theoretical reasons why this is a questionable practice, which are addressed later in the book. Here I discuss balancing sample size and data quality in order to maximize the quality of research.

The developed nations—particularly if non-Western ones such as Japan are excluded—share similar legal systems and definitions. They also have fairly advanced mechanisms of crime data collection and record keeping and have had so for a long period of time. Thus, research focusing exclusively on these nations is reasonably certain to be based on comparable data of good quality. Of course, the research issues which can be addressed and the generalizability of results are both highly limited.

If the focus of research is to have a sample representing all nations or only developing nations, then INTERPOL would seem to be the best choice. Similarly, if the focus of research is any subsample of economically, geographically, or culturally similar nations other than developed or Latin American nations, current INTERPOL information is the only viable choice. Data are available for too few developing nations, African nations, Asian nations, Islamic nations, and so on from UNCS and WHO for meaningful analysis. This may change with future UNCS data, as the number of nations reporting is likely to increase. If the focus of research is homicides in Latin American nations, then WHO data prior to the 1993 report are a good choice, as they are available for a large number of Latin American nations and are probably the most valid and reliable source of homicide data.

Earlier, I mentioned that multiyear averages have often been used to compensate for random yearly fluctuations. This also increases the sample of nations. Generally, a subset of years is used when data are not available for a nation for all years, and thus the sample includes all nations for which data are available for any of the years. Messner (1992) has done research indicating this procedure is unlikely to alter the results of research, particularly for recent time periods.

Another method for increasing sample size is to combine data sets. In the case of homicides, INTERPOL and UNCS use virtually identical definitions. For most nations, the reported rates are identical or similar for the same years. Thus, a larger sample can be created either by averaging INTERPOL and UNCS rates when they are available from both sources or by using the INTERPOL or UNCS rates when available from one source. WHO homicide rates should not be combined with INTERPOL or the UNCS, as they are defined differently and based on the number of bodies not incidents. In INTERPOL and the UNCS, burglary, robbery, motor vehicle theft, assault, and rape are also similarly defined, although the rates differ more frequently between the two sources for these offenses than for homicides, making combining data sets questionable.

While combining data sets increases sample size and representativeness, it also adds a source of error and noncomparability of data. If sample size is thus expanded, data analysis should be carried out on the individual samples and rates as well as the combined samples and rates, with results compared and contrasted.

Special consideration must be given to official crime data provided by the nations of sub-Saharan Africa. Data from most of these nations are of such questionable quality, they should not be used in cross-national comparisons or analysis. As noted earlier, data for very few of these nations are available in UNCS or WHO data, probably because the reporting, recording, and archiving of crime and other data in these nations are haphazard and subject to bias. In recent years, an increasingly large number of these nations reports to INTERPOL, but the data are likely to be highly inaccurate.

Inspection of crime data for these nations reveals gross inconsistencies and contradictions. For example, the third UNCS reports 340 intentional homicides for Lesotho in 1986, while the fourth UNCS reports 40 for this same year. The fourth UNCS reports 6 intentional homicides committed in Botswana in 1990, while INTERPOL reports 152.

General crime reports—rather than specific rates for specific crimes—are available from OSAC, U.S. State Department *Consular Information Sheets*, the *Library of Congress Country Studies*, as well as the Foreign and Commonwealth Office of the United Kingdom via the WWW (see Appendix A for all sites cited in this section). For most nations these crime reports generally agree with official police crime data as to which nations are low or high on crime, but for sub-Saharan African nations there are extreme disagreements for many nations. For example, INTERPOL crime data indicate Guinea to have among the lowest rates of homicides and thefts in the world, whereas a recent OSAC report refers to "critical" rates of violent and property crimes in Guinea. Police data reported in the *World Factbook of Criminal Justice Systems* indicate Nigeria to have very low crime rates, whereas the Library of Congress study on Nigeria refers to serious crime growing to "nearly epidemic proportions" during the 1980s. Conversely, the Foreign and Commonwealth Office report for Swaziland refers to it as a "generally peaceful nation" with little violence, whereas recent INTERPOL data indicate it has homicide rates between 50 and 90. There are numerous sub-Saharan African nations where official police data and general crime reports are in great disagreement.

I could not locate research focusing on reasons for the poor quality of police crime data in sub-Saharan African nations other than that which discusses problems in developing nations in general. I was able to ascertain the likely reasons by reports available in various WWW locations and e-mail contact via discussion lists with people who have lived in or visited these African nations.

Apparently, most of the sub-Saharan nations have not yet developed reliable methods for collecting and recording crime data. As these nations have been primarily concerned with economic survival, the development of efficient and centralized record keeping has not been a high priority. Often, data are collected for only part of a nation, but rates are calculated using the entire population. Also, many crimes go unreported due to fear and distrust of the police. For example, the *World Factbook of Criminal Justice Systems* states regarding Nigeria that "published crime statistics were probably grossly understated, because most of the country was virtually unpoliced—and public distrust of the police contributed to underreporting of crimes."

In many nations there are more modern and traditional tribal systems of justice existing side-by-side, which, of course, confounds official statistics. The volatile political situation in many of these nations not only further interferes with systematic record keeping but makes it difficult to determine which acts are criminal and which are political or revolutionary. INTERPOL data indicate a homicide rate for Rwanda of 2.9 in 1991 and an absurdly high 1,250 in 1994. Clearly, the latter includes deaths due to the ethnic conflicts in Rwanda rather than criminal acts as they are normally defined.

As the nations of this region modernize and stabilize, more accurate crime data should become available. Currently, however, qualitative general crime assessments are probably more accurate than official police data.

CONCLUSION

Official crime data have many inherent flaws which make their use in cross-national comparisons and research questionable. Also, the samples of nations for which data have been available have not accurately represented the nations of the world. Much past research using official data has not adequately addressed these problems and is thus of questionable validity and value. While many problems remain in these data, the quality has improved and continues to improve. And we now know more about controlling and reducing the errors. Also, particularly in the case of INTERPOL data, the number of nations for which data are available has increased greatly. Thus, it is only in recent years that quality research using official data has been possible.

As the developing nations modernize, they should continue to become more proficient and complete in the collection and reporting of crime data. In recent years, the United Nations has made a concerted effort to help developing nations improve their efficiency in crime data collection and record keeping. This should contribute to continued improvement in the quality of data (Lynch, 1993). With each survey in the UNCS data, the U.N. increases its effort to validate the data collected and increase the number of nations reporting.

WHO recently inquired of its member states that routinely report data which factors might affect comparability. They expect future WHO reports to have better quality data that show fewer discrepancies in national figures and are more comparable across nations (WHO, 1995). WHO is also going to publish standard errors of their estimates.

The nations of Europe have recently made it a priority to improve and standardize the collection and reporting of crime data. The *European Sourcebook of Crime and Criminal Justice* reflects the concern for quality data and should contribute to better data as there are plans to issue the

Sourcebook on a regular basis (Council of Europe, 1995). The Economic and Social Council of the United Nations (ECOSOC) is in the process of setting up a crime and criminal justice data book for Eastern-Central European nations. And the first *Asia Crime Report* promises to expand and improve crime data collection in future reports (Asia Crime Prevention Foundation, 1993). Thus, efforts are underway in many parts of the world to improve the quality and quantity of official crime data.

While some problems in official crime data will never be resolved—such as the lack of uniform crime definitions in all nations—there has been and should continue to be substantial improvement in these data. If they are used with care, they will contribute greatly to our understanding of why nations vary in the amount and causes of crime.

REFERENCES

Akman, D. & Normandeau, A. (1968). Toward the measurement of criminality in Canada: A replication study. *Acata Criminologica*, 1, 135–260.

Ali, B. (1986). Methodological problems in international criminal justice research. *International Journal of Comparative and Applied Criminal Justice*, 10 (2), 163–176.

Archer, D. & Gartner, R. (1984). *Violence and crime in cross-national perspective.* New Haven, CT: Yale University Press.

Arthur, J. (1991). Development and crime in Africa: A test of modernization theory. *Journal of Criminal Justice*, 19, 499–513.

Asia Crime Prevention Foundation. (1993). *Asia crime report no.1.* Tokyo, Japan: Author.

Baxi, U. (1990). Social change, criminality, and social control in India. In U. Zvekic (Ed.), *Essays on crime and development* (pp. 227–261). Rome, Italy: UNICRI.

Bayley, D. H. (1969). *The police and political development in India.* Princeton, NJ: Princeton University Press.

Bennett, R. (1976). The effect of police personnel on crime clearance rates: A cross-national analysis. *International Journal of Comparative and Applied Criminal Justice*, 6, 177–193.

Bennett, R. (1991). Development and crime: A cross-national, time-series analysis of competing models. *The Sociological Quarterly*, 32, 343–363.

Bennett, R. & Lynch, J. (1990). Does a difference make a difference? Comparing cross-national crime indicators. *Criminology*, 28, 153–181.

Bennett, R. & Wiegand, R. (1994). Observations on crime reporting in a developing nation. *Criminology*, 32 (1), 135–148.

Biderman, A. & Lynch, J. (1991). *Understanding crime incidence statistics: Why the UCR diverges from the NCS.* New York: Springer-Verlag.

Black, D. (1970). Production of crime rates. *American Sociological Review*, 35 (4), 733–748.

Block, R. (Ed.). (1984). *Victimization and fear of crime: World perspectives.* Washington, D.C.: U.S. Department of Justice.

Bottomley, A. K. & Coleman, C. (1981). *Understanding crime rates: Police and public roles in the production of official statistics.* Gower, Wales: Westmead.

Breen, R. & Rottman, D. (1985). *Crime victimisation in the Republic of Ireland.* Dublin, Ireland: The Economic and Social Research Institute, paper no. 121.

Clifford, W. (1983). Criminology in developing nations—African and Asian examples. In E. Johnson (Ed.), *International handbook of contemporary development* (pp. 83–97). Westport, CT: Greenwood Press.

Clinard, M. & Abbott, D. (1973). *Crime in developing countries: A comparative perspective.* New York: John Wiley & Sons.

Council of Europe. (1995). *European sourcebook of crime and criminal justice statistics: Draft model.* Strasbourg, France: Author.

Deane, G. (1987). Cross-national comparison of homicide: Age/sex-adjusted rates using the 1980 U.S. homicide experience as a standard. *Journal of Quantitative Criminology,* 3 (3), 215–227.

Durkheim, E. (1966). *Suicide.* New York: Free Press.

Durkheim, E. (1973). *Moral education.* New York: Free Press.

Eisner, M. (1995). The effect of economic structures and phases of development on crime. *Criminological Research,* 32, 17–43.

Ember, C. & Ember, M. (1995). Issues in cross-cultural studies of interpersonal violence. In B. Ruback & N. Weiner (Eds.), *Interpersonal violent behaviors: Social and cultural aspects* (pp. 25–42). New York: Springer-Verlag.

Evans, S. S. & Scott, J. E. (1984). The seriousness of crime cross-culturally: The impact of religiosity. *Criminology,* 22, 39–59.

Franke, H. (1994). Violent crime in the Netherlands: A historical-sociological analysis. *Crime, Law, and Social Change,* 21 (1), 73–100.

Gartner, R. (1995). Methodological issues in cross-cultural large-survey research. In B. Ruback & N. Weiner (Eds.), *Interpersonal violent behaviors: Social and cultural aspects* (pp. 7–24). New York: Springer-Verlag.

Gartner, R., Baker, K., & Pampel, F. (1990). Gender stratification and the gender gap in homicide victimization. *Social Problems,* 37, 593–612.

Groves, W. B., McCleary, R., & Newman, G. (1985). Religion, modernization, and world crime. *Comparative Social Research,* 8, 59–78.

Groves, W. B., Newman, G., & Corrado, C. (1987). Islam, modernization, and crime: A test of the religious ecology thesis. *Journal of Criminal Justice,* 15, 495–503.

He, N. & Marshall, I. H. (1995). *Problematic issues in Chinese official crime statistics.* Paper presented at the American Society of Criminology meeting, Boston, MA, November 15–18.

Hindelang, J. J. (1974). The uniform crime reports revisited. *Journal of Criminal Justice,* 2, 370–381.

Hoebel, E. A. (1954). *The law of primitive man.* Cambridge, MA: Harvard University Press.

Hsu, M. (1969). A study of the differential response to the Sellin-Wolfgang index of delinquency. *Sociological Commentator* (spring), 41–50.

Huang, W. S. & Wellford, C. F. (1989). Assessing indicators of crime among international crime data series. *Criminal Justice Policy Review,* 3, 28–47.

INTERPOL. (1992). *International crime statistics for 1991 and 1992.* Lyons, France: General Secretariat.

Junger-Tas, J. (1994). The international self-report delinquency study: Some method-
ological and theoretical issues. In J. Junger-Tas, G. Terlouw, & M. Klein (Eds.),
Delinquent behavior among young people in the western world (pp. 1–14).
Amsterdam, Netherlands: Kluger.

Junger-Tas, J. (1996). Youth and violence in Europe—A quantitative review. *Studies
on Crime and Crime Prevention*, 5 (1), 31–58.

Kalish, C. (1988). *International crime rates*. Washington, D.C.: U.S. Department of
Justice, Bureau of Justice Statistics.

Kangaspunta, K. (1995). *Crime and criminal justice in Europe and North America
1986–1990*. Helsinki, Finland: HEUNI.

Kick, E. & LaFree, G. (1985). Development and the social context of murder and
theft. *Comparative Social Research*, 8, 37–57.

Kohn, M. L. (1989). Cross-national research as an analytic strategy. In M. L. Kohn
(Ed.), *Cross-national research in sociology* (pp. 77–102). Beverly Hills, CA:
Sage.

Krahn, H., Hartnagel, T., & Gartrell, J. (1986). Income inequality and homicide rates:
Cross-national data and criminological theories. *Criminology*, 24, 269–295.

Krohn, M. (1976). Inequality, unemployment, and crime: A cross-national analysis.
The Sociological Quarterly, 17, 303–313.

Krohn, M. (1978). A Durkheimian analysis of international crime rates. *Social
Forces*, 57, 654–670.

Krohn, M. & Wellford, C. (1977). A static and dynamic analysis of crime and the
primary dimensions of nations. *International Journal of Criminology and
Penology*, 5, 1–16.

Lynch, J. (1993). Secondary analysis of international crime survey data. In A. Alvazzi
del Frate, U. Zvekic, & J. van Dijk (Eds.), *Understanding crime: Experiences of
crime and crime control* (pp. 175–192). Rome, Italy: UNICRI.

Lynch, J. (1995a). Building data systems for cross-national comparisons of crime and
criminal justice policy: A retrospective. *ICPSR Bulletin*, 15, 1–6.

Lynch, J. (1995b). Crime in international perspective. In J. Wilson & J. Petersilia
(Eds.), *Crime* (pp. 11–37). San Francisco, CA: ICS Press.

Marenin, O. (1993). *The dynamics of development and crime: A critical review of the
routine activities approach*. Paper presented at the Academy of Criminal Justice
Sciences meeting, Pittsburgh, PA, March 16–20.

Marshall, I. H. (1996). How exceptional is the United States? Crime trends in Europe
and the U. S. *European Journal on Criminal Policy and Research*, 4 (2), 7–34.

Messner, S. F. (1982). Societal development, social equality, and homicide: A cross-
national test of a Durkheimian model. *Social Forces*, 61, 225–240.

Messner, S. F. (1989). Economic discrimination and societal homicide rates: Further
evidence on the cost of inequality. *American Sociological Review*, 54, 597–611.

Messner, S. F. (1992). Exploring the consequences of erratic data reporting for cross-
national research on homicide. *Journal of Quantitative Criminology*, 8 (2), 155–
173.

Mulvihill, D. J. & Tumin, M. M. (1969). *Crimes of violence, Vols.11, 12, 13*. Washington D.C.: Government Printing Office.

Mushanga, T. (1992). *Criminology in Africa*. Rome, Italy: UNICRI.

Neapolitan, J. L. (1996). Cross-national crime data: Some unaddressed problems.
Journal of Crime and Justice, 19, 95–112.

Neuman, L. & Berger, R. (1988). Competing perspectives on cross-national crime: An evaluation of theory and evidence. *The Sociological Quarterly*, 29, 281–313.

Newman, G. (1976). *Comparative deviance: Perception and law in six cultures*. New York: Elsevier.

Newman, G. (1979). *Understanding violence*. New York: Harper & Row.

Putting crime in perspective. (1995, January). *The Economist*, 42–43.

Riedel, M. (1990). Nationwide homicide data sets: An evaluation of the uniform crime reports and National Center for Health statistics data. In D. L. MacKenzie, P. J. Baunach, & R. R. Roberg (Eds.), *Measuring crime: Large-scale, long-range efforts*. Albany, NY: SUNY-Albany Press.

Sawyer, J. (1967). Dimensions of nations: Size, wealth, and politics. *American Journal of Sociology*, 73, 145–172.

Schmalleger, F. (1994). *Criminal justice today*. Englewood Cliffs, NJ: Prentice Hall.

Scott, J. E. & Al-Thokeb, F. (1977). The public's perception of crime: Scandinavia, West Europe, the Middle East, and the United States. In C. R. Huff (Ed.), *Contemporary corrections*. Beverly Hills, CA: Sage.

Scott, J. E. & Al-Thokeb, F. (1980). Crime statistics and the perception of crime. In G. Newman (Ed.), *Crime and deviance: A comparative perspective* (pp. 42–67). Beverly Hills, CA: Sage.

Skogan, W. (1974). The validity of official crime statistics: An empirical investigation. *Social Science Quarterly*, 55, 25–38.

Souryal, S. (1990). Religious training as a method of social control: The effective role of Sharia law in Saudi Arabia. In U. Zvekic (Ed.), *Essays on crime and development* (pp. 261–298). Rome, Italy: UNICRI.

Sparks, R. F. (1976). Crimes and victims in London. In W. G. Skogan (Ed.), *Sample surveys of the victims of crime* (pp. 43–71). Cambridge, MA: Ballinger.

Sparks, R. F., Glenn, H. G., & Dodd, D. J. (1977). *Surveying victims*. New York: John Wiley & Sons.

Tanner, R. E. (1970). *Three studies in East-African criminology*. Uppsala, Sweden: The Scandinavian Institute of African Studies.

Teske, R. & Arnold, H. (1982). Comparison of the criminal statistics of the United States and the Federal Republic of Germany. *Journal of Criminal Justice*, 10, 359–374.

Tonry, M. (1995). *Malign neglect: Race, crime, and punishment in America*. New York: Oxford University Press.

U.N. (1993). *Crime trends and criminal justice operations at the regional and interregional levels*. Vienna, Austria: Author.

U.N. (1995). *Ninth United Nations Congress on the prevention of crime and the treatment of offenders*. Cairo, Egypt: Author.

Valez-Diaz, A. & Megargee, E. (1971). An investigation of differences in value judgments between youthful offenders and nonoffenders in Puerto Rico. *Journal of Criminal Law, Criminology, and Police Science*, 61, 549–556.

van Dijk, J. & Mayhew, P. (1993). Criminal victimisation in the industrialised world: Key findings of the 1989 and 1992 International Crime Surveys. In A. Alvazzi del Frate, U. Zvekic, and J. van Dijk (Eds.), *Understanding crime: Experiences of crime and crime control* (pp. 1–50). Rome, Italy: UNICRI.

Vigderhous, G. (1978). Methodological problems confronting cross-cultural criminological research using official data. *Human Relations*, 31, 229–247.

Wellford, C. (1974). Crime and the dimensions of nations. *International Journal of Criminology and Penology*, 2, 1–10.

WHO. (1962–1981). *The world health statistics annual: 1960–1980*. Geneva, Switzerland: Author.

WHO. (1979, 1980, 1981, 1982, 1989, 1990, 1991, 1992). *The world health statistics annual: 1978, 1979, 1980, 1981, 1988, 1989, 1990, 1991*. Geneva, Switzerland: Author.

WHO. (1995). *The world health statistics annual: 1994*. Geneva, Switzerland: Author.

Wilkins, L. T. (1980). World crime: To measure or not to measure? In G. Newman (Ed.), *Crime and deviance: A comparative perspective*. Beverly Hills, CA: Sage.

Williamson, J., Karp, D., Dolphin, J., Dorr, R., Barry, S., & Ravels, W. (1977). *The research craft*. Boston, MA: Little Brown.

Wolf, P. (1971). Crime and development: An international analysis of crime rates. *Scandinavian Studies in Criminology*, 3, 107–120.

3

Evaluation of Unofficial Crime Data

VICTIMIZATION DATA

Some analysts believe that the problems and errors affecting police data make their use in comparisons and cross-national crime research of limited value (Junger-Tas, 1994; van Dijk & Mayhew, 1993). Even those of us who believe police data have improved to where they are of some value—if properly inspected and analyzed—recognize the necessity of other types of cross-national crime data. The major alternative to police data in the United States has been the National Crime Survey, which collects data on personal and household victimizations through a survey of sampled households. Many European nations have also conducted victimization surveys since the early 1970s (Beirne & Messerschmidt, 1991; Block, 1992; Clinard, 1978; Kaiser, Kury, & Albrecht, 1991; Marshall, 1996). A few developing nations of the world have conducted limited victimization surveys (e.g., Bennett & Wiegand, 1994; Block, 1992; Brillon, 1975; Clinard, 1978; Clinard & Abbott, 1973; van Dijk, Mayhew, & Killias, 1990).

While some cross-national crime research has used victimization rates from surveys in different nations, the results are of limited value. This is due to substantial differences in the methodologies used and the wording of questions as well as the small number of nations for which data were available. The United Nations Interregional Crime and Justice Research Institute (UNICRI) has conducted the first three victimization surveys that use the same survey instrument across a number of nations. The first International Victimization Survey (IVS) was completed in 1989, the second in 1992, and the third in 1997. The essence of the IVS is its standardization, as the same questions are asked in roughly the same manner in all nations (Mayhew, 1993). The IVS includes questions on common crimes—such as, burglary, larceny, and assault—fear of crime, attitudes about punishment, and so on. Surveyed nations are more fully described in Chapter 1.

Advantages of IVS Data

The most obvious advantage of IVS data over that of police is that they include the "dark" figures of crime, that is, crime that does not become known to police or is not recorded by police in official reports. Thus, IVS crime rates are not dependent on or biased by cross-national differences in the reporting of crimes to police, nor by how they are recorded and classified once reported. IVS data may thus more accurately indicate the actual amount of crime in nations and be more comparable across nations.

Legal definitions and codes differ across nations and therefore also across the INTERPOL and UNCS categories in which crimes are placed by nations. The IVS asks respondents not only the same questions in all nations but also for descriptions of the crime rather than using labels such as robbery or burglary. Thus, all respondents are reporting whether they were victimized in the same manner rather than whether they were the victims of a certain crime label. Furthermore, there are indications that people around the world tend to have similar understandings and definitions of common criminal behavior (Braithwaite, 1989; Newman, 1976).

Compared to police data, IVS data provide much more information about the crime incident and the context in which it occurred. Thus, IVS data can be reorganized into much more meaningful aggregates, such as neighborhoods, minority group members, urban areas, and so on. The factors that directly affect people do not operate at the national level but at the regional, city, community, neighborhood, and household levels. While police data can be analyzed only at the national level, IVS data can be analyzed at many different levels and aggregates. Furthermore, IVS data can be used to study the associations of variables to crime both within and across nations as well as to compare and contrast these.

Police data provide information only on the incidence of crime per year, while IVS data provide information on both the incidence and prevalence of victimizations. Thus, IVS data inform us not only of the rate of victimization in a year but also the number of people/households victimized. As multiple victims likely account for a fairly large proportion of the overall victimization rates, prevalence data can be highly useful (Skogan, 1992). Incidence and prevalence of victimizations may vary across crimes and nations, and analysis of these differences might be highly informative. Particularly interesting would be analysis of whether the associations of relevant variables to incidence differed from their associations to prevalence across and within nations.

The IVS provides much information that police data cannot regarding not only the circumstances of crimes but also people's attitudes toward crime and criminal justice. Respondents are questioned about law enforcement, fear of crime, crime prevention, sentencing, police, and so on. This information can be studied in relation to the crime in nations—both as indicated by IVS and police data—as well as other national and subnational attitudes. If, as frequently stated, a major goal of cross-national crime research is to assist effective public policy regarding crime, then understanding how crime and attitudes concerning crime are associated may be of great importance.

The IVS queries respondents who report victimizations as to whether they were reported to the police. Thus, as shown in Chapter 2, the IVS is valuable in ascertaining for which crimes police data are likely to be most valid. Crimes such as burglary—which the IVS indicates are almost always reported—are likely to be indicated accurately by police data. Crimes not found to be reported frequently—such as minor larcenies—are probably not accurately indicated by police data (Lynch, 1993).

There are, of course, problems and sources of error in victimization data and thus with IVS data.[1] Lynch (1993) argues that a major advantage of IVS over police data is that it is easier to identify the sources of error in IVS data. It is then also easier to account for errors in analysis and thereby reduce their effect. In contrast, Beirne and Perry (1994) argue that the reliability of victimization surveys as sources of data for studying cross-national crime has not been established.

Problems with IVS Data

Just as some people do not report some crimes to the police, some people are unwilling to respond to the survey. If those who respond differ systematically from those who do not, then victimization rates will be systematically biased. There is some evidence that those who are most heavily victimized are most likely to respond, which would exaggerate the amount of victimizations (Block, 1993; Young, 1988). Even if response bias renders victimization rates inaccurate, the problem is not great if all nations are similarly affected, as cross-national comparisons would then remain valid.

Response rates to the IVS varied greatly across nations, ranging from just over 30 percent to greater than 90 percent. However, analysis of victimization rates across nations has shown no systematic associations to variations in response rates (van Dijk & Mayhew, 1993). Also, those who did not respond at first but did on second contact did not differ significantly from those who initially responded (Mayhew, 1993). Van Dijk and Mayhew (1993) argue that analysis of response problems suggests that they do not bias results to any great degree, but the researchers admit the evidence is inconclusive.

The likelihood that people will respond and report certain victimizations may also vary over time, confounding trend analysis. As noted in Chapter 2, there has been a higher sensitivity to, and less tolerance of, violence in Western nations in recent years. Thus, people who have been attacked or assaulted might be more likely to report such victimizations in more recent surveys. Similar changes might occur in developing nations.

The accuracy of victimization data depends on the ability of respondents to remember victimizations and on their honesty in reporting them. Some respondents probably suffer memory decay, that is, forget victimizations, particularly those that are minor or that occurred in the more distant past (Lynch, 1993; Skogan, 1986). This will have two biasing effects. First, the amount of less serious crime will be underestimated, and second, it will create a recency bias indicating more crime in the most recent year than in past years.

If memory decay tends to be similar across nations, then cross-national comparisons will not be affected by memory decay. Minor thefts and larcenies may be perceived as more serious in developing than developed nations, as people who have less are more affected when they lose possessions. Skogan (1981) has done research indicating that within nations people from lower socioeconomic status are more likely to recall and report minor crimes. Thus, it is likely there are also differences in recalling and reporting victimizations between developed and developing nations, which, in turn, might invalidate comparisons of victimizations between nations at different levels of development.

There is also evidence of telescoping effects in victimization surveys, that is, the tendency to recall events occurring outside the time period of interest into the more recent past (Block, 1993; Lynch, 1993). This is more likely to occur with more serious crimes, as they will remain more vivid in people's memories. This has the effect of overestimating the number of both serious victimizations and victimizations of the recent past. Telescoping can be reduced by using boundary procedures, which is done in the NCS, but the IVS did not use such procedures (Block, 1993). As with other factors, telescoping will not adversely bias cross-national comparisons unless telescoping effects vary among nations.

In addition to failure to remember crimes properly, some respondents may intentionally omit certain victimizations in their answers. For some of the same reasons people are reluctant to report crimes to the police, they may be reluctant to report them in surveys. This may be particularly true for sexual offenses (Lynch, 1993; Skogan, 1981; Young, 1988). There are indications that the IVS had particular problems getting accurate responses for sexual victimizations in the developing nations (Zvekic & Alvazzi del Frate, 1995a). As reluctance to report certain crimes on the IVS is probably influenced by cultural values and political attitudes, honesty errors may vary substantially among nations, particularly between developing and developed nations or nations from different geographic regions.

In research using samples there is always some sample error, and the amount of error is likely to be great when samples are small and the event of interest is relatively rare. The IVS samples are generally not very large, with most being between one and two thousand, and crime victimizations are rare events. Thus, a small amount of sample error can have a large effect on the rate of victimizations.

For example, 1,009 Norwegians were surveyed in 1989, with fewer than 1 percent reporting having been a burglary victim in 1988. Thus, the number of households reporting a burglary in Norway in 1988 was fewer than ten. A difference of only five burglaries in another sample would increase or decrease the indicated rate of burglary by more than 50 percent. Thus, the possibility of one nation having a lower or higher rate of victimizations for a given crime in a given year due to sample error rather than an actual difference is substantial. Killias (1990) argues that given the crime rates in Western Europe, samples of fewer than 5,000 people are insufficient for reliable analysis.

Lynch (1993) suggests that sample size can be increased by the pooling of data. For those nations surveyed more than once, data can be pooled from several surveys. Of course, this negates any trend analysis in these nations. He also suggests that nations be grouped according to important economic, political, and cultural characteristics, and the samples pooled. Thus far, analysis of IVS data has not used pooled samples.

IVS data analysis done by those who conducted the surveys used samples which had been weighted to make them as representative as possible of actual national populations aged sixteen or more in terms of gender, regional population distribution, age, and household composition. Data from Japan were unweighted, although the sample fit the national population profile well (van Dijk & Mayhew, 1993). The practice of weighting data should be continued in future analysis using IVS data.

Even if there is minimal sample error in IVS samples, they would still not accurately indicate all criminal victimizations in the nations surveyed. Since the IVS includes only crimes against people residing in households, crimes against commercial establishments, government agencies, transients, and tourists are not included. There is evidence that the volume of crime against commercial establishments varies among nations (Lynch, 1995). Also, the IVS did not gather information on victims under sixteen years old. As a result, the IVS underestimates the amount of crime in nations, and this underestimation may vary across nations. This might particularly be the case between developing and developed nations, as the latter will have a greater number of commercial establishments and the former more young people.

Comparisons between developing and developed nations are also problematic due to samples in developing nations being taken in just one large city in each nation, whereas the entire nation was sampled for developed nations. To make data comparable, special victimization rates were calculated for urban areas with more than 100,000 population for the developed nations. Since all the cities in the developing nations sampled had populations over 600,000—twelve of fourteen, over 1 million; and ten of fourteen, over 3 million—it is questionable that urban areas of more than 100,000 provide a proper basis of comparison between developed and developing nations. Also, as the cities in developing nations vary in population from 600,000 to over 11 million, comparisons among the developing nations may not be appropriate.

Most of the samples in developing nations were somewhat smaller than those in developed nations. In developing nations, only two samples were greater than 2,000, and several were less than 1,000. In developed nations, most samples were greater than 2,000 and all were greater than 1,000. Thus, the probability of sample error and lack of accurate representation is greater in the developing nations.

Earlier I suggested that an advantage of IVS over official data is that in all nations respondents are asked the same questions which describe specific criminal acts, whereas official data are recorded and classified according to legal codes and customs that vary substantially cross-nationally. Even with all respondents answering the same questions, however, there is the possibility of differences in the subjective interpretation of questions; and these might be systematic across nations. Research on past victimization surveys has found that differential interpretations of the same question can influence how people respond to that question (Crawford, Jones, Woodhouse, & Young, 1992; Glenn, 1988; Sparks, 1992). The interpretation of and responses to questions about sexual incidents are particularly likely to vary among respondents and across nations (Hanmer & Saunders, 1984; Skogan, 1981). There has also been some criticism of the comprehensiveness of questions included in the IVS surveys (Beirne & Perry, 1994; Marshall, 1996).

Prior to constructing the IVS instrument, research was done to word questions in a manner to make them universally understood (van Dijk & Zvekic, 1993). This probably is not entirely possible, and some differences in interpretation and response among respondents and across nations remain. The amount of variation introduced by differential interpretations is likely to be small, and some of this small amount is probably random within and across nations. There may be more bias introduced by differential interpretations between developing and developed nations than among the nations in either category.

Computer-Assisted Telephone Interviewing (CATI) was used for the IVS in the developed nations, while face-to-face interviews were used in developing nations. Also, in the developed nations, samples were based on random digit dialing; while in the developing nations, it was based on three residential areas: rich, medium, and poor. There is evidence that CATI increases victimizations reported due to increased control and consistency in interviews (Hubble & Wilder, 1988; de Leeuw & van der Zouwen, 1988). Dillman and Tarnai (1988), in a review of this issue, argue the differences between CATI and face-to-face interviews are small and not significant. Still, given the other factors that might confound comparisons of IVS data from developing and developed nations, another possible source of bias is troubling.

The use of CATI in developed nations means people who do not own phones are not included in samples. Research in the United States indicates that poverty is inversely related to phone ownership and directly related to victimizations (Block, 1993). Thus, use of CATI may miss the segment of the population most likely to be victimized. If nations vary in phone ownership and/or the association of phone ownership to victimizations, the victimization rates in the IVS may not be comparable.

Mayhew (1993) argues that phone ownership is high and similar across developed nations, and thus any bias or error introduced by differential phone ownership is not very great. Research done prior to the IVS indicated that there were differences in phone ownership among the nations involved, in some cases being greater then 10 percent (van Dijk & Mayhew, 1993). Given the already discussed possibility of large sample error, this additional source cannot be so readily dismissed as irrelevant. It further indicates the need to view the IVS victimization rates with some skepticism and suggests differential phone ownership be included in analysis as a control variable.

Like police data, the IVS can only inform us on cross-national variation in conventional crimes and cannot inform us on corporate crime, white-collar crime, transnational crime, and so on. Unlike police data, victimization data cannot provide information on the crime of most concern to people— homicide. In general, people of most nations are more concerned with violent than with property crimes, and victimization research is of limited value in measuring serious violent crime (Lynch, 1993; Reiss & Roth, 1993). The IVS also does not include questions on such victimless crimes as drug use and prostitution. Also, victimization research can provide no information on the offenders, whereas police data at least provide gender and age status.

Lynch (1993:175) called the IVS "a quantum leap in international statistics on crime and justice issues." The foregoing discussion of some of the problems with these data, and with the limited number of nations surveyed, indicates that the IVS to date falls short of a quantum leap. The third IVS, however, will include more nations than the first two, around forty. There are numerous problems inherent in victimization research and more are introduced when the research is cross-national. Thus, extremely high quality cross-national victimization data may not be attainable. However, given what has been learned in the past, future IVS surveys should provide better data, especially if they are better funded and include more nations and larger samples.

How useful are the IVS data currently available? This depends on the degree to which errors and problems systematically bias data or are largely random and not of great magnitude. UNICRI brought together a number of experts for the International Conference on Understanding Crime to analyze and discuss the error structures of the IVS data (van Dijk & Zvekic, 1993).

The consensus was that while errors make estimates of the absolute numbers of victimizations questionable, they probably do not invalidate comparisons across nations or over time.

Comparisons across nations showed that the ratio of various types of crimes to each other did not vary much among nations (Block, 1993). Analysis also found that the correlates of victimization risks, such as age, were fairly constant across nations (van Dijk, 1991). As previously noted, victimization rates showed no systematic association to response rates (van Dijk & Mayhew, 1993). These studies and more subjective evaluations convinced those most intimately involved with the IVS that the data are of sufficient quality for cross-national comparisons (Block, 1993; Lynch, 1993; Mayhew, 1993).

Most of the analysis indicating the comparability of IVS data across nations was done with data from only the developed nations. The comparability of data between developed and developing nations—and to a lesser degree among developing nations—is more questionable. I have already noted comparability problems between developed and developing nations that might result from smaller samples in developing nations, differing sampling techniques, only one major city being sampled in developing nations, and different interviewing modes being used in developed and developing nations. There may also be systematic differences in how respondents remember victimizations and respond to the same questions between developed and developing nations.

Van Dijk and Zvekic (1993) argue that urban dwellers in nations at all levels of development are similar, with similar problems and perceptions. Therefore, as long as comparisons between developed and developing nations—or among developing nations—are of urban dwellers, data should be comparable. There is little hard evidence that this is the case, with some research suggesting the data are not comparable. Interviewers found the more wealthy people hard to reach in many developing nations, and thus samples in these nations are weighted toward the less wealthy (Zvekic & Alvazzi Del Frate, 1995a). As noted earlier, due to lack of phone ownership by some poor people, samples in developed nations are likely weighted against the less wealthy. If victimization risk is related to wealth in either or both types of nations, data may not be comparable.

With the exception of Japan, the developed nations share a similar Western culture. The developing nations have cultures which differ from each other and from developed nations. It is possible that cultural variations will result in systematic variations in the remembering and reporting of victimizations, particularly those regarding sexual offenses. Also, theft or damage of less expensive items might frequently be forgotten or ignored by respondents in developed nations, whereas this might not be the case in developing nations where such items are relatively more valuable.

The number of factors that may bias comparisons of IVS data between the developed and developing nations makes such comparisons of questionable validity. And there is more reason to doubt the validity of comparisons among developing than among developed nations.

Recommendations for Use of IVS Data

Despite the problems discussed, IVS data do provide a valuable alternative to police data for a number of purposes. And IVS data should improve in quality in future surveys, further increasing their value in cross-national research. Efforts are underway to improve methodology, increase sample sizes, and increase the number of nations surveyed.

The third IVS—completed but not available at this writing—should be superior to the first two in quality. Analysis of past surveys was used to refine both the methodology and the questionnaire (UNICRI, 1996). Developing nations and nations in transition particularly were provided with more assistance in face-to-face interviewing and data entry. Also, with eighteen nations having participated twice and nine thrice, trend analysis has become possible. Until IVS data are of higher quality and include more nations, however, great care must be taken in their analysis and interpretation.

The confidence we can have in IVS data depends on the crimes and nations under analysis. We can have greater confidence in research focusing on those offenses which are least likely to be strongly affected by sample response, recall, honesty, and differential interpretations problems. Therefore, serious violent crime is probably not very accurately indicated in IVS data, with homicides not included at all. As police and WHO data provide fairly good measures of homicides cross-nationally—homicide being a good general indicator of violent crime—cross-national research on violence is probably best done with official data.

Burglaries and motor vehicle thefts appear to be well reported to police and are thus likely to be accurately indicated by police data. As police data include commercial establishments—which IVS data do not—and are available for many more nations, they are probably better for research on burglaries and motor vehicle thefts. Comparisons between police and IVS data in terms of the rank order of nations on these offenses and the association of relevant variables might also prove interesting.

Sexual offenses are probably not very accurately indicated by either police or IVS data. Research on sexual offenses should probably use both sources and compare results. Thus, the crimes for which IVS data are probably most valuable are larcenies of various types and minor assaults, as these are likely to be fairly accurately indicated in IVS but not police data.

The quality of IVS data is almost certainly highest for the Western nations, of lesser quality for the nations of Eastern-Central Europe, and of the least quality for developing nations. Thus, research could be done in waves, with first analysis done on only the Western nations, and then adding the Eastern-Central European nations, and finally including developing nations. Whenever a new set of nations is added, a dummy variable could be included representing this set of nations. It should be remembered that comparisons which include developing nations must use comparable urban areas for the other nations.

An interesting area for future research is exploring an inconsistency. While all past research using police data has found a strong positive associa- tion between development and property crimes (e.g., Bennett, 1991; Kick & LaFree, 1985; LaFree & Kick, 1986; Shichor, 1990), IVS data indicate that developing nations have higher rates of property crime (Zvekic & Alvazzi Del Frate, 1995b). The reasons for this paradox and which type of data is correct are extremely important in explaining how and why property crime varies cross-nationally and over time.

Even when IVS data are not superior to police data, they allow for research police data cannot. IVS data can be used to compare not only crime across nations but also the correlates of crime within nations and whether these correlates vary across nations. IVS data can also address aspects of the crime problems of nations for which police data provide no information.

Lynch (1993) has suggested some ways to check the quality of IVS data and partially control for some error sources. Earlier I covered his suggestions for increasing sample size. He proposes that the representativeness of samples can be checked by comparing demographic data from the IVS samples to demographic data from other sources. Similarly, he recommends checking the accuracy of the victimization data by ranking nations on victimization rates and comparing that to rankings based on other crime indicators. Lynch further suggests comparing one- and five-year victimization rates to check for period and/or recall effects. Finally, as previously discussed, he recommends the inclusion of variables in models to account for suspected sources of error, for instance, response rate and interview mode differences.

SELF-REPORT CRIME DATA

Another method frequently used for measuring the incidence and prevalence of crime is the self-report survey. Self-report surveys solicit from a sample of respondents information on the offenses they have committed, as well as information about the circumstances of the offenses and about themselves. They are usually carried out anonymously or with the promise of confidentiality. Most self-report surveys are conducted with juveniles rather than adults, and the majority have been conducted in school settings (Junger-Tas, 1989; Reuband, 1989). Self-report surveys were first carried out in the 1940s, gained popularity in the 1950s, and became an important way of measuring delinquency in the 1960s (Jensen & Rojek, 1992; Nye & Short, 1957; Porterfield, 1943). Rather crude in methodology in early years, they have become increasingly sophisticated. While still flawed, self-report surveys are now considered a legitimate alternative to other measures of delinquency (Jensen & Rojek, 1992; Junger-Tas, 1994).

The great majority of self-report studies have been conducted in the United States, as has most of the work on instrument construction and methodology (Block, 1984; Klein, 1989). Other Western nations have conducted some self-report studies, with Germany and the Netherlands having fairly solid histories of developing and refining self-report research (Klein, 1989). There has also been very limited self-report research in some developing nations (e.g., LaFree & Birkbeck, 1991; Priyadarsini & Hartjen, 1981). With a few exceptions where two nations could be compared, the self-report surveys done in the past were not useful for cross-national comparisons due to substantial differences in sample frames, research designs, instruments, and so on. The first attempt to obtain cross-nationally comparable self-report delinquency data was the International Self-Report Delinquency study (ISRD). This study was conducted in the early 1990s under the auspices of the Research and Documentation Center of the Dutch Ministry of Justice (Junger-Tas, Terlouw, & Klein, 1994).

Advantages of Self-Report Data

Self-report data have many of the same advantages as victimization data over police data: (1) they are not influenced by definitional, reporting, and classification differences among nations; (2) they can be disaggregated in more meaningful ways than can police data; and (3) they have further advantages over victimization data. Victimization data are not useful in indicating juvenile crime, as victims rarely know the age of offenders (Lynch, 1986). Victimization research misses victimless crimes, nonpersonal crimes, and crimes against commercial establishments. Self-report research includes these as well as other types of crime. Thus, self-report research includes the "dark" figures of crime missed by police and victimization data.

Self-report data are likely to be more accurate in indicating minor offenses, as they are generally more salient to the offender than the victim (Hagan, Gillis, & Simpson, 1985, 1987; Hindelang, Hirschi, & Weis, 1979; Junger-Tas, 1989). Self-report research is particularly useful in providing data on the extent of minor deviance among the basically normal population, for example, recreational drug use and alcohol abuse. Sexual offenses are also more accurately indicated, as offenders—particularly if anonymous—are less likely to be inhibited about reporting these than are victims.

Probably the greatest advantage of self-report data over those of police or victimization surveys is that they can provide a great deal of information on the differences between offenders and nonoffenders. Victimization surveys provide no information on offenders, and cross-national police data give only age and gender information. Data on the personal, social, and economic characteristics of offenders as compared to nonoffenders can most directly address which conditions and traits contribute to offending, which is the primary goal of criminological research. Cross-national self-report data can help identify which national characteristics are associated with variations in criminal behavior across nations, which factors are associated with criminal behavior within nations, and whether the associations to criminal behavior are similar across nations.

Furthermore, self-report data add another basis of comparison for the accuracy of official and victimization data as to the relative rankings of nations for some types of crimes. If for a particular category of crime a set of nations has a similar rank for official, victimization, and self-report data, we can have confidence not only that the order is correct but also in the validity of all three types of data. Differences between police and other official data and self-report data can also be analyzed to identify cross-national differences in the functioning of official crime control systems.

Within the United States, self-report data have indicated that official crime data greatly underestimate the prevalence and incidence of delinquency and greatly overstate the differentials in delinquency by age, sex, race, and social class (Elliott & Huizinga, 1983; Elliott, Huizinga, & Morse, 1987; Hirschi, 1969; Klein, 1986). Analysis of cross-national self-report data can reveal whether this is true in other nations and in which nations it is more or less the case. For those types of crimes which are likely accurately measured by self-report data—such as, drug use and minor property crime—these data might more accurately indicate inter- and intranational associations to variables such as age, sex, race, and social class.

Neither INTERPOL nor UNCS crime data provide information on the race or social class of offenders. Thus, in order to examine whether and how the associations of race and class to offending vary between official and self-report data, official data would have to be requested from individual nations. As both INTERPOL and UNCS do provide information on gender and age status of offenders, comparisons can be made for these between police and self-report data. Differences between the two can be looked at within nations and compared across nations.

Problems with Self-Report Data

The general problems influencing the reliability and validity of self-report data have been fully discussed elsewhere (e.g., Elliott & Ageton, 1980; Jensen & Rojek, 1992; Junger-Tas, 1989). These include the honesty of respondents both in terms of exaggeration and underreporting, systematic nonresponse, memory errors, differential understandings of questions, and nonrepresentative sample frames.

Past research indicates that honesty and memory variations among respondents contribute to a significant amount of underreporting of offenses and some exaggeration of offending (Clark & Tifft, 1966; Gold, 1970; Junger-Tas, 1989; Reiss & Rhodes, 1959). Research also indicates, however, that there are no significant differences in memory and honesty by race or social class, and thus the use of these data for research may not be compromised by errors introduced by honesty and memory (Gold, 1970; Hindelang, Hirschi, & Weis, 1979; Junger-Tas, 1989). Other research has found that involvement in delinquency as indicated by self-report surveys is highly correlated with police, court, and institutional data (Elliott & Voss, 1974; Erickson & Empey, 1963; Hindelang, Hirschi, & Weis, 1981). Two quite thorough analyses on the quality of United States self-report data found reliability measures to be impressive and validity in the moderate-to-strong range (Hindelang, Hirschi, & Weis, 1981; Hirschi, Hindelang, & Weis, 1980).

Despite most research indicating self-report data to be reasonably reliable and valid, their usefulness is still limited. Self-report surveys generally miss the most serious, chronic offenders due to the sample frames used and response problems (Cernkovich, Giordano, & Pugh, 1985; Hagan, Gillis, & Simpson, 1985, 1987; Hindelang, Hirschi, & Weis, 1979). This is particularly true of self-report surveys using school samples, which is often the case (Baerveldt, 1987; Junger-Tas, 1977; Mutsaers, 1987). Even in the best, most representative samples, those who commit the most serious offenses—murder and rape—are not sufficiently included due to the rarity of these acts (Jensen & Rojek, 1992). Also, most self-report research has been limited to juveniles, and there are indications that sampling and other problems would make quality self-report research on adults virtually impossible (Reuband, 1989).

The problems affecting self-report data are amplified when attempting to collect and analyze cross-national self-report data. Interpretation and the understanding of questions, response rates, degree of honesty, and so forth might all vary among nations and possibly systematically. If this is the case, cross-national comparisons of the incidence, prevalence, and distribution of delinquency as measured by self-report surveys would be of little value. Since the age of majority varies across nations, cross-national self-report research is immediately confronted with the problem that the populations sampled do not include the same age range unless adjustments are made.

Ideally, a cross-national self-report survey would employ a common questionnaire, nationally representative samples, and the same procedures for obtaining and interviewing subjects. While many comparative problems would remain, they would be minimized. Unfortunately, the first attempt at a large-scale cross-national, self-report study—the ISRD—falls short of this ideal.

The International Self-Report Delinquency Study (ISRD)

The ISRD was conducted in twelve studies in these nations: Belgium, Finland, Germany, Greece, New Zealand, Portugal, Spain, Switzerland, Italy, the United Kingdom, the Netherlands, and the United States.[2] Within the United Kingdom, studies were conducted in England, Wales, and Northern Ireland. New Zealand and West Germany used only part of the common questionnaire and had considerably different sampling frames, so they are not strictly comparable to the other studies (Junger-Tas, 1994).

The ISRD questionnaire evolved over a series of pilot studies and involved considerable negotiation and compromise before the nations reached a consensus (Junger-Tas, 1994; Klein, 1994). The ISRD instrument was developed from the most carefully designed self-report instrument available, the National Youth Survey questionnaire developed by Elliott and his associates (Elliott, Huizinga, & Ageton, 1985). It has been argued that for self-report data to be useful, the questionnaire must parallel legal codes, while remaining comprehensible to respondents (e.g., Albrecht, 1989; Elliott & Huizinga, 1989).

This is very difficult in a cross-national study, as legal codes, languages, and respondents vary substantially. The ISRD instrument used a common core operationalization of delinquent behavior, including only acts which would be considered crimes if committed by adults in all participating nations. This first ISRD included only Western nations, so economic, social, and cultural variations that might result in differential understandings and interpretations of questions were limited.

The ISRD instrument covered five groups of variables: (1) prevalence and frequency of offending, (2) circumstances of delinquent acts, (3) social reactions to delinquent acts, (4) social and demographic variables, and (5) theoretical variables related to social control theory. Several nations performed reliability tests—repeating earlier questions at the end of the interview—and found high levels of reliability (Junger-Tas, Klein, & Zhang, 1992). In order to maximize validity, care was taken to have high item specificity, and filtering questions were used prior to going into the exact details of the delinquent act and its circumstances (Junger-Tas, 1994). Despite these precautions, the possibility of respondents from different nations interpreting questions differently must be considered as possibly biasing results. This will become a greater problem if and when the study is expanded to include non-Western and developing nations.

Ideally, the ISRD would have used nationally representative samples in all nations. However, only four nations had sufficient funds for nationally representative samples: Portugal, Switzerland, the Netherlands, and the United Kingdom. Spain used a stratified national sample of cities. Two studies were conducted in only one city in the nation involved—Mannheim, Germany and Belfast, Northern Ireland. Two studies were in one city only and used school samples—Omaha, the United States and Helsinki, Finland. In Italy, school samples were used in three cities: Genoa, Messina, and Siena. In Liege, Belgium, a mixed school and random sample was completed. A cohort study was conducted in Dunedin, New Zealand. Nonscientific surveys using only part of the core questionnaire were conducted in East and West Germany.

The age range of the populations from which respondents were sampled also differed among the various studies. In some studies the youngest subjects were fourteen, while in others they were fifteen. The upper age limit ranged from eighteen to twenty-one. Those nations that used school samples would miss those who quit school at younger ages, and they would likely systematically differ in their delinquent behaviors from those who remain in school.

The amount and types of delinquent behavior by juveniles probably vary by age, city versus noncity residence, and school versus nonschool population. Thus, the samples from the different nations in the ISRD are not strictly comparable. Some nations used various methods to increase the number of high-risk juveniles in samples, while others did not. This further increases the lack of comparability of some samples.

Past research on self-report surveys indicates that response rates vary between juveniles who have and have not had prior contact with police and/or the juvenile justice system (e.g., Angenent, 1984; Veendrick, 1976). Contact with the juvenile justice system might vary across nations independent of delinquent behavior, which would result in systematic differences in the types of juveniles responding to surveys in different nations. There might also be social, cultural, and economic differences among juveniles from different nations which systematically influence how many and which type of juveniles respond to the survey. The large degree of variation in response rates among nations—61 to 98 percent—also gives reason for concern (Junger-Tas, 1994).

Information in the ISRD studies was collected on all potential respondents, so comparisons could be made between those who did and did not respond. Nonresponse can then be analyzed with respect to such variables as race, age, gender, and socio-economic status, and then taken into account in models making cross-national comparisons.

The mode of data collection also differed among the nations surveyed. Some surveys used face-to-face interviews, some were self-administered, and others a mix of the two. As past research indicates the mode of interview may not greatly influence responses; differences in the mode may not greatly affect cross-national comparisons either (Hindelang, Hirschi, & Weis, 1981).

When the ISRD data from Finland, the Netherlands, and the United States were compared to self-report data from other sources, a high degree of similarity was found in all three nations (Junger-Tas, 1994). Delinquency prevalence rates, the social distribution of delinquency, and the correlates of delinquency were found to be similar in all the nations (Junger-Tas, 1994).

Thus, despite the differences in sample frames, response rates, data collection techniques, and so on, the ISRD data appear to be quite robust. Still, it is clear that the many differences among the studies limit the types of research for which the data can be used.

Direct cross-national comparisons of the prevalence and incidence of self-reported delinquency—and analysis of the national characteristics that explain variations in these—should probably be restricted to the four nations that used nationally representative samples. Comparisons across nations of the correlates and spatial distribution of delinquency within nations can be done if results are interpreted with care, taking into consideration differing sample frames and response patterns. Subunits within national studies, such as, urban areas, can be used to increase comparability among nations. Disaggregation and reaggregation of data might also be done to enhance the comparability of data. Differences among studies might also be entered into explanatory models as variables, for example, whether a school sample was used.

Thus far the ISRD data have not been made available to researchers outside those involved in the original studies. Their analyses have been restricted to within-nation distributions and correlates of delinquent behavior, although there have been some cross-national comparisons of these results. The research is reported in *Delinquent Behavior Among Young People in the Western World: First Results of the International Self-Report Delinquency Study* (Junger-Tas, Terlouw, & Klein, 1994). More complex cross-national comparisons are underway, and a second book with the results of these should be available by the time this book is in print. The ISRD data will be made generally available after their publication in the second book.

As the ISRD data constitute the only cross-national self-report crime data that can be used for comparisons of a number of nations, self-report crime data lag behind official and victimization crime data in both quality and quantity. ISRD data are available for only a small number of nations, all Western. Official and victimization data for these same nations are likely to be of higher quality than the self-report data, and data are available for many more nations. As there has been only one ISRD, no analysis of delinquency trends can be done, while both official and victimization data allow for some trend analysis.

This pioneering effort in cross-national self-report research should set the stage for better work in the future, wherein many of the problems and errors in the ISRD are eliminated or controlled. However, just as in official and victimization data, some problems are inherent in the method and the nature of national differences. International self-report data will probably always be limited to juveniles, given the many problems in getting acceptable adult samples and responses, and given that it is generally young adults who commit the most serious offenses. Also, self-report research cannot provide data for cross-national comparisons of the most serious offenses, particularly homicides. And yet these are crimes of most concern to the citizens of most nations. The sampling, response, interpretation problems, and so on, will be amplified if the studies are extended to developing and non-Western nations.

Self-report data do tap dimensions of the crime problems of nations that official and victimization data cannot. Also, by providing substantial information on offenders and the circumstances of offenses, self-report data can most directly address the questions of who commits crimes and why, which are central to most research. They also provide information on such important issues as age at onset of offending, specialization versus general-ization in offending, chronic versus casual offenders, and so forth.

There is currently discussion about replicating the ISRD or even making it a regular event. Future surveys should include more nations and improve on standardization of sampling frames and modes. Some analysis of the ISRD results has revealed problems in the application of certain items (Junger-Tas, 1994). More psychometric work is underway to evaluate and improve the instrument. If future ISRD studies are conducted, they will use a refined and improved survey instrument.

Some nations have used the survey instrument on their own in national surveys (Poland, Hungary, Cyprus, Malta, the Czech Republic, Sweden, Estonia, and the Dutch Antilles), and more nations are considering its use. Whether the data from these surveys can be coordinated with other ISRD data remains to be seen.

NOTES

1. For a more critical and complete discussion of the IVS data and methodology, see the Travis et al. (1995) article. While the article is in response to an IVS report that Australia ranks first among industrialized nations in sexual crimes, it is a thorough and highly critical review of the shortcomings of the IVS.

2. For a more complete discussion of the methodology used in the ISRD, see Junger-Tas (1994).

REFERENCES

Albrecht, H-J. (1989). Comparative research on crime and delinquency: The role and relevance of national penal codes and criminal justice systems. In M. W. Klein (Ed.), *Cross-national research in self-reported crime and delinquency* (pp. 227–248). Norwell, MA: Kluwer Academic Publications.

Angenent, M. (1984). Medewerking aan enquetes over niet-geregistreerde criminal-iteit. *Tiljkschrift Voor Criminologie*, 6.

Baerveldt, C. (1987). *School en delinquentie*. The Hague: WODC (Ministerie of Just-itie).

Beirne, P. & Messerschmidt, J. (1991). *Criminology*. San Diego, CA: HBJ.

Beirne, P. & Perry, B. (1994). Criminal victimization in the industrialized world. *Crime, Law, & Social Change*, 21, 155–165.

Bennett, R. (1991). Development and crime: A cross-national, time-series analysis of competing models. *The Sociological Quarterly*, 32, 343–363.

Bennett, R. & Wiegand, R. (1994). Observations on crime reporting in a developing nation. *Criminology*, 32 (1), 135–148.

Block, R. (Ed.). (1984). *Victimization and fear of crime: World perspectives.* Washington, D.C.: U.S. Department of Justice.

Block, R. (1992). Comparing national surveys of victims of crime. *International Journal of Victimology*, 1–20.

Block, R. (1993). Measuring victimisation: The effects of methodology, sampling, and fielding. In A. Alvazzi del Frate, U. Zvekic, & J. van Dijk (Eds.), *Understanding crime: Experiences of crime and crime control* (pp. 163–175). Rome, Italy: UNICRI.

Braithwaite, J. (1989). The state of criminology: Theoretical decay of renaissance. *Australian and New Zealand Journal of Criminology*, 22, 129–135.

Brillon, Y. (1975). Justice pénale moderne et traditionnelle en Côte d'Ivoire. *Internationale Journal de Criminologie et de Police Technique*, XXVII (3).

Cernovich, S. A., Giordano, P. C., & Pugh, M. D. (1985). Chronic offenders: The missing cases in self-report delinquency research. *Journal of Criminal Law and Criminology*, 76 (3), 705–732.

Clark, J. P., & Tifft, L. L. (1966). Polygraph and interview validation of self-reported deviant behavior. *American Sociological Review*, 31, 516–523.

Clinard, M. B. (1978). Comparative crime victimization surveys: Some problems and results. *International Journal of Criminology and Penology*, 6, 221–231.

Clinard, M. B. & Abbott, D. (1973). *Crime in developing countries: A comparative perspective.* New York: John Wiley & Sons.

Crawford, A., Jones, T., Woodhouse, T., & Young, T. (1992). Second Islington crime survey. In R. Matthews & J. Young (Eds.), *Issues in realist criminology.* Newbury Park, CA: Sage.

de Leeuw, E. D. & van der Zouwen, J. (1988). Data quality in telephone and face-to-face surveys: Comparative meta-analysis. In R. M. Groves, P. P. Biemer, L. E. Lyberg, J. T. Massey, W. L. Nichols II, & J. Waksberg (Eds.), *Telephone survey methodology* (pp. 283–299). New York: John Wiley & Sons.

Dillman, D. A. & Tarnai, J. (1988). Administrative issues in mixed mode surveys. In R. M. Groves, P. P. Biemer, L. E. Lyberg, J. T. Massey, W. L. Nichols II, & J. Waksberg (Eds.), *Telephone survey methodology* (p. 520). New York: John Wiley & Sons.

Elliott, D. S. & Ageton, S. (1980). Reconciling race and class differences in self-reported and official estimates of delinquency. *American Sociological Review*, 45, 95–110.

Elliott, D. S. & Huizinga, D. (1983). Social class and delinquent behavior in a national youth panel. *Criminology*, 21, 149–177.

Elliott, D. S. & Huizinga, D. (1989). Improving self-reported measures of delinquency. In M. W. Klein (Ed.), *Cross-national research in self-reported crime and delinquency* (pp. 155–186). Norwell, MA: Kluwer Academic Publications.

Elliott, D. S., Huizinga, D., & Ageton, S. (1985). *Explaining delinquency and drug use.* Beverly Hills, CA: Sage.

Elliott, D. S., Huizinga, D., & Morse, B. (1987). Self-reported violent offending. *Journal of Interpersonal Violence*, 1, 472–514.

Elliott, D. S. & Voss, H. L. (1974). *Delinquency and dropout.* Lexington, MA: D. C. Heath.

Erickson, M. L. & Empey, L. T. (1963). Court records, undetected delinquency, and decision-making. *Journal of Criminal Law, Criminology, and Police Science*, 54, 456–469.

Glenn, H. (1988). Multiple victiminzation. In M. Maguire & J. Pointing (Eds.), *Victims of crime: A new deal?* (pp. 90–100). Philadelphia, PA: Open University Press.

Gold, M. (1970). *Delinquency behavior in an American city.* Belmont, CA: Wadsworth.

Hagan, J., Gillis, A. R., & Simpson, J. (1985). The class structure of gender and delinquency: Toward a power-control theory of common delinquent behavior. *American Journal of Sociology*, 90, 1151–1178.

Hagan, J., Gillis, A. R., & Simpson, J. (1987). Class in the household: A power-control theory of gender and delinquency. *American Journal of Sociology*, 92, 788–816.

Hanmer, J. & Saunders, S. (1984). *Well-founded fear: A community study of violence to women.* London: Hutchinson.

Hindelang, M. J., Hirschi, T., & Weis, J. (1979). Correlates of delinquency: The illusion of discrepancy between self-report and official measures. *American Sociological Review*, 44, 995–1014.

Hindelang, M. J., Hirschi, T., & Weis, J. (1981). *Measuring delinquency.* Beverly Hills, CA: Sage.

Hirschi, T. (1969). *Causes of delinquency.* Berkeley, CA: University of California Press.

Hirschi, T., Hindelang, M. J., & Weis, J. (1980). The status of self-report measures. In M. W. Klein & K. Teilmann (Eds.), *Handbook of criminal justice* (pp. 473–488). Beverly Hills, CA: Sage.

Hubble, D. L. & Wilder, B. E. (1988). *Preliminary results from the National Crime Survey CATI experiment.* Proceedings of the American Statistical Association Section on Survey Methods Research, New Orleans, LA.

Jensen, G. F. & Rojek, D. S. (1992). *Delinquency and youth crime.* Prospect Heights, IL: Waveland Press.

Junger-Tas, J. (1977). Hidden delinquency and judicial selection in Belgium. In P. C. Friday & V. L. Stewart (Eds.), *Youth crime and juvenile justice* (pp. 70–94). New York: Praeger.

Junger-Tas, J. (1989). Self-report delinquency research in Holland with a perspective on international comparisons. In M. W. Klein (Ed.), *Cross-national research in self-reported crime and delinquency* (pp. 17–42). Norwell, MA: Kluwer Academic Publications.

Junger-Tas, J. (1994). The international self-report delinquency study: Some methodological and theoretical issues. In J. Junger-Tas, G. J. Terlouw, & M. W. Klein (Eds.), *Delinquent behavior among young people in the Western world* (pp. 1–14). New York: Kluger Publications.

Junger-Tas, J., Klein, M. W., & Zhang, X. (1992). *Problems and dilemmas in comparative self-report delinquency research.* Manuscript submitted for publication.

Junger-Tas, J., Terlouw, G. J., & Klein, M. W. (Eds.). (1994). *Delinquent behavior among young people in the Western world: First results of the International Self-Report Delinquency study.* New York: Kluger Publications.

Kaiser, G., Kury, H., & Albrecht, H. J. with the assistance of H. Arnold. (1991). *Victims and criminal justice.* Freiburg, Germany: Max Planck Institute.

Kick, E. & LaFree, G. (1985). Development and the social context of murder and theft. *Comparative Social Research,* 8, 37–57.

Killias, M. (1990). New methodological perspectives for victimization surveys: The potentials of computer-assisted telephone surveys and some related innovations. *International Victim,* 154.

Klein, M. W. (1986). Labeling theory and delinquency policy: An experimental test. *Criminal Justice and Behavior,* 13, 47–79.

Klein, M. W. (1989). Epilogue: Workshop discussion. In M. W. Klein (Ed.), *Cross-national research in self-reported crime and delinquency* (pp. 425–438). Norwell, MA: Kluwer Academic Publications.

Klein, M. W. (1994). Epilogue. In J. Junger-Tas, G. J. Terlouw, & M. W. Klein (Eds.), *Delinquent behavior among young people in the Western world* (pp. 381–386). New York: Kluger Publications.

LaFree, G. & Birkbeck, C. (1991). The neglected situation: A cross-national study of the situational characteristics of crime. *Criminology,* 29 (1), 73–98.

LaFree, G. & Kick, E. (1986). Cross-national effects of developmental, distributional, and demographic variables on crime: A review and analysis. *International Annals of Criminology,* 24, 213–235.

Lynch, J. (1993). Secondary analysis of international crime survey data. In A. Alvazzi del Frate, U. Zvekic, & J. van Dijk (Eds.), *Understanding crime: Experiences of crime and crime control* (pp. 175–192). Rome, Italy: UNICRI.

Lynch, J. (1995). Crime in international perspective. In J. Q. Wilson & J. Petersilia (Eds.), *Crime* (pp. 11–38). San Francisco, CA: ICS Press.

Marshall, I. H. (1996). How exceptional is the United States? Crime trends in Europe and the United States. *European Journal on Criminal Policy and Research,* 4 (2), 7–34.

Mayhew, P. (1993). Research issues. In A. Alvazzi del Frate, U. Zvekic, & J. van Dijk (Eds.), *Understanding crime: Experiences of crime and crime control* (pp. 381–85). Rome, Italy: UNICRI.

Mutsaers, M. (1987). Experiment criminaliteitspreventie in het LBO. *Justiele erkenningen,* June.

Newman, G. (1976). *Comparative deviance: Perception and law in six cultures.* New York: Elsevier.

Nye, F. I. & Short, J. (1957). Scaling delinquent behavior. *American Sociological Review,* 22, 326–331.

Porterfield, A. L. (1943). Delinquency and its outcome in court and college. *American Journal of Sociology,* 49 (3), 199–208.

Priyadarsini, S. & Hartjen, C. (1981). Delinquency and corrections in India. In G. F. Jensen (Ed.), *The sociology of delinquency* (pp. 109–123). Beverly Hills, CA: Sage.

Reiss, A. J. & Rhodes, A. L. (1959). *A socio-psychological study of adolescent conformity and deviation.* Report to the United States Office of Education.

Reiss, A. J. & Roth, J. A. (1993). *Understanding and preventing violence.* Washington, D.C.: National Academy Press.

Reuband, K. H. (1989). On the use of self-reports in measuring crime among adults: Methodological problems and prospects. In M. W. Klein (Ed.), *Cross-national research in self-reported crime and delinquency* (pp. 89–106). Norwell, MA: Kluwer Academic Publications.

Shichor, D. (1990). Crime patterns and socioeconomic development: A cross-national analysis. *Criminal Justice Review,* 15 (1), 64–78.

Skogan, W. (1981). *Issues in the measurement of victimization.* Washington, D.C.: Bureau of Justice Statistics.

Skogan, W. (1986). Methodological issues in the study of victimization. In E. Fattah (Ed.), *From crime policy to victim policy: Reorienting the justice system* (pp. 80–116). Basingstoke, England: Macmillan.

Skogan, W. (1992). *Innovations in the analysis of crime surveys.* Paper presented at conference on Measurement and Research Design in Criminal Justice, Griffith University, Queensland, Australia.

Sparks, R. F. (1992). *Research on victims of crime: Accomplishments, issues, and new directions.* Rockville, MD: U. S. Department of Health and Human Services.

Travis, G., Egger, S., O'Toole, B., Brown, D., Hogg, R., & Stubbs, J. (1995). The International Crime Surveys (ICS): Some methodological concerns. *Current Issues in Criminal Justice,* 6 (3), 346–361. (N.B.: ICS = IVS)

UNICRI. (1996). *International (crime) victim survey.* Rome, Italy: Author.

van Dijk, J. (1991). *The international crime survey (ICS): Some organisational and methodological issues and results.* Leiden, Netherlands: Criminological Institute of Leiden University.

van Dijk, J. & Mayhew, P. (1993). Criminal victimisation in the industrialised world: Key findings of the 1989 and 1992 international crime surveys. In A. Alvazzi del Frate, U. Zvekic, and J. van Dijk (Eds.), *Understanding crime: Experiences of crime and crime control* (pp. 1–50). Rome, Italy: UNICRI.

van Dijk, J., Mayhew, P., & Killias, M. (1990). *Experiences of crime across the world: Key findings of the 1989 international crime survey.* Deventer, Netherlands: Kluwer.

van Dijk, J. & Zvekic, U. (1993). Surveying crime in the global village. In A. Alvazzi del Frate, U. Zvekic, & J. van Dijk (Eds.), *Understanding crime: Experiences of crime and crime control* (pp. 365–380). Rome, Italy: UNICRI.

Veendrick, L. (1976). *Verborgen en geregistreerde criminaliteit in Groningen.* Groningen, Netherlands: Criminologisch Instituut.

Young, J. (1988). Risk of crime and fear of crime: A realist critique of survey-based assumptions. In M. Maguire & J. Pointing (Eds.), *Victims of crime: A new deal?* (pp. 164–176). Philadelphia, PA: Open University Press.

Zvekic, U. & Alvazzi del Frate, A. (1995a). International crime survey in the developing world. In U. Zvekic & A. Alvazzi del Frate (Eds.), *Criminal victimization in the developing world* (pp. 3–14). Rome, Italy: UNICRI.

Zvekic, U. & Alvazzi del Frate, A. (1995b). Overview of the main findings. In U. Zvekic & A. Alvazzi del Frate (Eds.), *Criminal victimization in the developing world* (pp. 15–48). Rome, Italy: UNICRI.

II

Theoretical Perspectives
and Past Research

4

Theoretical Orientations

Any theoretical perspective that can guide research on crime within nations can also be used to guide research across nations, such as, strain, social disorganization, anomie, and control theories. This is true insofar as the concepts in these microlevel theories can be operationalized to indicate variation among nations across time and/or space. Research based on such perspectives can help us learn which national traits or trends are associated with variations in crime and crime patterns. The major advantages of such microlevel perspectives are that they suggest specific hypotheses, are based on a small set of concepts, and can be closely linked to empirical results.

Microlevel perspectives, however, do not explain why nations vary across time and/or space as to the traits and trends that are associated with crime. Thus, we might discover that variations in inequality are associated with cross-national crime variation and yet have no explanation of why inequality varies. For this, theories at a higher level of abstraction are needed.

Grand theories operate at this higher level of abstraction, assuming that the forces which influence crime apply similarly to all, or at least broad categories of, nations. They have been criticized, however, for presupposing universality and for ignoring the diversity of nations and their circumstances (Ember & Ember, 1995; Groves & Newman, 1989). The link between grand theories' highly abstract concepts and variables as they are operationalized is often unclear; it is a leap to conclude that empirical associations provide theoretical support. Microlevel theories provide a small set of concepts, which can be more closely tied to empirical observations.

This chapter discusses the two major grand theories that attempt to explain cross-national crime—modernization and dependency.[1] It also discusses the most important of the microlevel theoretical perspectives that have been used to explain cross-national crime variation.

GRAND THEORIES

Modernization Theory and Related Perspectives

The dominant grand theory addressing cross-national variation in crime has been modernization. With roots in Durkheimian thought, modernization theory is based on changes in crime patterns being associated with changes resulting from the modernization and development of nations. Durkheim (1964) proposed that development results in a more complex division of labor which weakens mechanic solidarity and the control of the collective conscience. The result is anomie and a normative system that no longer controls people's desire for material goods and creates systematic frustrations.

In the original formulation, anomie results from rapid social change which creates a cultural lag, as culture changes at a slower pace than technology (Ogburn, 1923, 1964). Eventually, anomie recedes as mechanic solidarity is replaced by organic solidarity which develops out of mutual interdependence. Thus, in this perspective, crime would be associated with the speed—rather than level—of development. In Durkheim's later work, organic solidarity never fully replaces the mechanic. So, in this perspective, some degree of anomie and thus increased crime become permanent features of developed nations (Durkheim, 1964, 1973).

While Durkheim's was not primarily a theory of crime, it would suggest rapid increases in crime as nations develop and permanently higher rates of crime once developed. In the last twenty-five years, Durkheim's general theory of social development has been used to devise a grand theory of cross-national crime variation called modernization theory (Clinard & Abbott, 1973; Shelley, 1981). This theoretical perspective explains cross-national crime in terms of industrialization, urbanization, and the resultant social disorganization and anomie.

Shelley's 1981 book *Crime and Modernization: The Impact of Industrialization and Modernization on Crime* is generally seen as the first full formulation of this theory (Shelley, 1981). In its perspective, all nations go through the same developmental stages and thus also the same changes in crime patterns. The developmental process and resultant changes in crime patterns which occurred in developed nations established a model for the relationship between crime and development applicable to all nations. Developing nations are seen as going through the same "natural" evolution as the developed nations did in the nineteenth century.

The societal forces of industrialization and urbanization are proposed to explain more about the pattern of property and violent crimes than do the unique features of individual nations or groups of nations. Development also systematically alters the nature of the offender population in terms of age, gender, and social class. Industrialization and urbanization disrupt traditional family and community patterns, weakening both formal and informal social controls. Of particular importance is the migration of many young people from a peasant, unskilled social world into a technically demanding one. Incoming migrants lack the cultural background to solve disputes nonviolently; and anomie, poverty, and unemployment breed property crimes.

As in Durkheim's work, both rapidity of change and level of development influence crime rates. Level of development is more important, as nations eventually reach a modern state with crime patterns permanently different from premodern times. Modernization theory has been widely criticized for its inability to explain trends in different types of crime, particularly regarding predictions of violent and property crime (e.g., Bennett, 1991; LaFree & Kick, 1986; Neuman & Berger, 1988). While Durkheim's work did not distinguish among different types of deviance, modernization theory has always distinguished between violent and property crime (Clinard & Abbott, 1973; Shelley, 1981).

The modernization perspective proposes that in the early stages of development all crime increases, as traditional structures of social integration and control break down. Violent crime increases due to the migration of rural youths to the city, who bring with them the tradition of settling disputes violently. Eventually, development of social equality and organic solidarity result in a large decline in violent crime, since it is associated with a rural way of life. Property crime continues to grow due to increasingly materialistic values, abundance of wealth, and material aspirations that outpace growth in affluence. Overall crime rates increase, with property crime being the dominant form; crime patterns and rates converge as nations converge in their economic and social structure (Clinard & Abbott, 1973; Shelley, 1981; Stack, 1982, 1984; Thome, 1992).

According to modernization perspective, poverty and crime are closely linked early in the developmental process. Eventually, however, rising material aspirations and values affect the entire society, and crime is committed by people in all social classes. There is also increased criminality by women and juveniles in the latter stages of development. This expanded pool of potential offenders further contributes to increased property crime. Thus, modernization theory predicts that development results in nations having greater amounts of total crime, increased property crime, decreased violent crime following a short-term increase, and a greatly increased ratio of property to violent crime.

More recently, modernization theory has been adapted to include insights from the routine activities or opportunity theoretical perspective (Cohen, 1982; Cohen & Felson, 1979). The basic predictions remain the same—development results in increased property and decreased violent crime—but the reasons for these are expanded and refined.[2] Opportunity theory does not attempt to explain variation in crime by differences or changes in social controls or motivating forces but rather in terms of differential opportunities (Cohen & Felson, 1979; Cohen, Felson, & Land, 1980; Felson & Cohen,

1980). Kick and LaFree (1985) adapted the ideas of opportunity theory to explain changes in the crime patterns of nations as they develop. Others have since used the same ideas in addressing cross-national variation in crime across time and space (e.g., Bennett, 1991; LaFree & Kick, 1986; Ortega, Corzine, Burnett, & Poyer, 1992).

The increasing economic prosperity which accompanies development is a key component of this perspective. Thefts increase as nations develop, largely because of the increase in desired, valuable, and portable commodities. Furthermore, the establishment of retailing institutions make these readily available to both consumers and thieves. Accompanying the increase in desired objects available for theft is a decrease in guardianship, as household size becomes smaller and people are away from home more often. Lastly, this theory suggests that as thieves generally commit their crimes against strangers (Belson, 1975; Petersilia, Greenwood, & Lavin, 1978; Repetto, 1974; West, 1978) and development results in increased impersonal contacts and short-term relationships, development also results in a social context conducive to theft. Thus, development is seen as contributing to increased thefts by: increasing availability of desired goods, reducing guardianship, and decreasing personal restraints.

Violent crime, particularly murder, is most frequently committed against people known to the offender, and most often intimates (Emovan & Lambo, 1978; Lundsgaarde, 1977; Wolfgang, 1966). Development lessens daily contact among intimates, as people spend more time outside the home. Geographic mobility and the impersonal nature of modern relationships reduce the number of intimates and close acquaintances, as does smaller family and household size (Kick & LaFree, 1985). Thus, development— resulting in fewer close relationships and less personal interaction time— should also result in less violent crime and fewer homicides (e.g., Wikström, 1985, 1992).

Combining the ideas of early modernization theory with the ideas of the opportunity perspective, current modernization theory explains both property and violent crimes in terms of social control, motivation, and opportunity. Social control is lessened by the normlessness and reduced collective conscience that accompany development, thus contributing to increased property and violent crime. Property crime is motivated by increased goals, materialistic values, and decreased fatalism about poverty and inequality. At the same time, the availability of desired goods increases and guardianship decreases, providing much greater opportunity for theft.

Interdependence eventually results in organic solidarity and increased respect for the individual, promoting social control of violent but not property crime. Development also reduces the motivation to commit violent acts by increasing social equality, and it reduces the opportunity for violent crimes by lessening interpersonal contact and relationships. Thus, development results in increased property and decreased violent crime.

Civilization theory can also be subsumed under the umbrella of the modernization perspective, although it is important to note that the former distinguishes between development and modernization (Elias, 1976; Heiland & Shelley, 1992).[3] In this perspective, nations might industrialize and urbanize but not modernize, as modernization includes political and cultural changes that do not necessarily accompany development. Still, the basic underlying hypothesis of this perspective is that the overall direction of change in all societies is toward becoming increasingly civilized, with differences only in the rate and degree of civilization.

The key hypothesis of civilization theory is that as nations modernize, structural changes engender personality changes, resulting in the control of individual behavior shifting from external sanctions to internal self-control (Elias, 1976, 1982; Heiland & Shelley, 1992). The expansion of capitalism produces an unprecedented degree of functional differentiation and mutual interdependency in the absence of intensive personal knowledge. Monopolization and centralization of state and economic power result in growing formal control as well as a stable and comprehensive arrangement for human action. People are free to act and pursue opportunities in society without interfering or conflicting with others.

Private vengeance and punishments are replaced with external systems of justice which are more restorative than vengeful (Braithwaite, 1989; Chesnais, 1992). A civilizing process takes place whereby impulsive, violent behavior becomes subject to internal constraints, informal controls, and formal systems of justice. Capitalism contributes to a reduction in violence because violence is dysfunctional for the operation of markets based on mutual trust. Furthermore, a high degree of self-control is an important resource for participation in capitalist markets and modern society. Shame becomes more important in crime control, as success is dependent on being held in high regard by others (Elias, 1976; Gurr, 1981).

Civilization theory proposes that the civilizing of the human personality and the internalization of constraint result in dramatic decreases in violence but increases in self-inflicted harm such as drug abuse. Also, civilized societies develop greater tolerance of deviant behavior, fewer and less severe sanctions in the criminal justice system, and decriminalization of penal law (van Dijk, 1989). Self-control and informal social control among individuals as well as a criminal justice system based on tolerance with a therapeutic orientation are all seen as "civilized" alternatives to the use of physical force and punishment.

Another theoretical perspective that can be subsumed under the modernization perspective is the currents of lethal violence or stream analogy. While this theoretical tradition predates Durkheim (Ferri, 1882; Morselli, 1879), it has been dormant until a recent revival (Unnithan, 1983; Unnithan & Whitt, 1992, 1994; Whitt, 1985). In this perspective, suicide and homicide are seen as two currents in a stream of lethal violence, with some variables affecting the size of the stream and others affecting which current is predominant. The two major dependent variables are the lethal violence rate (LVR—murders plus suicides) and the suicide-murder ratio (SMR—suicides divided by suicides plus murders).

The current version of the theory as described by Unnithan and Whitt (1992, 1994) proposes that inequality should be positively associated with the LVR because it contributes to frustration, increasing the overall stream of violence; it should be positively associated to the SMR because it diverts blame from self, thus increasing the proportion of violence expressed as homicides. Development is proposed to reduce inequality and thus contribute to a lower LVR. Development is also seen as increasing the sense that people control their own fates, which will increase the proportion of violence expressed as suicides and the SMR, as more violence will be internally directed. Development is further proposed to weaken social support systems, thus increasing suicide rates, the SMR, and the LVR. Development would reduce the LVR due to less inequality but also increase it due to less social support, and therefore should have a null effect on the LVR, while substantially increasing suicides and the SMR.

The basic explanations and predictions concerning the development-crime association are similar for all the foregoing theoretical perspectives, which is why all can be subsumed under the general modernization theory umbrella. Those that are concerned with property crimes—such as thefts—agree that as nations develop, property crime rates increase and will remain higher than they were prior to development. The original modernization perspective addresses both the process and rate of development—which creates social disruption and a cultural lag that contribute to property crimes—and the permanent conditions and values of modern nations that continue to motivate property crimes and also result in less social control. The opportunity perspective also proposes that the more developed a nation is, the more property crime it will have due to increased opportunities for such crimes.

All the foregoing perspectives addressing violent crime agree that as nations develop, they will experience declines in violent crimes—particularly homicides—and less violent crime should be a permanent feature of highly developed nations. The original modernization perspective sees violent crime increasing in the early stages of development but declining in the latter stages due to increased social equality and the development of organic solidarity. The stream analogy also proposes a reduction in violent crime due to the decreased inequality that should accompany modernization. The opportunity perspective proposes reduction in violence with development due to decreased opportunities. The civilization perspective suggests violence is lower in developed nations because such societies create arrangements that result in people having more internal control of violent tendencies.

Both the stream analogy and civilization perspective see development resulting in social changes that contribute to increases in self-inflicted harm. The stream analogy focuses on suicide, whereas civilization theory focuses on drug use.

Overall, the above theories predict permanently increased property crime, increased self-inflicted harm, and decreased violent crime as nations develop. Also, total crime should increase with development, due to the large increase in property crime as all social classes become involved.

The major criticism of the modernization perspective is its claim that all nations go through the same developmental process resulting in the same changes in crime patterns.[4] First, this ignores other possible sources of variation in crime across time and space that might be as, or more, important than the effects of development (Newman & Ferracuti, 1980). For example, two nations at similar stages of development might both experience increases in property crime as they develop, but there might still be a very great difference in the absolute rates of property crime or in the degree of increase. The amount of property crime in the nations and the degree of change may well be due to factors unrelated to modernization, even if modernization is responsible for increases in both nations.

A more severe criticism of the claim of similar developmental advancement of all nations is that it ignores historical specificity and the historical, cultural, and political traditions of nations (Groves & Newman, 1989; Shelley, 1986; Vagg, 1995). Nations currently developing are doing so in substantially different historical and situational contexts and with different traditions from the already developed nations and from each other. These conditions and traditions may result in development's having different effects on crime (Lopez-Rey, 1970; Sumner, 1982; Vagg, 1995; Zvekic, 1990). Development now is more rapid, thus creating a greater lag between industrialization and cultural change. Nations may develop economically yet not modernize in terms of political and cultural development. Urbanization and industrialization do not necessarily occur together. The age structure cannot adapt so quickly, resulting in a large proportion of the population in the high-crime age categories of adolesence and young adulthood.

Regarding civilization theory, Braithwaite (1993) has argued there is no unidirectional historical trend across all nations toward or away from shame-based social control. He notes that there are aspects of modernization that can contribute to both increased and decreased importance of shaming in crime control.

Arthur and Marenin (1995) have noted that modernization theory is both oversimplified and unclear as to what concepts it subsumes. Rogers (1989) argues that both development and crime are diverse and complex concepts, and the association between the two can take many forms, depending on historical and contextual terms.

Shelley (1986) herself, in reexamining modernization, acknowledged that the theory overstates the effect of urbanization and industrialization on crime patterns, particularly noting that developing nations are not following the same evolutionary model as developed nations. She also acknowledged that development has no consistent effects on the crimes of women and juveniles. She further stated that urbanization, industrialization, and modernization do not always proceed at the same pace—in some instances, changes in one realm might be very different from those in another. And finally, she suggested that focusing on more limited social changes may be more productive in explaining changes in crime patterns. She did still maintain that the impact of large-scale economic and social change on crime is of critical importance.

Dependency Theory

Dependency, the other major grand theory, argues that currently developing nations do so more in terms of external influences than internal ones as did the already developed nations.[5] More specifically, developing nations are dependent on and exploited by already developed nations. In contrast to modernization theory, nations do not move along a unilinear track toward development, with dependence and underdevelopment being temporary states. Exploitation, at the very least, results in more uneven development both within and across nations, creating inequalities which were not present when the developed nations modernized. This grand theory sees the dependence of developing nations on the developed as the central factor in the crime patterns of the former.

Dependency theory is largely based on a Marxist perspective on crime, wherein conventional crime is due to inequities resulting from class conflict and exploitation (Bonger, 1916). In this view, the real crimes of exploitation, oppression, and so on are not included in most analyses. Since this issue is beyond the scope of this book, whose focus is conventional crime, the discussion here is restricted to how dependency theory explains variation in conventional crimes across time and space. In recent years, dependency theory has incorporated the ideas of world system theory into explanations of cross-national crime variation. Dependency theory mainly focuses on the internal processes of dependence, whereas world system theory is more concerned with the broader world economic order.

In the dependency perspective, development remains the key factor in explaining the differing crimes rates of nations across space and time. However, development is not seen as having similar effects in all nations, and consideration must be given to the historical and situational context of development (Greenberg, 1981; Sumner, 1982). The different conditions of currently developing nations result in very different associations between development and crime. Nations currently developing are dependent on the technology, products, and consumer demand of developed nations (Vagg, 1995).

The dependency perspective argues that the analysis of crime in developing nations must begin with colonialism, its consequences, and the continuing dependence of developing nations on the developed (Lopez-Rey, 1970; Quinney, 1977; Sumner, 1982). The spread of the capitalist mode of production and accompanying exploitation is seen as driving development in developing nations. In the world system perspective, the uneven advance of global capitalism produces three categories of nations: core, periphery, and semiperiphery (Wallerstein, 1974).

The core contains the highly developed nations, the periphery contains the economically dependent and least developed nations, and the semiperiphery contains the partially developed nations which serve as an economic and political buffer between the core and periphery. Development in nations now developing—particularly those in the periphery—is not internally driven as in the past. Rather, it is driven externally through exploitation by the core nations (Evans, 1979; Frank, 1969; Mandel, 1977; Sumner, 1982; Walton, 1982).

Core nations—through multinational corporations—exploit periphery nations for raw materials and cheap labor. So the surplus created by development is removed from these nations, rather than remaining internal as was the case with already developed nations (Mandel, 1977; Sumner, 1982, Vagg, 1995). Development is much more uneven than in the past, with substantial inequality created both within and across nations. Core nations make alliances with elites in periphery nations to promote economic, political, and monetarist policies that exploit and penalize the poor while making the elites quite wealthy. Shivji (1976:114) has referred to this as the "development of underdevelopment," wherein the majority of the population is worse off than they were prior to capitalist-driven development.

In this view, crime in developing nations results from the poverty, inequality, and political oppression that accompany development which is based on exploitation and dependency (Platt & Takagi, 1981; Quinney, 1977; Schwendinger & Schwendinger, 1970, 1983; Sumner, 1982). Crime is the product of the economic and social miseries produced by capitalist exploitation and the continuing influence of colonialism.

As in classic Marxist theory, the economic realm influences all other segments of society. Thus, development in these nations is seen as causing cultural alienation, a spiritual malaise, values of selfishness, and political oppression—all of which also contribute to criminal behavior (Arthur & Marenin, 1995; Chambliss, 1974; Quinney, 1977; Schwendinger & Schwendinger, 1970, 1983; Sumner, 1982). Capitalism is seen as breeding individualistic value systems, acquisitiveness, and competition, which directly contribute to crime. It further indirectly increases crime by encouraging abuse of the power of local elites and their international sponsors. The criminal justice system—developing out of colonialism, exploitation, and the neocolonial order—is also seen as protecting the elites and treating the poor unjustly (Adeyemi, 1990; Baxi, 1990; van Onselen, 1976). This leads to disrespect for the law and the settlement of disputes outside the legal system (Queloz, 1990; Sumner, 1982).

Three forms of crime are generated by inequities in developing nations: crimes of accommodation, interpersonal violence, and crimes of rebellion (Gurr, Grabosky, & Hula, 1977; Michalowski, 1985; Quinney, 1977). These are crimes generated in the subordinate classes and do not include crimes of the elites.

Crimes of accommodation include property and entrepreneurial offenses—such as, drug sales, prostitution, and gambling—and are motivated by the desire for survival and material goods among people who lack legal access to these. Interpersonal violence—such as, murder, rape, and assault—is the result of frustration and misdirected anger created by deprivation and demoralizing living conditions (Balkan, Berger, & Schmidt, 1980; Blau & Blau, 1982; Messner, 1989; Quinney, 1977). Crimes of rebellion are illegal political actions—such as, protests, riots, and strikes—that result from frustration and alienation. These include both irrational and rational attempts to promote class interests and redress grievances.

A major problem with crime theories derived from a Marxist conflict orientation is the difficulty of operationalizing variables and the resultant lack of empirical verification. On the one hand, dependency theory is based on a nation's place in the economic order of the world and its economic dependency on other nations. Thus, predicted associations to crime should involve inequality among nations regarding the degree of underdevelopment, the amount of debt, import/export ratios, penetration by multinational corporations, and so forth. On the other hand, dependency has more commonly been interpreted as predicting an association between the results of dependency—not dependency itself—and crime (Neuman & Berger, 1988). Thus, the key causal variable has been economic inequality within nations, which is seen as resulting from capitalist exploitation, uneven expansion, and resultant class divisions. At the micro level, dependency theory sees inequality as a primary causal variable and proposes that it increases as the capitalist mode of production penetrates developing nations. Modernization theory considers inequality of secondary importance and proposes that it decreases as nations develop economically and otherwise.

It is not clear in the general dependency perspective what role absolute poverty should play in explaining cross-national variation in crime. Which should have higher crime rates—the least-developed nations with the lowest standards of living or those nations that have begun to develop and become more capitalist? Is the number of people living in absolute poverty or a nation's degree of relative inequality of greater importance? Does it matter if the poor and/or relatively deprived live in urban or rural areas? Not only are these difficult empirical questions to answer, but also it is not clear what dependency theory would predict.

Even if national variation in traits such as inequality, poverty, and so forth are found to be associated with crime, it does not necessarily mean these traits primarily result from dependency on and exploitation by other nations. Full support for dependency theory would need to show that dependency and exploitation result in inequality and poverty, which in turn result in crime. A full test of dependency theory would also require operationalizing variables to indicate amounts of political oppression and/or mobilization. The former should be positively associated to crime and the latter negatively. Both, in turn, should be associated with economic exploitation and dependency. Most difficult to operationalize would be variables indicating cross-national variation in such values as self-interest and materialism, which are proposed to accompany capitalism and contribute to crime.

Heiland and Shelley (1992) suggest that a theoretical orientation be developed around the triad of modernization, civilization, and centralization of power in government and the corporate world. They suggest that the power dimension and conflicts between national elites and the powerless will complement development approaches and enhance understanding of changing patterns and levels of crime. They see this as providing a macrostructural explanatory framework, the starting point for an improved conceptual orientation to explaining cross-national crime.

OTHER PERSPECTIVES

Culture and Historical Traditions

While it is generally accepted that there is a relationship between development and crime, it is also generally accepted there is no universal theoretical framework to explain and predict this relationship in all nations (Queloz, 1990; Vagg, 1995; Zvekic, 1990). It is quite likely this is because development takes place in nations which vary substantially in their histories and cultural configurations. The cultural context is likely to influence crime both directly and indirectly by moderating how crime is affected by modernization and/or dependency. Cultural explanations of crime variation do not constitute a unified theory as do modernization and dependency. Rather, they provide a number of perspectives which are similar due to their concern with culture over structure.

In both modernization and dependency orientations, local cultural traditions and ideologies are seen as secondary to long-term economic processes and resultant social changes. In modernization theory, they are seen as being of little importance relative to the overriding effects of development; in dependency theory, precedence is given to the changing place of nations in the world order and their economic relationships.

Cultural norms, values, and ideologies can directly influence national crime rates by motivating and facilitating criminal behaviors, as well as by mediating the effects of development and structural variables. Shelley (1986) herself has acknowledged that modernization theory both exaggerated the universality of the effects of urbanization and industrialization on crime and underestimated the importance of historical and cultural traditions in explaining crime. A number of analysts have argued that the cultural effects of colonization and exploitation of developing nations may be as important in causing crime as the economic effects (e.g., Adeyemi, 1990; Hafercamp & Ellis, 1992; Neapolitan, 1994; Schwendinger & Schwendinger, 1983).

While modernization and dependency perspectives focus primarily on changes in crime patterns and rates, cultural perspectives focus more on consistency of rates and national variations over time. Cultural traditions develop and are shaped slowly through the historical experiences of nations and are then transmitted from generation to generation. As Shaw and McKay (1942) have noted, the norms and values conducive to crime can outlive the circumstances which created them. For example, one nation may have a homicide rate of around 2/100,000 and another around 7/100,000. Both may change due to development and/or dependency, yet one remains substantially higher than the other due to long-term cultural differences. Of course, culture and transmitted norms change, but generally this occurs much more slowly than structural changes.

Culture influences crime in two ways. Nations may differ in having norms that motivate, allow, or even prescribe certain crimes as responses to certain situations, problems, or conflicts. Nations may also differ in having integrated systems of norms and values that control criminal behaviors and bind their people to the social order. While developmental and structural perspectives generally ignore the former effect, they do address changes in the latter, crime-controlling effect of culture.

A cultural perspective that addresses the integrative, controlling aspect of culture from stable—rather than changing—attributes of nations is called *synnomie* (Adler, 1983, 1996; Helal & Coston, 1991). This perspective has focused on nations with low crime rates and why they remain low throughout the course of development. The opposite of anomie, synnomie is the state of the sharing of norms and a system of social controls which assure such sharing.

In this view, nations have and maintain low crime rates because they maintain or create culturally harmonious social controls. These social controls not only preserve and transmit shared values, they also provide a strong sense of community and social support. In all cases, the social control agencies include the family and at least one other agency. Synnomie in a nation both directly controls criminal behavior and mediates the influence of factors which might otherwise result in cultural changes that would increase criminal behavior.

Nijboer (1995) has suggested that the overall guiding principal on which a nation is integrated may be a factor in the amount of crime in a nation. Specifically, he distinguishes between cultures which primarily emphasize guilt to exercise social control and those which primarily emphasize shame. And he suggests that the latter will experience more violent crime than the former.

Since the seminal work of Durkheim (1966), religious ecology has been considered not only a good indicator of cultural variation among nations but also a factor related to crime and deviance within nations. Most theoretical linking of religious ecology to crime has used concepts which relate to social integration and anomie. Christianity, particularly Protestantism, is seen as fostering cultures with an emphasis on individualism, or more descriptively what Tocqueville (1956) called "competitive individualism." This undermines solidarity and social cohesion, which, in turn, results in higher criminality in Protestant/Christian nations (Groves, McCleary, & Newman, 1985; Groves, Newman, & Corrado, 1987; Haferkamp & Ellis, 1992).

Conversely, Islamic religions are seen as fostering cultures which value tradition, community, and a unified collective conscience (Groves, McCleary, & Newman, 1985; Groves, Newman, & Corrado, 1987; Newman, 1976). Thus, nations which are strongly Islamic are predicted to have less criminal behavior than other nations. Haferkamp and Ellis (1992) similarly argue that the low crime rates in Japan are largely due to the religious traditions of Buddhism, Shinto, Taoism, and Confucianism, all of which emphasize the importance of community and social obligation over individualism and freedom.

Souryal (1987, 1990) goes even further, arguing that the Islamic nations, such as Saudi Arabia, which use Shariah law should have even lower crime rates than other Islamic nations. According to Souryal, basing the laws of a nation on divine law contributes to a unified set of beliefs and norms that permeate the culture, creating a noncriminogenic environment. Hansmann and Quigley (1982) have conversely argued that an excessive religious homogeneity can result in too high a level of social integration and too powerful a collective conscience. This fosters low respect for the value of any single person and strong social passions. The predicted result is more homicides in nations with homogenous, permeating religious ecologies.

Culture has more often been theoretically linked to violent than property crime. The dominant perspective is that violence breeds violence. Thus, legitimate or official violence such as warfare or capital punishment is proposed to contribute to criminal violence through modeling, norm creation, and desensitization (Bowers, 1984; Ember & Ember, 1995; Gartner, 1990; Landau & Pfefferman, 1988). Similarly, violence in developing nations is theoretically linked to their violent histories of colonization, slavery, oppression, and postcolonial violence (Ferguson & Whitehead, 1992; Haferkamp & Ellis, 1992; Messerschmidt, 1993; Neapolitan, 1994).

Others have argued that it is not simply the violence of colonization that contributes to crime in developing nations but also the destruction of the indigenous culture and traditional methods of social control (Brillon, 1986; Greenberg, 1981; Neapolitan, 1997; Sumner, 1982). Arthur (1991) calls this perspective flawed in that many developing nations—particularly in the Caribbean and South America—have high crime rates and yet are not recent victims of colonization. However, this ignores the enduring aspects of culture which can be transmitted over many generations, even when the conditions creating these aspects are no longer present. It also ignores the postcolonial oppression and violence which resulted from colonial oppression and continuing external interference.

Hansmann and Quigley (1982) have argued that the moral authority of a culture and the sanctions and social controls it supports can lose strength when its people are continually exposed to other cultures. They suggest that this is particularly true if the other cultures are perceived as superior. This is, of course, the situation generally created by colonization and subjugation. Neapolitan (1997) has suggested that the destruction of the indigenous religious institution is of particular importance in loss of social control, as religion is central to the culture and moral authority of tribal peoples.

Cultural variation among nations has also been suggested to contribute to variation in rape rates. One perspective argues that cultural norms and values which devalue women and support male dominance contribute to rapes in such nations (Baron & Straus, 1989; Brownmiller, 1975; Cherry, 1983). The cultural orientation of excessive masculinity generally known as *machismo* has also been linked to colonization (Messerschmidt, 1993; Neapolitan, 1994; Rivera, 1978). Another cultural perspective suggests that sexually permissive norms contribute to male sexual frustration and thus increased rapes (Chappell, 1989). This would suggest, for example, that Islamic nations have fewer rapes.

While the general cultural theories of synnomie and individualism apply to all types of crime, there has been little direct linking of culture specifically to property crimes. It is generally acknowledged in both modernization theory and dependency theory that development, particularly capitalist-driven development, contributes to more materialistic values and goals (Clinard & Abbott, 1973; Shelley, 1981; Sumner, 1982). Sklair (1991) specifically suggests that the spreading of Western culture through global capitalism contributes to the creation of a culture of consumerism and greed. Shichor (1990) proposes that the importance placed on the consumption of material possessions is associated with the amount of thefts in a nation.

A major problem with all cultural approaches to crime is finding ways to measure and operationalize cultural values and context (see Chapter 7). Even if a way is found to indicate cultural traits and their variation, the sources of cultural traits may be impossible to identify. As noted earlier, culture is developed and transmitted over long periods of time and therefore may be long divorced from the events which created many of its aspects.

Microlevel Perspectives

The earlier grand theories clearly suggest a number of microlevel theories and concepts. As noted, the link between empirical results and grand theories is not always clear. Thus, it may be better to approach explaining cross-national crime variation by focusing on the microlevel concepts without reference to a grand theory. Much of the research on cross-national crime has been guided by the inequality, relative deprivation perspective (Blau, 1977; Blau & Blau, 1982; Messner, 1980). From this perspective, inequality—generally indicated by income inequality—generates frustrations and desires which motivate criminal behavior.

Stack (1984) has proposed that inequality in nations should contribute to property crime, which is seen as a primitive form of income and wealth redistribution. He further suggests that the strength of this relationship will depend on whether the culture of a nation promotes the viewpoint that inequality is illegitimate.

Most theories and research linking inequality with cross-national crime variation have been concerned with violent crime. This perspective suggests economic inequality generates frustration, anger, and aggression, which are often expressed as violent crimes (Hansmann & Quigley, 1982; Krahn, Hartnagel, & Gartrell, 1986; Messner, 1980; Nettler, 1984). These crimes are often misdirected at those who are in people's immediate environment.

Other factors are seen as interacting with or exacerbating the effects of inequality on violent crime. Blau (1977) proposes diversity among people in a society has not only a vertical dimension—inequality—but also a horizontal one—heterogeneity. The latter includes areas that differentiate among people but do not rank them, such as, religion, race, ethnicity, and language.

It is suggested that people are inclined to feel antagonistic toward those who are culturally and/or physiologically different. Thus, horizontal heterogeneity contributes to interpersonal conflict (Blau, 1977; Hansmann & Quigley, 1982). When inequality is based on cultural, ethnic, or racial differences, the deprivation engendered by inequality is more salient and concentrated. It thus generates greater forces toward violent crime (Avison & Loring, 1986; Messner, 1989). Therefore, this perspective proposes that cultural heterogeneity and economic inequality have independent and interactive effects on violent crime. Stephens (1994) proposes that increased immigration, cultural pluralism, and political democratization have resulted in increased anomie and heterogeneity in many nations, and that this is the major reason for the recently increased crime in these nations.

Gartner (1990) has suggested focusing on various contexts relevant to explaining cross-national variation in crime rather than on a grand, all-encompassing theory. She specifically addresses violent crime, but the contexts can also be relevant to crime in general, with degree of relevance depending on the specific context. The four structural and cultural contexts are material, integrative, demographic, and cultural.

Some aspects of these contexts are relatively enduring in nations and thus should pertain primarily to cross-sectional variation in crime. Others vary over shorter periods and should be primarily associated with crime trends. Also, some aspects pertain more to factors that motivate crime, while others to those that control crime. All of these suggest a variety of concepts and variables which can be examined in relation to variation in crimes across time and space.

The material context involves primarily the economic aspects of nations, particularly inequality and poverty. This context is mainly concerned with motivations toward crime. The integrative context involves the concepts previously discussed in synnomie theory, that is, social integration, norm consensus, and so on. It is mainly concerned with social control preventing crime.

The demographic context involves factors such as age structure, as well as factors suggested by opportunity theory, that is, females in labor force, household size, and so on. This context primarily addresses opportunities to commit crimes rather than motivations or controls. Gartner (1990) does not distinguish opportunity as an approach separate from motivational and control approaches. Finally, the cultural context involves prescriptive and proscriptive norms which can encourage or discourage criminal behavior, respectively.

Other theorists attempt to explain cross-national variation in crimes involving specific categories of people. They focus on concepts directly relevant to the category of interest. For example, South and Messner (1986) propose that an undersupply of women in a nation increases their value and thus decreases their victimization. Fiala and LaFree (1988) suggest that crimes against children should be associated with female labor force participation that is not supported societally, as this combination creates stress that contributes to child abuse.

FINAL COMMENTS

Ideally, a theory addressing variation in crime in nations across space and time would meet a number of criteria. It would explain both unities and diversities in amounts of crime and crime patterns. The theory would apply to both crime differences among nations and changes in crime over time. The concepts and variables proposed to explain crime variation would suggest individual, cumulative, and interactive associations. A good theory should not separate itself from history but rather consider historical context and influence. Finally, the theory would be able to be linked to empirical results. Obviously, these are ideal goals toward which to strive.

A grand theory is desirable in that it provides a unifying perspective and attempts to explain not only variation in crime but also variation in the national traits that contribute to crime. Microlevel theories are more easily tied to operationalized concepts and empirical results. Research should eventually link the two types of perspectives.

A major question in cross-national crime research is how nations should be grouped for analysis. Classic modernization theory suggests all nations should be included in one model, while dependency theory suggests developing and developed nations be analyzed separately. World system theory would suggest that there should be an even further division into core, periphery, and semiperiphery nations. Also, should the nations in transition of Eastern-Central Europe and the former U.S.S.R. be included in analysis with other nations, or is their recent history and situation so different as to require separate analysis? The cultural perspective suggests that cultural variation must be taken into account, either by including variables indicating culture or grouping nations by culture. This issue is further addressed in Chapter 7.

NOTES

1. Other analysts who have categorized the theories used to explain cross-national crime variation have not distinguished between grand and microlevel theoretical perspectives. Neuman and Berger (1988) suggest these theoretical perspectives: modernization, ecological-opportunity, and Marxian-world system. LaFree (1997) also suggests three theoretical perspectives, but his are social disorganization, situational, and economic distress.

2. Neuman and Berger (1988) propose what they call ecological-opportunity theory as distinct from modernization theory. Similarly, LaFree (1997) sees this as a distinct perspective, using the term *situational* perspective. I subsume this perspective under the modernization umbrella because its predictions regarding change in crime patterns are identical to those of modernization theory; changes engendered by the development of nations are seen as the driving force in changing crime patterns.

3. Civilization theory is also seen as a distinct perspective from modernization theory (Eisner, 1994; Heiland & Shelley, 1992). I subsume it under modernization due to the similarity of its predictions and its claim of universal application.

4. For a more complete critical analysis of the claims of universality of modernization theory, see Groves and Newman, 1989.

5. Neuman and Berger (1988) refer to this perspective as Marxian-world system theory; while LaFree (1997) uses the generic term *radical criminology*. I use the term *dependency theory* because it is widely used internationally and is not as constrained by the inevitability of capitalist contradictions of Marxist theory (Zvekic, 1990).

REFERENCES

Adeyemi, A. A. (1990). Crime and development in Africa: A case study on Nigeria. In U. Zvekic (Ed.), *Essays on crime and development* (pp. 135–194). Rome, Italy: UNICRI.

Adler, F. (1983). *Nations not obsessed with crime*. Littleton, CO: Fred B. Rothman.

Adler, F. (1996). Our American society of criminology, the world, and the state of the art. *Criminology*, 34 (1), 1–10.

Arthur, J. (1991). Development and crime in Africa: A test of modernization theory. *Journal of Criminal Justice*, 19, 499–513.

Arthur, J. & Marenin, O. (1995). Explaining crime in developing countries: The need for a case study approach. *Crime, Law, and Social Change*, 23 (3), 191–214.

Avison, W. & Loring, P. (1986). Population diversity and cross-national homicide: The effects of inequality and heterogeneity. *Criminology*, 24, 733–750.

Balkan, S., Berger, R. J., & Schmidt, J. (1980). *Crime and deviance in America: A critical approach*. Belmont, CA: Wadsworth.

Baron, L. & Straus, M. (1989). *Four theories of rape in American society*. New Haven, CT: Yale University Press.

Baxi, U. (1990). Social change, criminality, and social control in India. In U. Zvekic (Ed.), *Essays on crime and development* (pp. 227–261). Rome, Italy: UNICRI.

Belson, W. A. (1975). *Juvenile theft: The causal factors*. New York: Harper & Row.

Bennett, R. (1991). Development and crime: A cross-national, time-series analysis of competing models. *The Sociological Quarterly*, 32, 343–363.

Blau, P. (1977). *Inequality and heterogeneity*. New York: Free Press.

Blau, J. & Blau, P. (1982). Metropolitan structure and violent crime. *American Sociological Review*, 47, 114–128.

Bonger, W. A. (1916). *Criminality and economic conditions*. Boston, MA: Little, Brown.

Bowers, W. J. (1984). *Legal homicide*. Boston, MA: Northeastern University Press.

Braithwaite, J. (1989). *Crime, shame, and reintegration*. New York: Cambridge University Press.

Braithwaite, J. (1993). Shame and modernity. *The British Journal of Criminology*, 33 (1), 1–18.

Brillon, Y. (1986). Les incidences du développement sur la criminalité Africaine. *International Annals of Criminology*, 24 (2), 23–38.

Brownmiller, S. (1975). *Against our will: Men, women, and rape*. New York: Simon and Schuster.

Chambliss, W. (1974). The political economy of crime: A comparative study of Nigeria and the United States. In S. F. Sylvester & E. Sagarin (Eds.), *Politics and crime*. New York: Praeger.

Chappell, D. (1989). Sexual criminal violence. In N. A. Weiner and M. E. Wolfgang (Eds.), *Pathways to criminal violence* (pp. 68–108). Newbury Park, CA: Sage.

Cherry, F. (1983). Gender roles and sexual violence. In E. R. Allgeier and N. B. McCormick (Eds.), *Challenging boundaries: Gender roles and sexual behavior*. Palo Alto, CA: Mayfield.

Chesnais, J. C. (1992). The history of violence: Homicide and suicide through the ages. *International Social Science Journal*, 44, 217–234.

Clinard, M. B. & Abbott, D. (1973). *Crime in developing countries: A comparative perspective*. New York: John Wiley & Sons.

Cohen, S. (1982). Western crime control models in the third world. *Research in Law, Deviance, and Social Control*, 4, 185–199.

Cohen, L. & Felson, M. (1979). Social change and crime rate trends: A routine activities approach. *American Sociological Review*, 44, 588–608.

Cohen, L., Felson, M. & Land, K. (1980). Property crime rates in the United States: A macrodynamic analysis. *American Journal of Sociology*, 86, 90–118.

Durkheim, E. (1964). *The division of labor in society.* New York: Free Press.

Durkheim, E. (1966). *Suicide.* New York: Free Press.

Durkheim, E. (1973). *Moral education.* New York: Free Press.

Eisner, M. (1994). Gewaltkriminalität und stadtentwicklung in der schweiz. *Schweizerische Zeitschrift für Soziologie*, 20 (1), 179–204.

Elias, N. (1976). *Über den prozess der zivilisation.* Frankfurt am Main, Germany: Suhrkamp.

Elias, N. (1982). *The civilizing process, volume 2: Power and civility.* New York: Pantheon.

Ember, C. & Ember, M. (1995). Issues in cross-cultural studies of interpersonal violence. In B. Ruback & N. Weiner (Eds.), *Interpersonal violent behaviors: Social and cultural aspects* (pp. 25–42). New York: Springer-Verlag.

Emovan, A. & Lambo, T. (1978). Survey of criminal homicide in Nigeria. *Scandinavian Journal of Social Medicine*, 6, 55–58.

Evans, P. (1979). *Dependent development: The alliance of multinational, state, and local capital in Brazil.* Princeton, NJ: Princeton University Press.

Felson, M. & Cohen, L. (1980). Human ecology and crime: A routine activity approach. *Human Ecology*, 8, 389–406.

Ferguson, R. & Whitehead, N. (1992). *War in the tribal zone.* Santa Fe, NM: School of American Research Press.

Ferri, E. (1882). *L'omicidio-suicidio:Responsibilita giuridica.* Turin, Italy: privately published.

Fiala, R. & LaFree, G. (1988). Cross-national determinants of child homicide. *American Sociological Review*, 53, 432–445.

Frank, A. (1969). *Latin America: Underdevelopment or revolution?* NewYork: Monthly Review Press.

Gartner, R. (1990). The victims of homicide: A temporal and cross-national comparison. *American Sociological Review*, 55, 92–106.

Greenberg, D. F. (Ed.). (1981). *Crime and capitalism.* Palo Alto, CA: Mayfield.

Groves, W. B., McCleary, R., & Newman, G. (1985). Religion, modernization, and world crime. *Comparative Social Research*, 8, 59–78.

Groves, W. B. & Newman, G. (1989). Against general theory in comparative research. *International Journal of Comparative and Applied Criminal Justice*, 13 (1), 23–29.

Groves, W. B., Newman, G., & Corrado, C. (1987). Islam, modernization, and crime: A test of the religious ecology thesis. *Journal of Criminal Justice*, 15, 495–503.

Gurr, T. (1981). Historical trends in violent crime: A critical review of the evidence. In M. Tonry & N. Morris (Eds.), *Crime and justice: An annual review of research, volume 3* (pp. 295–353). Chicago: University of Chicago Press.

Gurr, T., Grabosky, P., & Hula, R. (1977). *Politics of crime and conflict: A comparative history of four cities.* Beverly Hills, CA: Sage.

Hafercamp, H. & Ellis, H. (1992). Power, individualism, and the sanctity of human life: Development of criminality and punishment in four cultures. In H. Heiland, L. Shelley, & H. Katoh (Eds.), *Crime and control in comparative perspectives* (pp. 261–280). New York: Walter de Gruyter.

Hansmann, H. & Quigley, J. (1982). Population heterogeneity and the sociogenesis of homicide. *Social Forces, 6,* 206–224.

Heiland, H. & Shelley, L. (1992). Civilization, modernization, and the development of crime and control. In H. Heiland, L. Shelley, & H. Katoh (Eds.), *Crime and control in comparative perspectives* (pp. 1–20). New York: Walter de Gruyter.

Helal, A. & Coston, C. (1991). Low crime rates in Bahrain: Islamic social control—Testing the theory of synnomie. *International Journal of Comparative and Applied Criminal Justice,* 15 (1), 125–144.

Kick, E. & LaFree, G. (1985). Development and the social context of murder and theft. *Comparative Social Research,* 8, 37–57.

Krahn, H., Hartnagel, T., & Gartrell, J. (1986). Income inequality and homicide rates: Cross-national data and criminological theories. *Criminology,* 24, 269–295.

LaFree, G. (1997). Comparative cross-national studies of homicide. In M. D. Smith & M. Zahn (Eds.), *Homicide studies: A sourcebook of social research.* Beverly Hills, CA: Sage.

LaFree, G. & Kick, E. (1986). Cross-national effects of developmental, distributional, and demographic variables on crime: A review and analysis. *International Annals of Criminology,* 24, 213–235.

Landau, S. & Pfefferman, D. (1988). A time-series analysis of violent crime and its relation to prolonged states of warfare. *Criminology,* 26, 489–504.

Lopez-Rey, A. M. (1970). *Crime: An analytical appraisal.* New York: Praeger.

Lundsgaarde, H. P. (1977). *Murder in space city.* New York: Oxford University Press.

Mandel, E. (1977). *From class society to communism.* London: Ink Links.

Messerschmidt, J. W. (1993). *Masculinities and crime: Critique and reconceptualization of theory.* Lanham, MD: Rowman & Littlefield.

Messner, S. F. (1980). Income inequality and murder rates: Some cross-national findings. *Comparative Social Research,* 3, 185–198.

Messner, S. F. (1989). Economic discrimination and societal homicide rates: Further evidence on the cost of inequality. *American Sociological Review,* 54, 597–611.

Michalowski, R. J. (1985). *Order, law, and crime.* New York: Random House.

Morselli, J. (1879). *Suicide: An essay in comparative moral statistics.* New York: Appleton.

Neapolitan, J. L. (1994). Cross-national variation in homicide rates: The case of Latin America. *International Criminal Justice Review,* 4, 4–22.

Neapolitan, J. L. (1997). Homicides in developing nations: Results of research using a large, representative sample. *International Journal of Offender Therapy and Comparative Criminology,* forthcoming.

Nettler, G. (1984). *Explaining crime.* New York: McGraw-Hill.

Neuman, L. & Berger, R. (1988). Competing perspectives on cross-national crime: An evaluation of theory and evidence. *The Sociological Quarterly,* 29, 281–313.

Newman, G. (Ed.). (1976). *Comparative deviance: Perception and law in six cultures.* New York: Elsevier.

Newman, G. & Ferracuti, F. (1980). Introduction: The limits and possibilities of comparative criminology. In G. Newman (Ed.), *Crime and deviance: A comparative perspective* (pp. 7–16). Beverly Hills, CA: Sage.

Nijboer, J. (1995). Trends in violence and homicides in the Netherlands. In C. Block & R. Block (Eds.), *Trends, risks, and interventions in lethal violence: Proceedings of the third annual spring symposium of the Homicide Research Working Group (HRWG)*. Atlanta, GA: HRWG.

Ogburn, W. F. (1923). *Social change*. New York: Huebsch.

Ogburn, W. F. (1964). *On culture and social change: Selected papers 1886–1959*, O. D. Duncan (Ed.). Chicago: University of Chicago Press.

Ortega, S., Corzine, J., Burnett, C., & Poyer, T. (1992). Modernization, age structure, and regional context: A cross-national study of crime. *Sociological Spectrum*, 12, 257–277.

Petersilia, J., Greenwood, P., & Lavin, M. (1978). *Criminalcareers of habitual felons*. Washington D.C.: U. S. Department of Justice.

Platt, T. & Takagi, P. (Eds.). (1981). *Crime and social justice*. Totowa, NJ: Barnes and Noble.

Queloz, N. (1990). Changements sociaux, criminalité, et contrôle du crime. In U. Zvekic (Ed.), *Essays on crime and development* (pp. 23–42). Rome, Italy: UNICRI.

Quinney, R. (1977). *Class, state, and crime*. New York: McKay.

Repetto, T. J. (1974). *Residential crime*. Cambridge, MA: Ballinger.

Rivera, J. (1978). *Latin America: A sociocultural interpretation*. New York: Irvington Publishing Company.

Rogers, J. D. (1989). Theories of crime and development: An historical perspective. *Journal of Development Studies*, 25 (3), 319–330.

Schwendinger, H. & Schwendinger, J. (1970). Defenders of order or guardians of human rights? *Issues in Criminology*, 5, 123–157.

Schwendinger, J. & Schwendinger, H. (1983). *Rape and inequality*. Beverly Hills, CA: Sage.

Shaw, C. & McKay, H. (1942). *Juvenile delinquency and urban areas*. Chicago: University of Chicago Press.

Shelley, L. (1981). *Crime and modernization: The impact of industrialization and urbanization on crime*. Carbondale, IL: Southern Illinois University Press.

Shelley, L. (1986). Crime and modernization reexamined. *Annales Internationales de Criminologie*, 24, 7–21.

Shichor, D. (1990). Crime patterns and socioeconomic development: A cross-national analysis. *Criminal Justice Review*, 15 (1), 64–78.

Shivji, I. (1976). *Class struggles in Tanzania*. London: Heinemann Educational Books.

Sklair, L. (1991). *Sociology of the global system*. Baltimore, MD: Johns Hopkins University Press.

Souryal, S. (1987). The religionization of a society: The continuing application of Shariah law in Saudi Arabia. *Journal for the Scientific Study of Religion*, 26 (4), 429–449.

Souryal, S. (1990). Religious training as a method of social control: The effective role of Sharia law in Saudi Arabia. In U. Zvekic (Ed.), *Essays on crime and development* (pp. 261–298). Rome, Italy: UNICRI.

South, S. & Messner, S. (1986). The sex ratio and women's involvement in crime: A cross-national analysis. *The Sociological Quarterly*, 28, 171–188.

Stack, S. (1982). Social structure and Swedish crime rates: A time-series analysis. *Criminology*, 20, 499–513.

Stack, S. (1984). Income inequality and property crime. *Criminology*, 22, 229–258.

Stephens, G. (1994). The global crime wave. *The Futurist*, 28 (4), 22–29.

Sumner, C. (1982). Crime, justice, and underdevelopment: Beyond modernization. In C. Sumner (Ed.), *Crime, justice, and underdevelopment* (pp. 1–39). London: Heinemann Educational Books.

Thome, H. (1992). Gesellschaftliche modernisierung und kriminalität: Zum stand der sozialhistorischen kriminalitätsforschung. *Zeitschrift für Soziologie*, 21 (3), 212–228.

Toqueville, A. de (1956). *Democracy in America*. New York: Knopf.

Unnithan, N. (1983). *Homicide and the social structure: A cross-national analysis of lethal violence rates, 1950–1970*. Unpublished doctoral dissertation, University of Nebraska-Lincoln.

Unnithan, N. & Whitt, H. (1992). Inequality, economic development, and lethal violence: A cross-national analysis of suicide and homicide. *International Journal of Comparative Sociology*, 33 (3–4), 182–196.

Unnithan, N. & Whitt, H. (1994). *The currents of lethal violence: An integrated model of suicide and homicide*. Albany, NY: State University of New York Press.

Vagg, J. (1995). *Economic development and crime: Emerging patterns and new explanations*. Paper presented at the 47th annual conference of the American Society of Criminology, Boston, MA.

van Dijk, J. (1989). Penal sanctions and the process of civilization. *Annales Internationales de Criminologie*, 27, 191–204.

van Onselen, C. (1976). *Chibaro: African mine labor in Southern Rhodesia, 1900–1933*. London: Pluto Press.

Wallerstein, I. M. (1974). *The modern world-system*. New York: Academic Press.

Walton, J. (1982). The international economy and peripheral urbanization. In N. I. Fainstein and S. S. Fainstein (Eds.), *Urban policy under capitalism* (pp. 119–135). Beverly Hills, CA: Sage.

West, W. G. (1978). The short-term careers of serious thieves. *Canadian Journal of Criminology*, 20, 169–190.

Whitt, H. (1985). Comments on Steven Stack's paper "Suicide: A decade review of the sociological literature." *Deviant Behavior*, 6, 229–231.

Wikström, P-O. (1985). *Everyday violence in contemporary Sweden: Situational and ecological aspects*. Stockholm, Sweden: National Council for Crime Prevention.

Wikström, P-O. (1992). Context-specific trends for criminal homicide in Stockholm, 1951–1987. *Studies on crime and crime prevention*. Stockholm, Sweden: National Council for Crime Prevention.

Wolfgang, M. E. (1966). *Patterns in criminal homicide*. New York: John Wiley & Sons.

Zvekic, U. (1990). Development and crime in Yugoslavia: Results of the preliminary analysis. In U. Zvekic (Ed.), *Essays on crime and development* (pp. 299–342). Rome, Italy: UNICRI.

5

Past Research on Homicides

A separate chapter is devoted to past cross-national research on homicides for three reasons. First, the majority of cross-national crime research has focused on homicides, and thus there is much to review. Second, homicide data are generally considered the most valid and reliable of cross-national crime indicators, and thus homicide research is probably the best way to study cross-national comparisons of violence in general. Finally, homicide is considered the most serious of conventional crimes and therefore of the most concern and interest.[1]

Despite the general superiority of homicide data to other crime indicators, most past research is based on data of questionable quality and small, nonrepresentative samples. The majority of studies have used INTERPOL data without adjusting for percent of attempts (see Chapter 2). Most data used were collected prior to 1980 when the quality of data was generally much lower than it is now, regardless of the source. And most samples contain fewer than fifty nations and are heavily weighted toward developed Western ones, with a particular lack of African nations.

Thus, the research results reported here should be viewed more as being of heuristic value than as actually telling us much definitively about cross-national variation in homicides. All results in this chapter are based on official data, as victimization and self-report data do not address homicides. And research results are mainly organized around conceptual areas, relating to the theories discussed in Chapter 4.

Most past research has been theoretically based, with indicators chosen to represent concepts in these theories. It is not always clear which underlying concept or national attribute an indicator is tapping. Infant mortality, for example, has been used to indicate inequality (e.g., Conklin & Simpson, 1985), level of development (e.g., Shichor, 1990), the welfare of children (e.g., Savage & Vila, 1995), and the relative equality of women (e.g., Widom & Stewart, 1986). Other indicators have similarly been used to indicate different concepts and attributes.

Conversely, the same concept or national attribute has been operationalized by very different indicators. Social integration—or its reverse, individualism—has been operationalized by percent Protestant (e.g., Messner, 1982), Islamic predominance (e.g., Groves, McCleary, & Neuman, 1985), political and civil rights (e.g., Huang, 1995), divorce (e.g., Gartner, 1990), ethnic/linquistic heterogeneity (e.g., Hansmann & Quigley, 1982), and proportionate school enrollment (e.g., Messner, 1982). It is unlikely that these all tap the same underlying concept or attribute of nations. While the results of past research are primarily organized by theory and concepts, I also try to report the actual indicators used by investigators.

For many variables, some research will find associations to cross-national variation in homicides, while other research will not. In a few instances, one study will indicate a significant positive association, while another will indicate a significant negative association. These differences are due to variations in samples, indicators used for independent variables, sources of data for homicides, methods of analysis, and other variables included in the models. It is not possible to report variations among the studies in all of the above. I note differences when they are crucial to understanding what the studies as a whole appear to indicate.

DEVELOPMENT AND MODERNIZATION

The core proposition of modernization theory regarding homicides is that as nations reach higher levels of development there will be a decline in homicide rates. Level of development has most often been indicated by gross national or domestic product (GNP or GDP) per capita. Other indicators have been used, however, such as percent of labor force in agriculture, energy consumption, telephones per capita, and in some studies indices composed of several variables. Most of the indicators used correlate very highly with each other, as all somehow indicate economic development and change.

Most of this research has also been cross-sectional, examining whether nations at higher levels of development have systematically lower homicide rates than those at lower levels. This does not directly test modernization theory, as rates may well decline as nations develop—as the theory proposes—but other factors might greatly affect the actual level of rates.

The overwhelming majority of cross-sectional studies which include level-of-development indicators finds no significant association to homicides (e.g., Conklin & Simpson, 1985; Kick & LaFree, 1985; Krahn, Hartnagel, & Gartrell, 1986; Messner, 1989; Neapolitan, 1994; Unnithan & Whitt, 1992). A few older studies found the proposed negative association (Krohn & Wellford, 1977; LaFree & Kick, 1986; MacDonald, 1976; Quinney, 1965), but a more recent study actually found a positive association (Huang, 1995). Lester (1987) also found a positive association, but his research included only developed nations.

The most highly developed nations—with the exception of the United States—have relatively low homicide rates. However, when nations at all levels of development are analyzed, there appears to be no systematic association between development and homicides. Thus, cross-sectional analysis does not support modernization theory regarding homicides. The most highly developed nations progressed under different conditions from those of developing nations today, and most share a common Western culture. Perhaps future research should exclude the most developed nations from analysis or include a dummy variable to control for them.

In its original inception by Shelley (1981), urbanization played a central role in the changes in crime patterns resulting from development. Therefore, I look at research on urbanization and homicides separately from other indicators of development. The results of research including degree of urbanization are mixed. Some studies have found the negative association suggested by modernization theory (Conklin & Simpson, 1985; Krohn, 1978; Quinney, 1965; Wolf, 1971), while others have found no such association (Avison & Loring, 1986; Hansmann & Quigley, 1982; Kick & LaFree, 1985; MacDonald, 1976; Messner, 1980, 1982, 1986; Neapolitan, 1994). Looking at the studies as a whole, I do not believe there is much support for any significant association between urbanization and homicides.

It may be more appropriate to examine modernization theory by looking at the rate of development. Some research is still cross-sectional, but it includes such variables as change or growth in GDP/GNP in the years preceding the time period studied. These studies have not found an association between change in GDP/GNP and homicide rates and thus do not support modernization theory (Krahn, Hartnagel, & Gartrell, 1986; Krohn & Wellford, 1977; Neapolitan, 1994).

Bennett (1991), using pooled time-series analysis—which addresses both cross-sectional and temporal variation in homicides—found no association between GDP per capita, or growth in GDP per capita, and homicides. He did find a positive association between urbanization and homicides at lower levels of urbanization but not at higher levels. However, Ortega, Corzine, Burnett, and Poyer (1992) did find a positive association between GNP growth and homicides, using the same approach but controlling for the effects of geographic region. Neither study supports the modernization proposition of a negative association between development and homicides. Archer and Gartner (1984), looking at growth in city size and homicides, failed to find any association. They did find that the relative size of cities within nations was positively associated to homicides.

Also contradictory to the modernization perspective is Gurr's (1977) finding that from the late 1950s to the early 1970s many of the most developed nations experienced increasing homicides. However, rates in these nations remained well below those they had prior to modernization as well as those of many of the developing nations. Similarly, data from the United Nations Crime Surveys indicate that from 1970 to 1990 there has been a general upward trend in homicides and violent crime worldwide, particularly in the developing nations (U.N., 1992, 1993, 1995). The upward trend in violent crime in the majority of nations appears to be continuing in the 1990s (Stephens, 1994). If development resulted in lower rates, the trend should be downward.

Thus, the current state of research fails to support the modernization perspective that homicides decline as nations develop. The large declines in homicides and violence which occurred in European nations as they modernized do not appear to be occurring in many developing nations. Perhaps it will happen in the future, but it is clear that situational and historical contexts must be considered in examining the association between development and violent crime.

OPPORTUNITY AND DEMOGRAPHY VARIABLES

Demographic attributes of nations might affect homicide rates by influencing opportunities for homicides or the pool of potential offenders. Density of population should result in more contact among people and thus more situations where homicides might occur. Most past research has failed to find a positive association between population density and homicides (Avison & Loring, 1986; Hansmann & Quigley, 1982; Messner 1982, 1989; Neapolitan, 1994; Savage & Vila, 1995); and some research has found a small negative association (Conklin & Simpson, 1985; Huang, 1995). Krahn, Hartnagel, and Gartrell (1986) did find that income inequality had a much stronger association to homicides in high-density nations than in low ones. Thus, density may contribute to homicides only in conjunction with other factors that create stress or frustration.

The density of living conditions—that is, the number of people per household—might be more important than general density, as contact among intimates is more likely to result in homicides than other types of contact. Supporting this, Kick and LaFree (1985) found a positive association between household size and homicides. However, Neapolitan (1997b) failed to find an association when only developing nations were included in analysis. More research is needed on the association of household size to homicides to clarify if there is a relationship when level of development is considered.

One of the most well-documented findings in intranational crime research is that most homicides are committed by young adult males. Thus, we would expect that nations with a higher proportion of youths and/or males to have higher homicide rates, due to the larger pool of potential offenders. The majority of studies have failed to find an association of either youths or males to homicide rates (Avison & Loring, 1986; Gartner, 1990; Krahn, Hartnagel, & Gartrell, 1986; Messner, 1989; Neapolitan, 1994; Savage & Vila, 1995). Only Conklin and Simpson (1985) and Hansmann and Quigley (1982) have found a significant positive association between the proportion of youths and homicides.

Bennett (1991), using pooled time-series rather than cross-sectional analysis, actually found a negative association between youth population and homicides. Furthermore, research which has looked specifically at the proportion of young males in a nation has failed to find significant associations to homicides (Messner, 1989; Savage & Vila, 1995). Thus, there appears to be a paradox wherein young males commit most homicides, but the proportion of young males in a nation is not associated with homicide rates.

Population size and growth have often been included in models examining cross-national variation in homicides, although their inclusion is generally not warranted on theoretical grounds. Research has generally found no association between size and homicides (e.g., Krahn, Hartnagel, & Gartrell, 1986; Krohn, 1978; Krohn & Wellford, 1977; LaFree & Kick, 1986; Messner, 1989; Neapolitan, 1994). Conklin and Simpson (1985) did find a slight positive association.

Population growth has been found to have a positive association to homicides (Braithwaite, 1979; Krahn, Hartnagel, & Gartrell, 1986; LaFree & Kick, 1986; MacDonald, 1976; Messner, 1982). Other studies, however, have failed to find a significant association (Huang, 1995; Krohn & Wellford, 1977; Messner, 1989; Shichor, 1990). If there is a positive association, it is not clear why this should be. Neuman and Berger (1988) see population growth as an indicator of urbanism, and high-growth nations have more young people. However, one or both of these variables has been included in some of the research that still finds a positive association of population growth to homicides (e.g., Krahn, Hartnagel, & Gartrell, 1986; LaFree & Kick, 1986; Messner, 1982).

Rushton (1988, 1990, 1995a, b) has found that nations with predominantly African populations have higher rates of homicides and other violent crimes than those with predominantly Asian or Causasian populations. He suggests this is due to African people having smaller brains and higher levels of sex hormones.

Even if we accept the idea of race as a biological rather than social concept and that nations can be identified by their predominant race, Rushton's research. is severely flawed. He ignores all other research and variables which have been used to explain cross-national variation in violent crime. Thus, his one-way analysis of variance includes no variable other than the racial make-up of nations, never even considering the possibility of a spurious association. Several studies reanalyzing Rushton's data using more appropriate methods and including other explanatory variables found the association of racial make-up of nations to violent crime to be nonsignificant and negligible (Cernovsky & Litman, 1993; Neapolitan, 1997a).

ANOMIE AND SOCIAL INTEGRATION

Much of the research on cross-national crime variation revolves around the concepts of anomie and social integration. While there is substantial variation in the ways these are conceptualized and even more in how they are operationalized, there is a common core perspective. Crime, including homicides, is associated with the degree of social cohesion and value congruence in societies. Implied in this is that social conflict and individual-istic values contribute to lack of cohesion and congruence and, therefore, to more homicides.

Probably the most often used indicators of social cohesion and conflict used in cross-national research on crime are those that measure the degree of heterogeneity in nations, that is, race/ethnic, linguistic, and religious composition. The most commonly used indicators combine ethnic and linguistic heterogeneity into one measure. Most research using these has not found significant associations to homicides (Krahn, Hartnagel, & Gartrell, 1986; Messner, 1986, 1989; Neapolitan, 1994). Additionally, MacDonald (1976) found no association of homicides to indicators of racial or religious heterogeneity; Groves, Newman, and Corrado (1987) also found no associa-tion to religious heterogeneity.

Avison and Loring (1986) did find a positive association of homicides to ethnic/linguistic heterogeneity; and Braithwaite and Braithwaite (1980) found a positive association to an indicator of racial/ethnic heterogeneity. MacDonald (1976) found a small positive association between linguistic heterogeneity and homicides. Hansmann and Quigley (1982) found that indicators of linguistic, ethnic, and religious heterogeneity did not have significant associations to homicides individually, but that in combination they did.

Overall, the studies indicate at best a weak relationship between cultural heterogeneity and homicides. As we shall see later, cultural heterogeneity might be important in explaining cross-national variation in homicides only in combination with income inequality.

Several studies have used measures of occupational heterogeneity to indicate anomie, as Durkheim (1964) quite clearly proposed this to be important in the breakdown of mechanic solidarity. These studies have failed to find significant associations to homicides across nations (Krohn, 1978; Messner, 1986). Krohn (1978) also tried to operationalize anomie as a gap between material desires—indicated by literacy rate—and satisfaction of desires—indicated by four variables representing the availability of commodities. The resultant indicator was not associated with national variations in homicides.

Some investigators suggest divorce is both an indicator and a cause of lack of social integration. Several studies which included only developed, democratic nations have found positive associations between divorce rates and homicides (Gartner, 1990; Landau, 1984; Lester, 1987). Other research has failed to find a significant association when nations at all levels of development are included in analysis (Krahn, Hartnagel, & Gartrell, 1986; Rahav, 1990). In related research, Huang (1995) found that maternal absence—indicated by the percent of labor force composed by women—is positively associated to homicide rates. Thus, homicides may have more to do with lack of parental attention than divorce per se.

Central to Durkheim's (1964, 1966) thinking about deviance is that it is greater in societies with an overemphasis on individualism. Several studies propose that Protestantism emphasizes individualism and thus should be associated with less social control and more homicides. These studies have failed to find an association between Protestantism and national variations in homicides (Groves, McCleary, & Newman, 1985; Messner, 1982). Whitt, Gordon, and Hofley (1972) actually found Protestant nations to have somewhat lower homicide rates than Catholic or non-Christian nations. It should be noted, however, that this study included only six non-Christian nations. Also, all but one of the Protestant nations were highly-developed Western nations, whereas a high proportion of the other nations were developing nations.

Messner (1982) has proposed that education encourages individualism and thus might be associated with homicides. Groves, McCleary, and Newman (1985) conversely argue that education contributes to social integration by serving as a homogenizing force. Most research has not found significant associations between the educational levels of nations—generally indicated by proportionate school enrollment—and variations in homicides (Conklin & Simpson, 1985; Hansmann & Quigley, 1982; Messner, 1982, 1986). Groves, McCleary, and Newman (1985) found a small negative association. Thus, in general there is little support for either perspective.

Huang (1995) suggests that concern for the rights and welfare of others contributes to the development of organic solidarity. Therefore, nations that allow more political and civil rights and devote more resources to helping others should have lower homicide rates. Huang found a negative association of homicides to a combined measure of political and civil rights but none to government expenditures for social security and health. Neapolitan (1994) also found a negative association between political rights and homicides.

Gartner (1990), in a study of only developed nations, found homicides to be negatively related to social security expenditures. DeFronzo (1983) found that the amount nations spent on welfare expenditures reduced the amount of violent crime. Shichor (1990) found no association between homicides and public expenditures on education. Overall, the research suggests that political liberty does tend to depress homicide rates, while the research on welfare spending is inconsistent.

In general, the foregoing does not indicate that lack of social integration—regardless of how it is measured—is of great importance in explaining cross-national variation in homicides. More intensive, qualitative studies that focus on fewer nations indicate this may have more to do with poor operationalization of the concept than with an actual lack of importance. In an intensive study of ten nations with very low rates of crime, including homicides, Adler (1983) found the one common feature to be an intact social control system based on norm integration and social cohesion. She coined the term *synnomie*—in opposition to *anomie*—for this attribute of nations.

Helal and Coston (1991), in a test of synnomie, studied a very low crime rate nation, Bahrain, and found that religious solidarity, resulting in value sharing and social integration, accounted for the small amount of crime. Souryal (1987, 1990) similarly found that Saudi Arabia had less crime than other Islamic nations due to its adherence to Shariah law. He argues this adherence results in religious values permeating the culture to promote shared values and a unified collective conscience. In a study involving a larger sample of nations, Groves, Newman, and Corrado (1987) did not find an association of Islamic religion and homicides across nations. However, they did not actually study social integration as the more intensive studies have done. Intensive qualitative research on individual nations indicates that social integration (synnomie) probably plays an important role in the amount of crime in nations. Thus, an important task for future researchers is to find a way to measure this concept in an accurate and consistent manner for a large sample of nations.

POVERTY AND INEQUALITY

Theories of crime distinguish between absolute and relative deprivation as factors contributing to crime. Cross-nationally, there is little support for the former but substantial support for the latter in explaining homicides. Absolute deprivation or poverty has most often been indicated by GNP/GDP per person, with numerous studies finding no association to homicides (e.g., Kick & LaFree, 1985; Krahn, Hartnagel, & Gartrell, 1986; Messner, 1989; Neapolitan, 1994; Unnithan & Whitt, 1992).

Infant mortality rates have also been used to indicate cross-national differences in deprivation, and results have been mixed. One study found no association (Shichor, 1990); several found a positive one (Conklin & Simpson, 1985; Simpson & Conklin, 1992); and one a negative association (Rahav, 1990). Neapolitan (1997b) failed to find an association between absolute poverty—as indicated by Overseas Development Council data—and homicide rates in developing nations.

Relative inequality within nations has been operationalized by educational inequality (proportionate school enrollment), inflation, unemployment, and most frequently income inequality. Groves, McCleary, and Newman (1985) found educational equality to have the suggested negative association to homicides, but most research has failed to find a significant association (Conklin & Simpson, 1985; Hansmann & Quigley, 1982; Huang, 1995; Krahn, Hartnagel, & Gartrell, 1986; Messner, 1982, 1986). In pooled time series analysis, Bennett (1991) found a curvilinear relationship, with a negative association at lower levels of inequality but a positive one at higher levels.

Research does not support a strong association between unemployment and homicides when controlling for other variables (Avison & Loring, 1986; Krohn, 1976; MacDonald, 1976). Inflation and economic fluctuations can contribute to feelings of inequality by creating a gap between means and desires. Landau (1984), in research on fourteen highly developed nations, found a moderately positive association between inflation and violent crime. Eisner (1996) failed to find an association between economic fluctuations in Western European nations and homicides.

Results of studies have consistently shown a strong positive association between income inequality and homicides across nations (e.g., Braithwaite & Braithwaite, 1980; Kick & LaFree, 1985; LaFree & Kick, 1986; MacDonald, 1976; Messner, 1980, 1982, 1986; Neapolitan, 1994; Savage & Vila, 1995). Income inequality has most often been indicated by the Gini coefficient of income concentration, although other indicators have been used, such as the ratio of income of the upper ten percent to that of the lower twenty percent.

Some research indicates that income inequality has a strong association to homicides only if it is made salient by discrimination based on racial or cultural differences (Avison & Loring, 1986; Krahn, Hartnagel, & Gartrell, 1986; Messner, 1989). Krahn, Hartnagel, and Gartrell (1986) found that political democracy, size of the internal security force, and the development of capital relations of production exacerbated the effects of income inequality on homicides. There is also some evidence that the amount of money that nations devote to social welfare and to mitigating poverty can partially offset the effect of income inequality on violent crime (Archer & Gartner, 1986; Braithwaite, 1979; DeFronzo, 1983; Fiala & LaFree, 1988; Gartner, 1990). Messner and Rosenfeld (1997) found that the degree of decommodification of labor—as indicated by the ease of access to welfare benefits, their income replacement value, and the expansiveness of welfare coverage—is negatively related to cross-national homicide rates. They suggest that this is due to the decommodification of labor's insulating personal well-being from market forces.

The association of income inequality to homicides is generally seen as supportive of dependency theory, but this is not necessarily the case. Dependency theory is primarily concerned with the place of nations in the world economic order and considers both internal and external inequality. Income inequality is basically seen as an intervening variable between national economic dependence and homicides. However, we cannot assume that economic exploitation and dependence are the only or even the major causes of income inequality.

The few research efforts that have been made to link a nation's place in the world economic order and homicides directly have failed to find a significant association. Krahn, Hartnagel, and Gartrell (1986) found no significant association between development of capital relations of production and homicides. Simpson and Conklin (1992) did not find economic penetration by transnational corporations to influence homicides significantly. Also, as noted earlier, underdevelopment as indicated by GNP/GDP per person appears to have no association to homicides across nations. Clearly, more research and better indicators are needed to explore the associations among global economic relationships, inequality, and poverty within nations, and homicides and other crimes.

POLITICAL ORIENTATION

Research results regarding associations between the political orientations of nations and homicides are mixed, with no consistent results. Research by Huang (1995) and Neapolitan (1994) indicate a negative relationship between political rights and homicides, while Braithwaite and Braithwaite (1980) found a positive association. Similarly, Krahn, Hartnagel, and Gartrell (1986) found a positive relationship between a democracy index and homicides; while Messner (1989) found no significant association. Krohn and Wellford (1977) and Wellford (1974), using political orientation in terms of communist, neutral, or Western, did not find a relationship to homicides. However, Simpson and Conklin (1992) found nations with centralized political systems to have lower homicide rates.

CULTURAL VALUES AND NORMS

I have already discussed research relating to the probable role of social integration, value sharing, and so forth in the control of violent behavior in nations. Nations may also differ in violent behaviors due to differences in cultural values and norms that proscribe or promote violence. Groves, McCleary, and Newman (1985:60) have argued that research has "discounted or even ignored the possible effects of culture on cross-national variation in homicides." The situation has improved only marginally in recent years.

Some research shows a positive association between the involvement of nations in warfare and homicides (Archer & Gartner, 1981, 1984; Gartner, 1990; Landau & Pfefferman, 1988). Other research has found a positive relationship between the use of capital punishment and homicides (Bowers,

1984; Gartner, 1990; Hood, 1989). Archer, Gartner, and Beittel (1983), in research on the abolition of capital punishment in fourteen Western nations, found homicides declined after abolition to a greater degree than other crimes. Both warfare and capital punishment might promote and/or reflect norms and values that encourage violence as appropriate behavior, and thus they would encourage its use in the populace.

Even a casual examination of homicide rates indicates that nations with high rates tend to cluster in Latin America and sub-Saharan Africa. As nations in the same geographic region also tend to share similar histories and cultures, geographical clustering suggests a cultural contribution to cross-national variation in homicides. Of course, it is possible that nations in these regions share structural or demographic attributes that explain the high homicide rates. These nations do share similar warm climates, but Rotton (1986) failed to find an association between climate and homicides.

A number of studies of individual Latin American nations have found an important factor contributing to a large amount of violence to be a strong cultural emphasis on machismo (e.g., Herrera, 1965–1966; Toro-Calder, 1950; Wolfgang & Ferracuti, 1967). Neapolitan (1994) found that if the Latin American region is entered into models as a dummy variable, it is much more strongly related to homicides than income inequality or level of development. Similarly, Ortega, Corzine, Burnett, and Poyer (1992), using pooled time-series analysis, found regional effects more important than level of, or change in, development in explaining variation in homicides, with the Latin American region having particularly high rates.

Neapolitan (1997b), in an analysis of developing nations, found Christianity a very strong predictor of homicides. He suggests that this is because Christianity indicates the degree to which the indigenous cultures of these nations were destroyed by colonization and replaced by more violent cultures forged through conquest and postcolonial violence. Haferkamp and Ellis (1992), using historical analysis, explained the high levels of violence in Jamaica as being due to a history of colonization, slavery, and violence which devalued the sanctity of human life. Other historical analyses have linked violence in developing nations to the brutalities of colonization, slavery, and postcolonial conflicts (e.g., Cooper, 1980; Huggins, 1984; van Onselen, 1976).

An historical review by Brown (1994) explains the high levels of violence in the USA—as compared to other developed nations—as resulting from a history of turbulence and violence creating a cultural norm of "no duty to retreat." These studies of developing and developed nations all suggest the importance of historical experiences in the development of cultural values that promote violence and thus homicides.

While not including homicides, the IVS found that rates of violent victimizations were greater in Latin American and sub-Saharan African nations than in Asian, North African, or developed nations. This agreement with official homicide data as to the geographic clustering of violence further supports the cultural perspective.

While the research strongly suggests a cultural component to variation in homicide rates, there is still no direct support involving a large sample of nations. This is because no one has found a way to measure cultural values and norms conducive to violence in a consistent and systematic way for a large number of nations. Perhaps the best that can be done is more in-depth analysis of the culture and histories of individual nations, both violent and nonviolent. Friday (1995) argues that historical context may be the most important area for comparative criminology to address.

GUNS

Research on gun availability and ownership and variation in homicide rates has been restricted to highly developed nations. These studies find substantial associations between degree of gun ownership/availability and both gun-related and total homicides (Killias, 1992, 1993; Lester, 1991; Sproule & Kennett, 1989). The studies indicate displacement does not take place, as people do not tend to use other means if guns are not available. Research is needed which includes developing nations and more closely examines possible confounding factors as well as whether the association of guns to homicides is causal or simply reflects the same underlying cultural values.

WOMEN AND CHILDREN

Four studies have focused exclusively on infants and children as homicide victims. Hereafter, I shall use the term *children*, as associations of independent variables to infant and child homicides are nearly identical. Three of these included only highly developed nations, while one studied developing and developed nations separately. When focusing on developing nations, Fiala and LaFree (1988) failed to find significant relationships of any of their variables to homicide rates for children. They looked at GNP per person, income inequality, proportion of the labor force that is female, the ratio of females to males in professional occupations, and spending on social programs.

They also failed to find an association between income inequality and homicides of children in developed nations, as did Gartner (1990), who used pooled time-series rather than cross-sectional analysis. Gartner also found no association between ethnic/linguistic heterogeneity and homicides of children in developed nations. Conversely, Briggs and Cutright (1994), in research using the same approach but a slightly larger sample, found a positive relationship between ethnic/linguistic heterogeneity and homicides of children.

Both the Gartner (1990) and Briggs and Cutright (1994) studies found positive associations of battle deaths to child homicides. Gartner (1991), in a similar study, also agreed with Briggs and Cutright concerning the positive relationship of divorce to child homicides. All the studies on developed nations indicate that the proportion of the labor force that is female has a positive association, whereas spending on social programs has a negative one (Briggs & Cutright, 1994; Fiala & LaFree, 1988; Gartner, 1990, 1991).

Fiala and LaFree (1988) also indicated that low levels of female status— as indicated by the ratio of females to males in professional occupations— result in higher child homicide rates. Gartner (1991) found births to teenage mothers and illegitimacy rates to be positively related to child homicides, although these associations—as well as that of divorce—were conditioned by levels of government spending on social programs. Finally, the Briggs and Cutright (1994) study indicates that rape and child homicide rates are positively related.

Overall, these studies indicate that family disruption and negative treatment, or devaluing, of women tend to increase child homicides in developed nations. However, these effects can be offset in part by government spending on social programs.

Gartner, Baker, and Pampel (1990) did a pooled time-series analysis of highly developed nations, focusing on the female/male gap in homicide victimizations. They found that the proportion of women in nontraditional roles—for example, divorced, unmarried, in the labor force, in traditionally male occupations, having illegitimate children—decreased the gap; while higher female status, as indicated by enrollment in higher education, increased the gap. In other words, the adverse effects of non-traditional roles were evident only in contexts of low female status. In a similar study, Gartner (1990) also found divorce, women in the labor force, and income inequality to be positively associated to absolute rates of female victimizations, and welfare spending to be negatively related.

Much more research has focused on females as homicide offenders than as victims. Most of this research has centered around the emancipation hypothesis (Adler, 1975; Simon, 1975). This proposes that female offending increases and the male/female gap in offending decreases as nations modernize, gender roles change, and women pursue more opportunities outside the home. So, in some cases the research examines the female/male gap in offending and in others the absolute rate of female offending.

Clark (1989), in a study of female murder rates, failed to find significant associations to the variables of GNP per person, women in the labor force, urbanization, fertility, or the dependency theory variables of commodity concentration and investment dependence. Widom and Stewart (1986) found percent of illegitimate births and the child-to-woman ratio to have positive associations to female homicide rates. They suggest these are indicators of increased biological equality which creates stress on women.

Messner (1985) did not find stress in terms of income inequality to be related to female homicide rates, but he did find the proportion of never-married females to have a positive association. He sees this as supporting stress, or strain, theory in that the goal of marriage is more important to females than are financial goals. Conversely, Hartnagel and Mizanuddin (1986), using fertility rates as a measure of domestic role participation, found a moderately positive association to the female proportion of homicides. Thus, the relationship of females acting in traditional roles and homicides is unclear.

Most studies fail to support an association between the female/male gap in homicide offending and the level of development of nations (Hartnagel, 1982; Hartnagel & Mizanuddin, 1986; Steffensmeier, Allan, & Streifel, 1989). Only Bowker (1981) found the expected positive association.

Research specifically focusing on the changing role of women, in terms of labor force participation and occupational segregation, has yielded mixed results. A number of studies have indicated no association between various measures of these concepts and proportionate female offending (Bowker, 1981; Hartnagel, 1982; Simon & Baxter, 1989; Steffensmeier, Allan, & Streifel, 1989). However, both Hartnagel and Mizanuddin (1986) and Marshall (1982) found positive associations of level and type of female labor force participation to proportionate female homicide offending.

Most research also indicates that female educational achievement and equality, generally measured by proportionate enrollment in high schools or universities, does not have a significant association to proportionate female offending (Bowker, 1981; Hartnagel, 1982; Hartnagel & Mizanuddin, 1986; Steffensmeier, Allan, & Streifel, 1989; Widom & Stewart, 1986). An exception is the study by Simon and Baxter (1989), which found a positive association to the percent of female secondary school enrollment. Using the number of years women had the full vote as an indicator of political equality, Widom and Stewart (1986) found a positive association to proportionate female offending.

In total, these studies at best indicate mild support that increased homicides by females and decreased female/male gap in homicides accompany modernization and changing female status and roles. The female proportion of homicides may be greater in developed nations where females have more roles outside the home or where females are less valued; but it is not much greater. This is further supported by analysis indicating that over the thirty-year period from 1950 to 1980, female homicide rates did not change appreciably and may indeed have declined (Kruttschnitt, 1995).

TRENDS

If modernization theory is correct, then homicide rates, at least in developing nations, should generally decline as nations develop. Conversely, dependency theory would suggest increasing homicides in developing nations, as capitalist penetration and exploitation increases worldwide. As noted earlier, the United Nations analyzes its surveys for worldwide trends and has concluded homicides have been increasing since 1970, particularly in developing nations (U.N., 1992, 1993, 1995). Nijboer (1995) has found that after a long period of stable rates, homicides have recently increased in several Western European nations.

My own comparison of WHO and INTERPOL rates between the early 1980s and early 1990s indicates that as many nations experienced increased rates as decreased. However, Arthur (1991), in analyzing INTERPOL rates in eleven African nations from 1961 to 1984, found increased homicides in all. Research on various Latin American nations from the early 1960s to the early 1980s, using data internally collected, found no change in one, small increases in two, and a large increase in one (Birkbeck, 1992; Ellis, 1992).

Overall, there appears to be more support for increased than decreased rates in recent years, especially in developing nations. It is also true, however, that most nations have had relatively stable rates.

As noted earlier, Gurr's (1977, 1981) analysis of crime trends in eighteen developed, democratic nations from 1945 to 1975 indicated increased homicides in all but Japan. Eisner (1995) similarly has done analysis indicating increased homicides in most Western European nations from the 1960s into the 1990s. Recent research in Nordic nations and Scotland indicates moderate increases in homicides in recent years (Joutsen, 1992; McClintock & Wikström, 1990). Excepting the United States, homicide rates in all the developed, democratic nations remain relatively low, with no indication that they will increase to very high rates. Still, the increased homicides they have apparently experienced since the 1940s indicate that modernization may not permanently depress violence.

We are faced with an interesting paradox regarding development and homicides. When all nations or only developing nations are considered, there appears to be no systematic relationship between level of development and homicides. Also, homicide rates worldwide are in recent years at best stable and likely increasing. Yet the most highly developed nations—with the exception of the United States—experienced dramatic decreases in homicides as they modernized and their rates remain quite low today (Chesnais, 1992; Shelley, 1981).

Many developing nations do not have—and have not recently had—high homicide rates, and those that do have high rates are not experiencing declining rates. Apparently, the conditions which caused high rates in the developed nations in the past are not present in many developing nations today. Furthermore, the situation and conditions of development today differ greatly from those experienced by the already developed nations.

CONCLUSION

There is little support for the modernization theory perspective that lowered homicide rates accompany and follow modernization. There is also little support for associations of opportunity demographic differences among nations—such as, density, household size, and age structure—and differences in homicide rates. As the demographic features of nations change with development, this further contradicts modernization theory.

There is strong and consistent support for a positive relationship between income inequality and homicides, especially in combination with cultural heterogeneity and discrimination. This may not necessarily indicate support for dependency theory, as poverty and capitalist penetration do not appear to be associated with homicides.

There are strong indications that culture, both in terms of social integration and proviolent norms and values, plays an important role in the homicide rates of nations. It is crucial that better and more comprehensive ways are found to study the role of culture in explaining cross-national variation in homicides. As a corollary, it is also important to discover why nations differ in social integration and proviolent norms and values.

Studies regarding the association between political differences and homicides are few and have inconsistent results. Gun availability and ownership are consistently related to homicides, but this research has only included developed nations.

Research focusing exclusively on children and women as homicide victims seems to justify these as distinct areas of research. Family disruption and poor treatment of women are apparently important in the victimization of children. Variations in the roles and status of women appear to influence their likelihood of victimization.

Research focusing exclusively on women as homicide offenders does not indicate there is much difference in the causes of variation in female offending as compared to offending in general. Specifically, there is little support for the emancipation perspective that changes in the roles and status of women that accompany development contribute to increased offending.

Earlier discussed caveats concerning the data and samples used in most of the research reviewed in this chapter should be kept in mind when considering all these conclusions. As data and samples improve, all relevant theoretical perspectives and concepts should be reconsidered and studied anew.

NOTE

1. A chapter reviewing cross-national research on homicides by Gary LaFree is included in the book, *Homicide studies: A sourcebook of social research*, edited by M. Dwayne Smith and Margaret Zahn and published by Sage.

REFERENCES

Adler, F. (1975). *Sisters in crime.* New York: McGraw-Hill.

Adler, F. (1983). *Nations not obsessed with crime, Vol. 50.* Littleton, CO: Fred B. Rothman and Company.

Archer, D. & Gartner, R. (1981). Peacetime casualties: The effects of war on the violent behavior of noncombatants. In E. Aronson (Ed.), *Readings about the social animal* (pp. 236–248). San Francisco: W. H. Freeman.

Archer, D. & Gartner, R. (1984). *Violence and crime in cross-national perspective.* New Haven, CT: Yale University Press.

Archer, D. & Gartner, R. (1986). Violence and economy: A modest hypothesis on inequality, unemployment, and crime. *International Annals of Criminology*, 24 (1–2), 255–266.

Archer, D., Gartner, R., & Beittel, M. (1983). Homicide and the death penalty: A cross-national test of a deterrence hypothesis. *The Journal of Criminal Law and Criminology*, 74 (3), 991–1016.

Arthur, J. (1991). Development and crime in Africa: A test of modernization theory. *Journal of Criminal Justice*, 19, 499–513.

Avison, W. & Loring, P. (1986). Population diversity and cross-national homicide: The effects of inequality and heterogeneity. *Criminology*, 24, 733–750.

Bennett, R. (1991). Development and crime: A cross-national, time-series analysis of competing models. *The Sociological Quarterly*, 32, 343–363.

Birkbeck, C. (1992). Crime and control in Venezuela. In H. Heiland, L. Shelley, & H. Katoh (Eds.), *Crime and control in comparative perspectives.* (pp. 109–130). New York: Walter de Gruyter.

Bowers, W. J. (1984). *Legal homicide.* Boston: Northeastern University Press.

Bowker, L. H. (1981). The institutional determinants of international female crime. *International Journal of Comparative and Applied Criminal Justice*, 5, 11–28.

Braithwaite, J. (1979). *Inequality, crime and public policy.* London: Routledge & Kegan Paul.

Braithwaite, J. & Braithwaite, V. (1980). The effect of income inequality and social democracy on homicide: A cross-national comparison. *British Journal of Criminology*, 20, 45–53.

Briggs, C. & Cutright, P. (1994). Structural and cultural determinants of child homicide: A cross-national analysis. *Violence and Victims*, 9 (1), 3–16.

Brown, R. M. (1994). *No duty to retreat: Violence and values in American history and society.* Norman, OK: University of Oklahoma Press.

Cernovsky, Z. & Litman, L. (1993). Re-analyses of J. P. Rushton's crime data. *Canadian Journal of Criminology*, 35 (1), 31–36.

Chesnais, J. C. (1992). The history of violence: Homicide and suicide through the ages. *International Social Science Journal*, 44, 217–234.

Clark, R. (1989). Cross-national perspectives on female crime: An empirical investigation. *International Journal of Comparative Sociology*, 30 (3–4), 195–215.

Conklin, G. H. & Simpson, M. E. (1985). A demographic approach to the cross-national study of homicide. *Comparative Social Research*, 8, 171–186.

Cooper, F. (1980). *From slaves to squatters: Plantation labor and agriculture in Zanzibar and coastal Kenya.* New Haven, CT: Yale University Press.

DeFronzo, J. (1983). Economic assitance to impoverished Americans: Relationship to incidence of crime. *Criminology*, 21, 119–136.

Durkheim, E. (1964). *The division of labor in society.* New York: Free Press.

Durkheim, E. (1966). *Suicide.* New York: Free Press.

Eisner, M. (1995). The effect of economic structures and phases of development on crime. *Criminological Research*, 32, 17–43.

Eisner, M. (1996). *Modeling the effects of economic fluctuations on homicide rates in Europe, 1830–1993.* Paper presented at the European Social Science History Conference, May 9–11, Leeuwenhort, the Netherlands.

Ellis, H. (1992). Crime and control in the English-speaking Caribbean: A comparative study of Jamaica, Trinidad, Tobago and Barbados 1960–1980. In H. Heiland, L. Shelley & H. Katoh (Eds.), *Crime and control in comparative perspectives.* (pp. 131–162). New York: Walter de Gruyter.

Fiala, R. & LaFree, G. (1988). Cross-national determinants of child homicide. *American Sociological Review*, 53, 432–445.

Friday, P.C. (1995). The international division and international scholarship. *The Criminologist*, 20, 10–11.

Gartner, R. (1990). The victims of homicide: A temporal and cross-national comparison. *American Sociological Review*, 55, 92–106.

Gartner, R. (1991). Family structure, welfare spending, and child homicide in developed democracies. *Journal of Marriage and the Family*, 53 (1), 231–240.

Gartner, R., Baker, K., & Pampel, F. (1990). Gender stratification and the gender gap in homicide victimization. *Social Problems*, 37, 593–612.

Groves, W. B., McCleary, R., & Newman, G. (1985). Religion, modernization, and world crime. *Comparative Social Research*, 8, 59–78.

Groves, W. B., Newman, G., & Corrado, C. (1987). Islam, modernization, and crime: A test of the religious ecology thesis. *Journal of Criminal Justice*, 15, 495–503.

Gurr, T. (1977). Crime trends in modern democracies since 1945. *International Annals of Criminology*, 16, 41–85.

Gurr, T. (1981). Historical trends in violent crime: A critical review of the evidence. In M. Tonry & N. Morris (Eds.), *Crime and justice: An annual review of research, volume 3* (pp. 295–353). Chicago: University of Chicago Press.

Haferkamp, H. & Ellis, H. (1992). Power, individualism, and the sanctity of human life: Development of criminality and punishment in four cultures. In H. Heiland, L. Shelley & H. Katoh (Eds.), *Crime and control in comparative perspectives.* (pp. 261–280). New York: Walter de Gruyter.

Hansmann, H. & Quigley, J. (1982). Population heterogeneity and the sociogenesis of homicide. *Social Forces*, 61, 206–224.

Hartnagel, T. F. (1982). Modernization, female social roles and female crime: A cross-national investigation. *The Sociological Quarterly*, 23, 477–490.

Hartnagel, T. F. & Mizanuddin, M. (1986). Modernization, gender role convergence, and female crime: A further test. *International Journal of Comparative Sociology*, 27, 1–14.

Helal, A. & Coston, C. (1991). Low crime rates in Bahrain: Islamic social control—Testing the theory of synnomie. *International Journal of Comparative and Applied Criminal Justice*, 15 (1), 125–144.

Herrera, M. A. (1965-1966). Simulated combat. *Revista*, 9, 85–92.

Hood, R. (1989). *The death penalty: A world-wide perspective*. Oxford, England: Clarendon Press.

Huang, W. S. (1995). A cross-national analysis on the effect of moral individualism on murder rates. *International Journal of Offender Therapy and Comparative Criminology*, 39 (1), 63–75.

Huggins, M. (1984). *From slavery to vagrancy in Brazil: Crime and social control in the third world*. New Brunswick, NJ: Rutgers University Press.

Joutsen, M. (1992). Developments in delinquency and criminal justice: A Nordic perspective. In H. Heiland, L. Shelley, & H. Katoh (Eds.), *Crime and control in comparative perspectives* (pp. 23–44). New York: Walter de Gruyter.

Kick, E. & LaFree, G. (1985). Development and the social context of murder and theft. *Comparative Social Research*, 8, 37–57.

Killias, M. (1992). Gun ownership, suicide, and homicide: An international perspective. In A. Alvazzi del Frate, U. Zvekic, & J. van Dijk (Eds.), *Understanding crime: Experiences of crime and crime control* (pp. 289–302). Rome, Italy: UNICRI.

Killias, M. (1993). International correlations between gun ownership and rates of homicide and suicide. *Canadian Medical Association Journal*, 148 (10), 1721–1776.

Krahn, H., Hartnagel, T., & Gartrell, J. (1986). Income inequality and homicide rates: Cross-national data and criminological theories. *Criminology*, 24, 269–295.

Krohn, M. (1976). Inequality, unemployment, and crime: A cross-national analysis. *The Sociological Quarterly*, 17, 303–313.

Krohn, M. (1978). A Durkheimian analysis of international crime rates. *Social Forces*, 57, 654–670.

Krohn, M. & Wellford, C. (1977). A static and dynamic analysis of crime and the primary dimensions of nations. *International Journal of Criminology and Penology*, 5, 1–16.

Kruttschnitt, C. (1995). Violence by and against women: A comparative and cross-national analysis. In R. B. Ruback & N. A. Weiner (Eds.), *Interpersonal violent behaviors* (pp. 89–108). New York: Springer.

LaFree, G. & Kick, E. (1986). Cross-national effects of developmental, distributional, and demographic variables on crime: A review and analysis. *International Annals of Criminology*, 24, 213–235.

Landau, S. (1984). Trends in violence and aggression: A cross-cultural analysis. *International Annals of Criminology*, 22, 119–150.

Landau, S. & Pfefferman, D. (1988). A time-series analysis of violent crime and its relation to prolonged states of warfare. *Criminology*, 26, 489–504.

Lester, D. (1987). Cross-national correlations among religion, suicide, and homicide. *Sociology and Social Research*, 71, 103–104.

Lester, D. (1991). Crime as opportunity: A test of the hypothesis with European homicide rates. *British Journal of Criminology*, 31 (2), 186–191.

MacDonald, L. (1976). *The sociology of law and order*. Boulder, CO: Westview.

McClintock, F. H. & Wikström, P-O. (1990). Violent crime in Scotland and Sweden. *British Journal of Criminology*, 30 (2), 207–228.

Marshall, I. H. (1982). Women, work, and crime: An international test of the emancipation hypothesis. *International Journal of Comparative and Applied Criminal Justice*, 6, 25–37.

Messner, S. F. (1980). Income inequality and murder rates: Some cross-national findings. *Comparative Social Research*, 3, 185–198.

Messner, S. F. (1982). Societal development, social equality, and homicide: A cross-national test of a Durkheimian model. *Social Forces*, 61, 225–240.

Messner, S. F. (1985). Sex differences in arrest rates for homicide: An application of the general theory of structural strain. *Comparative Social Research*, 8, 187–201.

Messner, S. F. (1986). Modernization, structural characteristics, and societal rates of crime: An application of Blau's macrosociological theory. *The Sociological Quarterly*, 27 (1), 27–41.

Messner, S. F. (1989). Economic discrimination and societal homicide rates: Further evidence on the cost of inequality. *American Sociological Review*, 54, 597–611.

Messner, S. F. & Rosenfeld, R. (1997). Political restraint of the market and levels of criminal homicide: A cross-national application of institutional-anomie theory. *Social Forces, 75* (4), 1393–1416.

Neapolitan, J. L. (1994). Cross-national variation in homicide rates: The case of Latin America. *International Criminal Justice Review*, 4, 4–22.

Neapolitan, J. L. (1997a). Cross-national variation in homicides: Is race a factor? *Criminology*, forthcoming.

Neapolitan, J. L. (1997b). Homicides in developing nations: Results of research using a large, representative sample. *International Journal of Offender Therapy and Comparative Criminology*, forthcoming.

Neuman, L. & Berger, R. (1988). Competing perspectives on cross-national crime: An evaluation of theory and evidence. *The Sociological Quarterly*, 29, 281–313.

Nijboer, J. (1995). Trends in violence and homicides in the Netherlands. In C. Block & R. Block (Eds.), *Trends, risks and interventions in lethal violence: Proceedings of the third annual spring symposium of the Homicide Research Working Group (HRWG)*. Atlanta, GA: HRWG.

Ortega, S., Corzine, J., Burnett, C., & Poyer, T. (1992). Modernization, age structure, and regional context: A cross-national study of crime. *Sociological Spectrum*, 12, 257–277.

Quinney, R. (1965). Suicide, homicide, and economic development. *Social Forces*, 43, 401–406.

Rahav, G. (1990). Cross-national variations in violence. *Aggressive Behavior*, 16, 69–76.

Rotton, J. (1986). Determinism redux: Climate and cultural correlates of violence. *Environment and Behavior*, 18 (3), 346–368.

Rushton, J. P. (1988). Race differences in behavior: A review and evolutionary analysis. *Personality and Individual Differences*, 9, 1009–1024.

Rushton, J. P. (1990). Race and crime: A reply to Roberts and Gabor. *Canadian Journal of Criminology*, 32, 315–334.

Rushton, J. P. (1995a). Race and crime: An international dilemma. *Society*, 32 (2), 37–42.

Rushton, J. P. (1995b). Race and crime: International data for 1989–1990. *Psychological Reports*, 76, 307–312.

Savage, J. & Vila, B. (1995). *Lagged effects of nurturance on crime: A cross-national comparison*. Paper presented at American Society of Criminology meeting, Nov. 15–18, Boston.

Shelley, L. (1981). *Crime and modernization: The impact of industrialization and urbanization on crime*. Carbondale, IL: Southern Illinois University Press.

Shichor, D. (1990). Crime patterns and socioeconomic development: A cross-national analysis. *Criminal Justice Review*, 15 (1), 64–78.

Simon, R. J. (1975). *Women and crime*. Lexington, MA: D. C. Heath.

Simon, R. J. & Baxter, S. (1989). Gender and violent crime. In N. A. Weiner & M. E. Wolfgang (Eds.), *Violent crime, violent criminals* (pp. 171–197). Newbury Park, CA: Sage.

Simpson, M. E. & Conklin, G. H. (1992). *Homicide, inequality, political systems, and transnational corporations: A cross-national study*. Paper presented at American Sociology Association meeting, Aug. 24–27, Pittsburgh, PA.

Souryal, S. (1987). The religionization of a society: The continuing application of Shariah law in Saudi Arabia. *Journal for the Scientific Study of Religion*, 26 (4), 429–449.

Souryal, S. (1990). Religious training as a method of social control: The effective role of Sharia law in Saudi Arabia. In U. Zvekic (Ed.), *Essays on crime and development* (pp. 261–298). Rome, Italy: UNICRI.

Sproule, C. F. & Kennett, D. J. (1989). Killing with guns in the USA and Canada 1977–1983: Further evidence for the effectiveness of gun control. *Canadian Journal of Criminology*, 31 (3), 245–251.

Steffensmeier, D., Allan, E., & Streifel, C. (1989). Development and female crime: A cross-national test of alternative explanations. *Social Forces*, 68, 262–283.

Stephens, G. (1994). The global crime wave. *The Futurist*, 28 (4), 22–29.

Toro-Calder, J. (1950). *Personal crimes in Puerto Rico*. Unpublished M. A. thesis, University of Wisconsin-Madison.

U.N. (1992). *Trends in crime and criminal justice, 1970–1985, in the context of socio-economic change*. New York: Author.

U.N. (1993). *Crime trends and criminal justice operations at the regional and interregional levels.* Vienna, Austria: Author.

U.N. (1995). *Ninth United Nations Congress on the prevention of crime and the treatment of offenders*. Cairo, Egypt: Author.

Unnithan, N. & Whitt, H. (1992). Inequality, economic development, and lethal violence: A cross-national analysis of suicide and homicide. *International Journal of Comparative Sociology*, 33 (3–4), 182–196.

van Onselen, C. (1976). *Chibaro: African mine labor in southern Rhodesia, 1900–1933*. London: Pluto Press.

Wellford, C. F. (1974). Crime and the dimensions of nations. *International Journal of Criminology and Penology*, 2, 1–10.

Whitt, H. P., Gordon, C. C. & Hofley, J. R. (1972). Religion, economic development, and lethal aggression. *American Sociological Review*, 37, 193–201.

Widom, C. S. & Stewart, A. J. (1986). Female criminality and the status of women. *International Annals of Criminology*, 24, 137–162.

Wolf, P. (1971). Crime and development: An international analysis of crime rates. *Scandinavian Studies in Criminology*, 3, 107–120.

Wolfgang, M. E. & Ferracuti, F. (1967). *The subculture of violence: Toward an integrated theory in criminology.* London: Tavistock.

6

Past Research on
Property and Other Crimes

After homicides, most cross-national research has focused on property crimes, which include various types of thefts. Much of this research has used an overall theft rate which combines major and minor thefts; some have distinguished between major and minor thefts, and some have studied specific types of theft, such as breaking and entering or robbery. The problems in using combined theft rates and rates from before the 1980s were discussed in Chapter 2.

As most research has used combined and/or older theft rates, the results discussed here are of questionable value. They should therefore be seen more as having heuristic value than as actually explaining cross-national theft variation. Research on property crimes also suffers from the sample and indicator/concept problems discussed in the previous chapter.

There is very limited research on such crimes as sexual offenses, drug offenses, assaults, and so on as these suffer from extreme definitional, reporting, and recording variation among nations. Probably the best data on these types of offenses come from victimization rather than official data. Unlike homicides, for which only official data are available, there are victimization and self-report data for property and other crimes. Unfortunately, research using these data has been quite limited.

This chapter first addresses research on property crimes using a similar approach to that used in homicides, and then briefly addresses other crimes. This is followed by a brief summary and evaluation of where we are in cross-national crime research and how we might proceed.

PROPERTY CRIME

Modernization Theory

The fundamental proposition of modernization theory regarding property crime rates is that they increase as nations modernize and will remain high in highly developed nations. A very large body of cross-sectional research using a variety of indicators of development (most often GNP or GDP) and thefts based on arrests supports a strong positive association between level of development and property crime (Groves, Newman, & Corrado, 1987; Krohn, 1978; Krohn & Wellford, 1977; LaFree & Kick, 1986; Messner, 1986; Newman, 1990; Rahav, 1990; Shichor, 1990; Stack, 1984; Wellford, 1974). Neapolitan (1995) found a positive association of GDP to thefts even when only developing nations were included in analysis, indicating that the association of development to property crimes is not just due to the very high rates in the most developed nations. There have been two studies which failed to find a significant association between level of development and thefts (Kick & LaFree, 1985; MacDonald, 1976).

The association of GDP or GNP to thefts suggests that development and property crime are associated because of increased attractive and portable goods. Urbanization suggests that the proximity of offenders to targets might also be a factor. Some research indicates a positive relationship between degree of urbanization and the amount of property crime (Krohn, 1978; LaFree & Kick, 1986; MacDonald, 1976; Neapolitan, 1995; Wolf, 1971). However, several studies have not found a significant association (Hartnagel, 1982; Kick & LaFree, 1985).

Results including analysis of an association between development over time and increased property crime have been mixed. Krohn and Wellford (1977) found a positive association between change in GNP and change in rates of property crime over time. And pooled time-series analysis by Ortega, Corzine, Burnett, and Poyer (1992) also indicated a positive relationship between GNP and property crime. However, two other pooled time-series studies found the association of GDP and thefts to be curvilinear, with a positive association at lower levels but no—or even a negative—association at higher ones (Bennett, 1991; Bennett & Basiotis, 1991). Bennett found a similar curvilinear association between urbanization and theft rates.

Anderson and Bennett (1996) distinguished between minor theft rates in developing and developed nations as well as rates for males and females. Their pooled time-series analysis indicated no association of GDP to minor thefts for either males or females in either developing or developed nations. They found curvilinear associations between urbanization and thefts for both males and females in developed nations but no significant associations in developing nations. The association in developed nations went from negative to positive for males and the reverse for females.

The United Nations Crime Surveys (UNCS) indicate that minor thefts, burglaries, and robberies all increased from 1970 to 1990 (U.N., 1992, 1993, 1995). The increases were much greater in developed nations and for robberies. Studies focusing on Nordic, Latin American, and African nations also indicate increased property crimes in most nations in this same approximate time period (Arthur, 1991; Ellis, 1992; Joutsen, 1992). The increases were greater in the more developed Nordic nations than in other nations. Gurr's (1977) research also indicated greatly increased property crimes in all developed nations, except Japan, from the 1940s to the 1970s.

These trends indicate that as the nations of the world develop, property crimes increase; the higher the level of development, the greater the increase. However, the increase is not universal and a number of nations have experienced decreased property crime from 1970 to 1990, despite having become more developed (U.N., 1992, 1993, 1995). In a study of Western European nations, Eisner (1996) found that while property crimes have increased since 1960, they remained stable from 1900 to 1930 despite rapid development. Thus, trends in property crime do not unequivocally support modernization theory. And while the majority of research and trends supports a positive association between development and property crimes, research results are too inconsistent and mixed to draw any firm conclusions.

The results of the International Victimization Surveys (IVSs) further confuse the issue as they indicate developing nations have substantially higher rates of all types of theft victimizations—burglary, personal thefts, and robbery—than do developed nations (Zvekic & Alvazzi del Frate, 1995). Nations from Eastern-Central Europe have rates somewhat higher than the developed nations. Even considering the small sample of developing nations and the comparability problems of data from developed and developing nations, this is a very surprising finding.

Official arrest data have consistently shown that the most developed nations have much higher rates of all types of property crimes than virtually all developing nations. Yet victimization data indicate the opposite, and that includes burglary, which is not subject to much variation in reporting and thus should be accurately indicated by official data. Also, the sub-Saharan African nations—which tend to be among the most underdeveloped—had the highest property victimization rates; while the Latin American nations—which tend to be more developed—had the lowest rates. Resolving this paradox is one of the most important tasks of future cross-national crime researchers.

Among the developed nations, there is an association between level of affluence and property victimizations; and within all the developing nations, property crime victimizations are more likely in urban areas (van Dijk & Mayhew, 1993). Both findings may be seen as support for modernization theory in developing nations. However, other than for car thefts, the seven nations which participated in both the 1988 and 1991 surveys were as likely to have decreased as increased property crime victimization rates (van Dijk & Mayhew, 1993).

Opportunity and Demographic Variables

Opportunity theory suggests that crimes are more likely to occur when there are motivated offenders and unguarded targets. At a macrolevel, variations in these cannot be directly studied but rather suggested by some demographic variables. Households with working women and few people, for example, should be left unguarded more frequently than others. Bennett (1991), in pooled time-series analysis of thefts, found female labor force participation to have a positive association to theft rates until a moderately high level, diminishing to zero, and eventually becoming negative at a very high level. Bennett and Basiotis (1991), in a similar analysis of the same data but focusing on juvenile property crime, found that female labor force participation had a negative association to thefts, that is, opposite to that predicted by opportunity theory. Neapolitan (1995), in cross-sectional analysis of only developing nations, failed to find a significant association between female labor force participation and thefts.

Neapolitan (1995) also found no relationship between household size and thefts. In research which included nations at all levels of development, Kick and LaFree (1985) found the predicted negative association between household size and thefts. Anderson and Bennett (1996) argue that unemployment also increases guardianship and thus should have a negative association to theft rates. They found a curvilinear association going from positive to negative for male theft rates in developed nations and no association for females. In developing countries, there was no significant association to male rates but, opposite to expectations, a positive association to female theft rates.

As research within nations indicates young people commit a large proportion of property crimes, we would expect that the percent of young in nations would relate to property crime rates. Yet in pooled time-series analysis, Ortega, Corzine, Burnett, and Poyer (1992) failed to find an association between the proportion of juveniles in nations and property crimes. However, Bennett (1991), in a similar analysis, found a curvilinear association, with the percent of juveniles only having a positive association at higher levels. He suggests that a critical mass of young is needed before property crimes will increase. Neapolitan (1995) did not find a significant association between the percent of juveniles and thefts in developing nations.

Populations which are growing faster will have more young people than those growing more slowly. LaFree and Kick (1986) found the predicted negative association between growth and property crime, but Shichor's (1990) research did not indicate a relationship.

While not theoretically linked to property crime, size of population has sometimes been included in research models. These studies have not indicated population size to be a significant factor in property crime rates (Krohn, 1978; Krohn & Wellford, 1977; LaFree & Kick, 1986; Shichor, 1990; Wellford, 1974). Neapolitan (1995) also failed to find a relationship between population density and thefts in developing nations.

The IVS data provide more support for the opportunity perspective than studies using official arrest records. These studies indicate that burglaries and break-ins are more common in nations with higher proportions of people living in semi-detached and detached housing. They also indicate a strong association between levels of car ownership and car theft rates (van Dijk & Mayhew, 1993).

Analysis of the first survey by van Dijk (1991) found that young people were more likely to be victims in all nations, and that age structure is related to property victimization rates. He also found that in all developing nations the poor and urban were most likely to be victims, possibly because they are easier targets.

Anomie and Social Integration

Lack of social or cultural integration is proposed to contribute to crime in general, not just violent crime. The various indicators of this concept have already been discussed in Chapter 5. Two studies failed to find an association between ethnic/linquistic heterogeneity and property crimes (MacDonald, 1976; Messner, 1986). Several studies also indicated that the degree of division of labor or occupational heterogeneity is unrelated to property crimes (Krohn, 1978; Messner, 1986). Krohn's anomie indicator of a gap between material desires and availability of commodities was not associated with property crimes.

The proportion of people enrolled in school at various levels has not been found to relate to property crime rates, supporting neither the proposed individualizing nor homogenizing effect of education (Bennett & Basiotis, 1991; Messner, 1986; Rahav, 1990; Shichor, 1990). Political freedom has also been suggested to have both integrating and individualizing effects. Several studies have failed to find negative or positive associations of degree of political democracy or democratic orientation to property crimes (Krohn & Wellford, 1977; MacDonald, 1976; Stack, 1984). Neapolitan's (1995) research, focusing on developing nations and the degree of political freedom, found a positive association to thefts, indicating support for the perspective that political freedom promotes anomie, which contributes to thefts.

Neapolitan's research also indicated that the percent of Protestants is positively associated to thefts in developing nations, supporting the perspective that the emphasis on individualism in Protestantism promotes anomie and crime. While Groves, Newman, and Corrado (1987) did not find

Islamic nations to have lower rates of property crime, they did find that the Islamic religion may have impeded the growth of robberies.

Just as in the case of homicides, the foregoing summary shows little support for anomie or social integration as important in explaining cross-national variation in property crimes. Neapolitan's (1995) research on political rights and Protestantism is a notable exception. Also, as in the case of homicides, the more intensive, qualitative synnomie research of Adler (1983), Helal and Coston (1991), and Souryal (1987, 1990) suggests that anomie may be important to property crimes, we may just need better ways to operationalize the concept.

Poverty and Inequality

Earlier in this chapter, we saw that GNP/GDP is positively associated with property crime as indicated by official arrest data. This suggests that poverty at the national level does not have a positive association to property crime, as poorer nations have less property crime. Neapolitan (1995), using the Overseas Development Council indicator of absolute poverty, did not find a significant association to thefts in developing nations. Conversely, victimization data indicate developing nations to have more property victimization than the developed, and the least developed nations to have the most (van Dijk & Mayhew, 1993). The IVS data also indicate property victimization to be associated to socioeconomic status within nations. These findings suggest poverty may be an important factor in explaining property victimization variation across and within nations.

Theoretically, inequality, particularly income inequality, should be even more positively associated with property than with violent crimes. If people are deprived relative to others, the most direct pressure would be to rectify the deprivation through thefts. Research on the association of income inequality to property crime has indicated no such association (Kick & LaFree, 1985; MacDonald, 1976; Stack, 1984) or a negative one (Krohn, 1976; LaFree & Kick, 1986; Messner, 1986). These studies indicate a lack of support for income inequality promoting or motivating property crimes. Also, Messner (1986), using proportion of the labor force in professional-technical occupations to indicate occupational prestige equality, found a positive rather than negative relationship to property crimes.

Stack (1984) proposed that income inequality might only contribute to property crime in nations with egalitarian cultural systems. His research found no support for this proposition. It may be that developed nations have low levels of income inequality but high levels of property crime due to their affluence. Thus, the positive effect of income inequality on property crime might be masked by the high levels of crime in developed nations. However, Neapolitan (1995) failed to find an association between income inequality and thefts in research focusing on developing nations. Landau (1984), in research on developed nations, did find a positive relationship between inflation—which might contribute to relative deprivation—and robberies.

As already noted, educational inequality—as indicated by proportionate school enrollment—has not been found to be associated with property crimes. An exception is the pooled time-series study by Bennett (1991), which used a more sophisticated measure of educational inequality, that is, Ray and Singer's (1973) index of concentration. He found a curvilinear association, wherein at lower levels of inequality there is a negative association to property crimes but after passing a threshold the relationship turns positive. Anderson and Bennett (1996), using the same methodology and measure of inequality as Bennett (1991), also found curvilinear associations going from negative to positive for both male and female minor theft rates in both developed and developing nations.

Research relating infant mortality to property crimes has yielded mixed results. Shichor (1990) found no association, Rahav (1990) a negative one, and Savage and Vila (1995) a small positive one. In total, these results shed little light on whether inequality as indicated by infant mortality contributes to property crimes.

Overall, research using official data does not lend much support to either poverty or inequality as an important factor in explaining cross-national variation in property crimes. However, since victimization data indicate poverty may be important, we cannot reach any firm conclusions.

As noted in the previous chapter, research on inequality and poverty does not directly test dependency theory, which is more concerned with a nation's place in the world economic order. Chen (1992) found transnational corporate penetration and trade dependence to have positive associations to long-term, but not short-term, general crime levels in third world nations. More research is needed in this area.

Cultural Values and Norms

I have already noted the lack of support for Stack's (1984) proposition that egalitarian cultural values might increase the frustration due to a gap between goals and means, thus contributing to property crime. Other cultural values, such as materialism, might also motivate people to commit property crimes. There has been little cross-national research in this area, and thus there is little to support or reject the proposition that culture variation contributes to property crime variation.

Neapolitan (1995), using the ratio of per capita consumption to GDP as an indicator of materialism, failed to find an association to thefts in developing nations. As indicated earlier, he did find an association of the percent of Protestants—which might indicate Western materialist values—to thefts. Official arrest records clearly show that the developed Western nations have much higher rates of property crime than others, including such developed nations as Japan and Israel (INTERPOL, 1992; U.N., 1993, 1995). It has been suggested, but not empirically shown, that this is due to Western culture having high materialist values (Shichor, 1990; Sklair, 1991).

Ortega, Corzine, Burnett, and Poyer (1992) found regional effects on property crime, even when controlling for level of development, suggesting a possible cultural contribution. The IVS data also indicate that property crime victimizations tend to cluster geographically (van Dijk & Mayhew, 1993; Zvekic & Alvazzi del Frate, 1995). The IVS further indicate that beer-drinking nations have higher rates than wine-drinking ones, suggesting a cultural effect.

Other Research

Killias (1992) found that gun ownership in developed nations not only had a positive association to homicides but also to robberies. Stack (1984) did not find that the percent of property crimes cleared by arrest to be associated to rates of property crime.

Women and Property Crime

Both emancipation theory and opportunity theory suggest that as nations develop, women will have more motivation and opportunities to commit property crimes. Research on the association of development to female offending proportion and level of offending is inconsistent. Research using a variety of measures of development has found positive, negative, and no associations to both minor and major thefts, in terms of both proportionate female offending and level of female offending (Clark, 1989; Hartnagel & Mizanuddin, 1986; South & Messner, 1986; Steffensmeier, Allan, & Streifel, 1989; Widom & Stewart, 1986). Anderson and Bennett (1996), in pooled time-series analysis, concluded there is no strong interaction between development and gender as to rates of minor theft.

Research results for more direct measures of female emancipation and roles outside the home also have yielded mixed results. Clark (1989) found a positive association of female labor force participation to proportionate female offending for minor but not major thefts. Both Widom and Stewart (1986) and Hartnagel and Mizanuddin (1986) failed to find significant associations to proportionate offending for any type of theft.

Widom and Stewart (1986) found the higher the level of education for females in nations, the higher the level and proportion of property crimes. However, neither Steffensmeier, Allan, and Streifel (1989) nor Hartnagel and Mizanuddin (1986) found an association between female educational levels and proportionate female property crime offending.

Widom and Stewart (1986) did not find segregation by occupation to be associated to either proportionate theft offending or level of offending.

Steffensmeier, Allan, and Streifel (1989) also failed to find an association of occupational segregation to proportionate offending.

Widom and Stewart (1986) did find political equality—as indicated by the number of years women had the vote—to have positive associations to proportion and level of theft offending. South and Messner (1986) found female concentration in traditional domestic roles to be negatively associated to proportionate female offending. They also found a relative scarcity of women in nations to relate to lower theft rates.

In the years since Adler (1977) developed the emancipation hypothesis based on increased female offending in Western nations as they developed, several studies have attempted to test the hypothesis. Their results are inconsistent, and substantially more research is needed before we can reach any firm conclusions. Interactions among the economic, political, and cultural realms may make changes in female offending highly variable among nations as they develop.

Property Crime Summary

Cross-sectional analysis of official arrest records shows strong support for the modernization perspective of an association between level of development of nations and amount of property crime. There is also moderate support that as nations become more developed, they experience increased property crimes. Paradoxically, victimization data do not support the modernization perspective, as they indicate developing nations have more property crime than developed ones.

There is little support in analysis of official arrest records that opportunity variables indicating variation in guardianship or pool of offenders—such as, female labor force participation or proportion of youths—have much effect on property crimes. Conversely, victimization data indicate fairly strong support for opportunity theory in terms of suitable targets and age structure.

With the exception of one study on developing nations, which indicated positive associations of Protestantism and political rights to property crime, there was no support for variables attempting to indicate lack of social integration being associated with property crimes. As noted, more intensive research focusing on just a few nations does indicate synnomie to be important in controlling all types of crime. Research has also failed to support a positive association of inequality or poverty to property crimes. If there is an association, it appears to be a negative one. Cultural values have been little studied in relation to property crime, but they may well be significant in explaining differences among nations.

OTHER CRIMES

Rape and Sexual Offenses

There has been little research in cross-national variation in sexual offenses, owing to the questionable validity of data for these offenses. As discussed earlier, there are fairly severe problems with all cross-national crime data, with that for sexual offenses probably being of the lowest quality. This applies to both official and victimization data. Thus, the following research results should be viewed with great skepticism.

Modernization and the related opportunity perspective propose that sexual offenses against women should increase with development. This increase should result from a backlash against women as they challenge male status and power as well as from their increased vulnerability in spending more time outside the home.

Both Groves, Newman, and Corrado (1987) and Neapolitan (1996), using official arrest records, have found positive associations between GNP and sexual crimes/rapes. Neapolitan's research also indicates the proportion of women in university enrollment to be positively related to rape rates. Cultural factors and values may directly influence the amount of sexual offenses or mediate the relationship between other national attributes and sexual offenses. Kersten (1993), in research on Australia, Germany, and Japan, found differences in rates of violent sexual offenses to be related to the degree of hegemonic masculinity in a nation.

Conversely, IVS data indicate that developing nations have higher sexual victimization rates than developed nations or the nations of Eastern-Central Europe (Zvekic & Alvazzi del Frate, 1995). UNCS data from 1970 to 1990 also fail to support the modernization/opportunity perspective, as they indicate most nations have not experienced increases in rapes or sexual victimizations during this period (U.N., 1993, 1995).

Regional variations indicated by IVS data also suggest a possible cultural contribution to national variations in sexual offenses. Among the developing nations, those in Africa have substantially higher victimization rates than those in Latin America or Asia (Zvekic & Alvazzi del Frate, 1995). And among the developed nations, the Western European nations—Germany being the exception—have substantially lower rates than Australia, Canada, New Zealand, and the United States.

Further supporting a cultural contribution is Neapolitan's (1996) finding—using official data—that Christianity is positively associated with rapes in developing nations and that Protestantism is positively associated in developed nations. He attributes the first finding to the cultural influence of colonization and the latter to the individualism and permissiveness of Protestantism. In research contradicting a cultural perspective, Groves, Newman, and Corrado (1987) did not find that Islamic nations had fewer sexual offenses than non-Islamic nations when controlling for GNP.

There have been some other miscellaneous findings. In addition to the aforementioned results, Neapolitan (1996) failed to find income inequality or poverty to be associated to rapes. South and Messner (1986), using the sex ratio of males to females to indicate the value of women in nations, found it mildly related to the percent of rape cases solved. Kutchinsky (1991), in a study of four developed nations, did not find an association between pornography and rape.

Other, Nonsexual Crimes

There is little research on cross-national variation in crimes other than homicides, property crimes, and sexual offenses. Violence is generally considered to be best examined using homicide rates, and other offenses such as fraud and drug offenses vary greatly in terms of definitions, reporting, and recording across nations.

Similar to their results for property and sexual offenses, Groves, Newman, and Corrado (1987) found GNP to be positively related to drug and fraud arrests, with no differences between Islamic and non-Islamic nations. Widom and Stewart's (1986) research on levels and proportions of female offending indicated positive associations of GNP to drug and fraud offenses. An association between development and drug offenses indicates support for the civilization theory proposition that self-harm replaces harm of others as nations modernize.

Widom and Stewart (1986) also found higher levels of female education to relate to higher rates and proportion of female drug and fraud arrests, but they did not find significant associations for female labor force participation. Hartnagel and Mizanuddin (1986) failed to find significant associations of either level of female education or labor force participation to proportionate fraud offending.

UNCS data indicate that over the course of their surveys—1970 to 1990—crimes of all kinds were generally up worldwide, including fraud, drugs, kidnapping, and bribery (U.N., 1992, 1993, 1995). Stephens (1994) suggests this will continue into the twenty-first century. There is, however, substantial variation among nations, with many having experienced decreased rates for all or some offenses. In general, increases are more frequent and greater in the developed nations. Increases are also greater and more frequent for drug offenses. It is not clear whether this is due to actual changes in behavior or to changes in law enforcement concentration on drug offenses. Research using official arrest records from African, Asian, European, and Latin American nations also supports generally increased crime during the latter part of this century (Birkbeck, 1992; Ellis, 1992; Heiland, 1992; Joutsen, 1992; Shrivastava, 1992).

IVS data indicate that assault and threat rates vary little among developed, developing, and transitional Eastern-Central European nations.

However, among developing nations, those of sub-Saharan Africa are greater than those in other regions; and among developed nations, those of Australia, Canada, New Zealand, and the United States are greater than those of Western Europe. Consumer fraud victimizations were found to be highest in Eastern-Central European nations and lowest in the developed nations.

SELF-REPORT RESEARCH

International Self-Report Delinquency study (ISRD) data have not yet been analyzed from a cross-national perspective. Thus far, all analysis has been within each nation. A book on the results of cross-national analysis of this data is due in 1997. After that, the data will be made available to investigators other than those involved in its collection.

Some general findings from the intranation analyses of the thirteen nations have been made available (Junger-Tas, 1994). In all participating nations, boys committed more offenses than girls, with ratios in all nations being similar. For property offenses, the ratio was between 1.5 and 2, and for violent offenses about 2 to 4. The peak age for offending in all nations was similar at sixteen and seventeen, with violent offenses peaking at eighteen and nineteen, England being the exception at twenty.

Educational level did not relate to property offenses, but the lower the educational level, the more likely were violent offenses. School failure was also found to be related to violent offenses, and dislike of school to delinquency in general. Drug use was related to leaving school early.

In general, there was no association between socioeconomic status and delinquency, although a few of the studies indicated more violence in the lower social strata. In most of the nations, minority youths were equally or less likely to be involved in self-reported delinquency. An exception is the United States, where drug and violent offenses were most prevalent among Hispanics, followed by blacks, and then whites. Parental supervision and the relationship with the mother and father had strong associations to delinquency in all nations.

CONCLUSIONS

As already noted, the data and samples used in cross-national crime research have not been of sufficient quality to reach any firm conclusions about variation in crimes across space and time. This is particularly the case for research that has included developing nations. Furthermore, there are many contradictory findings, particularly between research results using different types of data. The following summarizes findings with the most support, the most important contradictory findings, and suggestions for where research should be directed. It is not intended to cover all avenues for research suggested in this and the final chapter.

The Western nations, with the exception of the United States, experienced great reductions in homicides as they developed, and their homicide rates remain relatively low in the present. In general, there is little evidence that the currently developing nations are experiencing lowered homicide rates as they develop, or that among developing nations, the more developed have lower rates. Thus, a different theoretical perspective from modernization must be used to explain variation in homicides across both space and time.

The Western nations also experienced great increases in property crimes as they developed, and the official rates remain high today. It appears that development and crime are associated even among developing nations, but it is not clear that there is a consistent pattern of growth in property crimes among developing nations. The biggest issue to be resolved in future property crime research is the paradox that victimization data not only fail to support a strong positive association between development and crime but actually indicate developing nations to have substantially higher rates.

The nations in transition of Eastern-Central Europe and the former U.S.S.R. probably need to be studied separately from other nations due to their unusual recent history and transitional situation. It is evident that the changes they have undergone in recent years have resulted in substantial increases in crime (e.g., Kangaspunta, 1995; Lotspeich, 1995). These increases indicate the problem of trying to apply the same paradigm to changes in crime patterns in all nations. Similarly, China has experienced greatly increased crime over the last fifteen or twenty years, probably due to its extreme social and economic changes (Wolfgang, 1996).

In general, research on homicides and property crimes must better address change over time. Nearly all the research that has done this has used pooled time-series analysis of the COC data set. As discussed in Chapter 2, these data are severely flawed. Also, pooled time-series analysis does not directly address the issue of change over time, particularly given the great variability in patterns of change. It is paramount that change in crime patterns over time be studied with better data and a wider variety of methodological approaches. More attention must be given to distinctions between change over time and cross-sectional variation.

There are tentative results indicating support for the civilization theory proposition of increased drug use with development. Further research in this area is needed but will have to wait for better official and self-report data.

Better measures of opportunity theory variables must be developed to examine properly how variations and changes in these influence crime. This is more likely to occur in increased and improved victimization research than in analyses of official data.

There has been little research on either violent or property crime which examines the dependency theory proposition that crime in developing nations relates to their economic dependency on other nations. Appropriate indicators of dependency must be developed to test properly the propositions of this perspective. Also, research must address how the position of nations in the world economic order relates to internal problems and stresses that contribute to crime. Economic dependency and possible associations to crime must also be studied in terms of differing cultural and political contexts.

Dependency theory suggests that inequality and poverty result from dependency and in turn result in crime. There is substantial evidence that income inequality does contribute to cross-national variation in homicides. More research is needed on other national characteristics that might mediate or exacerbate the influence of inequality on homicides. There is little evidence that poverty influences homicides or property crimes, but as yet the actual degree of poverty in nations has not been available for many nations or used in much research.

Inequality has not been found to contribute to property crimes. However, all the research on poverty and inequality on crime has used official data. Victimization data might indicate very different associations of poverty and inequality to property crimes, given how they differ from official data regarding level of development and crime.

It appears likely that culture, both in terms of social integration and values, plays an important role in both violent and property crime. More work must be done to resolve inconsistencies among the many concepts and indicators purporting to address the degree of social integration or anomie in nations. The concept of synnomie may be a good starting point, but we need a way to measure this characteristic for a large and varied sample of nations.

Similarly, we must find ways to measure more directly the differences among nations in cultural values and norms that are conducive to violent and/or property crime. Also, it is not enough to examine how values influence crime among nations, we must investigate why nations differ in these values. It should be particularly interesting to look further at the relationship between the two cultural perspectives. Ethnographic studies within nations support the idea that social disorganization and cultural anomie is conducive to the emergence of cultural value systems which allow and/or encourage crime (Sampson & Wilson, 1995).

In general, we need to recognize that crime is a complex phenomenon, which can only be explained and understood in terms of many types of development and the contexts in which they occur. Political, historical, social, demographic, economic, and cultural factors must all be considered.

There are more specific areas that past research indicates should be investigated. The role of guns in homicide rates outside of the developed nations needs study. The many contradictions as to factors that appear to relate strongly to crime within, but not among, nations need to be addressed. These include youth population, degree of urbanization, poverty, and a variety of opportunity theory variables. More attention must be paid to the possibility of curvilinear rather than linear associations, as well as to interactive rather than cumulative associations.

Past research suggests that female victimizations and offending are worthy of separate research, since they may be influenced by factors different from those that generally influence crime rates across nations. Certainly, hypotheses and concepts derived from the emancipation perspective need more research. Victimizations of children also appear to be worthy of research in their own right. Research on victimization or offending of specific categories of people must be careful to distinguish between absolute rates and the relative proportion of rates.

There is growing concern for transnational crime and the international-ization of crime in general. Drug trafficking in particular demonstrates the increasingly complex relationship among nations concerning crime. Drug trafficking transfers wealth to depressed economies, contributes to crime in both import and export nations, results in nations interfering in law enforcement in other nations, and so on (Shelley, 1990). Internationalization of world markets may make the dependency and interrelationships among nations of growing importance in both internal and transnational crime. As yet, there is little data to address this issue, but the United Nations has begun fledgling efforts (U.N., 1995).

REFERENCES

Adler, F. (1977). The interaction between women's emancipation and female crimin-lity: A cross-cultural perspective. *International Journal of Criminology and Penology*, 5, 101–112.

Adler, F. (1983). *Nations not obsessed with crime, Vol. 50*. Littleton, CO: Fred B. Rothman.

Anderson, T. & Bennett, R. (1996). Development, gender, and crime: The scope of the routine activities approach. *Justice Quarterly*, 13 (1), 31–56.

Arthur, J. (1991). Development and crime in Africa: A test of modernization theory. *Journal of Criminal Justice*, 19, 499–513.

Bennett, R. (1991). Development and crime: A cross-national, time-series analysis of competing models. *The Sociological Quarterly*, 32, 343–363.

Bennett, R. & Basiotis, P. (1991). Structural correlates of juvenile property crime: A cross-national time-series analysis. *Journal of Research in Crime and Delin-uency*, 28, 262–287.

Birkbeck, C. (1992). Crime and control in Venezuela. In H. Heiland, L. Shelley, & H. Katoh (Eds.), *Crime and control in comparative perspectives*. (pp. 109–130). New York: Walter de Gruyter.

Chen, D. (1992). *Third world crime in the world system: A cross-national study*. Unpublished dissertation, SUNY at Albany.

Clark, R. (1989). Cross-national perspectives on female crime: An empirical investigation. *International Journal of Comparative Sociology*, 30 (3–4), 195–215.

Eisner, M. (1996). *Modeling the effects of economic fluctuations on homicide rates in Europe, 1830–1993*. Paper presented at the European Social Science History Conference, May 9–11, Leeuwenhort, Netherlands.

Ellis, H. (1992). Crime and control in the English-speaking Caribbean: A comparative study of Jamaica, Trinidad, Tobago, and Barbados 1960–1980. In H. Heiland, L. Shelley, & H. Katoh (Eds.), *Crime and control in comparative perspectives.* (pp. 131–162). New York: Walter de Gruyter.

Groves, W. B., Newman, G., & Corrado, C. (1987). Islam, modernization, and crime: A test of the religious ecology thesis. *Journal of Criminal Justice*, 15, 495–503.

Gurr, T. (1977). Crime trends in modern democracies since 1945. *International Annals of Criminology*, 16, 41–85.

Hartnagel, T. F. (1982). Modernization, female social roles, and female crime: A cross-national investigation. *The Sociological Quarterly*, 23, 477–490.

Hartnagel, T. F. & Mizanuddin, M. (1986). Modernization, gender role convergence, and female crime: A further test. *International Journal of Comparative Sociology*, 27, 1–14.

Heiland, H. G. (1992). Modern patterns of crime and control in the Federal Republic of Germany. In H. Heiland, L. Shelley, & H. Katoh (Eds.), *Crime and control in comparative perspectives.* (pp. 45–68). New York: Walter de Gruyter.

Helal, A. & Coston, C. (1991). Low crime rates in Bahrain: Islamic social control— Testing the theory of synnomie. *International Journal of Comparative and Applied Criminal Justice*, 15 (1), 125–144.

INTERPOL. (1992). *International crime statistics for 1991 and 1992*. Lyons, France: General Secretariat.

Joutsen, M. (1992). Developments in delinquency and criminal justice: A Nordic perspective. In H. Heiland, L. Shelley, & H. Katoh (Eds.), *Crime and control in comparative perspectives* (pp. 23–44). New York: Walter de Gruyter.

Junger-Tas, J. (1994). The international self-report delinquency study: Some methodological and theoretical issues. In J. Junger-Tas, G. J. Terlouw, & M. W. Klein (Eds.), *Delinquent behavior among young people in the Western world* (pp. 1–14). New York: Kluger.

Kangaspunta, K. (1995). *Crime and criminal justice in Europe and North America 1986–1990*. Helsinki, Finland: HEUNI.

Kersten, J. (1993). Crime and masculinities in Australia, Germany, and Japan. *International Sociology*, 8 (4), 461–478.

Kick, E. & LaFree, G. (1985). Development and the social context of murder and theft. *Comparative Social Research*, 8, 37–57.

Killias, M. (1992). Gun ownership, suicide, and homicide: An international perspective. In A. Alvazzi del Frate, U. Zvekic, & J. van Dijk (Eds.), *Understanding crime: Experiences of crime and crime control* (pp. 289–302). Rome, Italy: UNICRI.

Krohn, M. (1976). Inequality, unemployment, and crime: A cross-national analysis. *The Sociological Quarterly*, 17, 303–313.

Krohn, M. (1978). A Durkheimian analysis of international crime rates. *Social Forces*, 57, 654–670.

Krohn, M. & Wellford, C. (1977). A static and dynamic analysis of crime and the primary dimensions of nations. *International Journal of Criminology and Penology*, 5, 1–16.

Kutchinsky, B. (1991). Pornography and rape: Theory and practice? Evidence from crime data in four countries where pornography is easily available. *International Journal of Law and Psychiatry*, 14 (1/2), 47–64.

LaFree, G. & Kick, E. (1986). Cross-national effects of developmental, distributional, and demographic variables on crime: A review and analysis. *International Annals of Criminology*, 24, 213–235.

Landau, S. (1984). Trends in violence and aggression: A cross-cultural analysis. *International Annals of Criminology*, 22, 119–150.

Lotspeich, R. (1995). Crime in the transition economies. *Europe-Asia Studies*, 47 (4), 555–589.

MacDonald, L. (1976). *The sociology of law and order*. Boulder, CO: Westview.

Messner, S. F. (1986). Modernization, structural characteristics, and societal rates of crime: An application of Blau's macrosociological theory. *The Sociological Quarterly*, 27 (1), 27–41.

Neapolitan, J. L. (1995). Differing theoretical perspectives and cross-national variation in thefts in less-developed nations. *International Criminal Justice Review*, 5, 17–31.

Neapolitan, J. L. (1996). *Cross-national variation in rapes: An examination of differing theoretical perspectives and samples*. Unpublished manuscript, Tennessee Technological University.

Newman, G. (1990). Crime and the human condition. In U. Zvekic (Ed.), *Essays on crime and development* (pp. 69–102). Rome, Italy: UNICRI.

Ortega, S., Corzine, J., Burnett, C., & Poyer, T. (1992). Modernization, age structure, and regional context: A cross-national study of crime. *Sociological Spectrum*, 12, 257–277.

Rahav, G. (1990). Cross-national variations in violence. *Aggressive Behavior*, 16, 69–76.

Ray, J. & Singer, D. (1973). Measuring the concentration of power in the international system. *Sociological Methods and Research*, 1, 403–437.

Sampson, R. & Wilson, W. (1995). Toward a theory of race, crime, and urban inequality. In J. Hagan & R. Peterson (Eds.), *Crime and inequality* (pp. 37–54). Stanford, CA: Stanford University Press.

Savage, J. & Vila, B. (1995). *Lagged effects of nurturance on crime: A cross-national comparison*. Paper presented at American Society of Criminology meeting, Nov. 15–18, Boston.

Shelley, L. (1990). The internationalization of crime: The changing relationship between crime and development. In U. Zvekic (Ed.), *Essays on crime and development* (pp. 119–134). Rome, Italy: UNICRI.

Shichor, D. (1990). Crime patterns and socioeconomic development: A cross-national analysis. *Criminal Justice Review*, 15 (1), 64–78.

Shrivastava, R. S. (1992). Crime and control in comparative perspective: The case of India. In H. Heiland, L. Shelley, & H. Katoh (Eds.), *Crime and control in comparative perspectives*. (pp. 189–208). New York: Walter de Gruyter.

Sklair, L. (1991). *Sociology of the global system*. Baltimore, MD: Johns Hopkins University Press.

Souryal, S. (1987). The religionization of a society: The continuing application of Shariah law in Saudi Arabia. *Journal for the Scientific Study of Religion*, 26 (4), 429–449.

Souryal, S. (1990). Religious training as a method of social control: The effective role of Sharia law in Saudi Arabia. In U. Zvekic (Ed.), *Essays on crime and development* (pp. 261–298). Rome, Italy: UNICRI.

South, S. & Messner, S. (1986). The sex ratio and women's involvement in crime: A cross-national analysis. *The Sociological Quarterly*, 28, 171–188.

Stack, S. (1984). Income inequality and property crime. *Criminology*, 22, 229–258.

Steffensmeier, D., Allan, E., & Streifel, C. (1989). Development and female crime: A cross-national test of alternative explanations. *Social Forces*, 68, 262–283.

Stephens, G. (1994). The global crime wave. *The Futurist*, 28 (4), 22–29.

U.N. (1992). *Trends in crime and criminal justice, 1970–1985, in the context of socio-economic change*. New York: Author.

U.N. (1993). *Crime trends and criminal justice operations at the regional and interregional levels*. Vienna, Austria: Author.

U.N. (1995). *Ninth United Nations Congress on the prevention of crime and the treatment of offenders*. Cairo, Egypt: Author.

van Dijk, J. (1991). *The International Crime Survey (ICS): Some organisational and methodological issues and results*. Leiden, Netherlands: Criminological Institute of Leiden University.

van Dijk, J. & Mayhew, P. (1993). Criminal victimisation in the industrialised world: Key findings of the 1989 and 1992 International Crime Surveys. In A. Alvazzi del Frate, U. Zvekic, and J. van Dijk (Eds.), *Understanding crime:Experiences of crime and crime control* (pp. 1–50). Rome, Italy: UNICRI.

Wellford, C. F. (1974). Crime and the dimensions of nations. *International Journal of Criminology and Penology*, 2, 1–10.

Widom, C. S. & Stewart, A. J. (1986). Female criminality and the status of women. *International Annals of Criminology*, 24, 137–162.

Wolf, P. (1971). Crime and development: An international analysis of crime rates. *Scandinavian Studies in Criminology*, 3, 107–120.

Wolfgang, M. (1996). Delinquency in China: Study of a birth cohort. *National Institute of Justice Research Preview*, May, 1–2.

Zvekic, U. & Alvazzi del Frate, A. (1995). Overview of the main findings. In U. Zvekic & A. Alvazzi del Frate (Eds.), *Criminal victimization in the developing world* (pp. 15–48). Rome, Italy: UNICRI.

III

Data and Analysis

7

Methodological Issues

This chapter addresses some of the methodological issues and problems in cross-national crime research. As most such research has involved official crime data and quantitative analysis, most of this chapter addresses these types of data and analysis. Furthermore, this type of research brings more questions on the suitability of various methodological practices. There is also some mention of case studies and qualitative approaches to data and issues.

Various statistical methods and tests are necessarily discussed and critiqued. However, this is not the place to discuss fully the complexity of issues involved in many statistical procedures, and in some cases I lack the expertise to cover these issues in great depth. I discuss the most important areas in question, briefly address these, make some recommendations, and provide information as to where more in-depth information is available.

SAMPLE SELECTION AND ISSUES

Most analysts have included as many nations as possible in their research on cross-national crime. Still, until recently, data have not been available for a sufficient number and diversity of nations to test hypotheses properly and to make generalizations. It is generally acknowledged that (1) sample size and composition can greatly influence results, (2) most research has not used sufficiently large or properly representative samples, and (3) studies have varied greatly in sample size and composition (Lynch, 1995; Messner, 1989; Neuman & Berger, 1988).

Small samples are less likely to represent accurately the populations of all nations, and many past studies have included a disproportionate number of Western nations. Small samples also may be highly dependent on only a few cases and limit the number of variables that can be included in analysis.

Thus, a case can be made for attempting to maximize the number of nations included in analysis or at least to include nations from all geographic regions, levels of development, and political and economic systems.

There are reasons that an approach of maximizing sample size and/or representativeness may not always be the best strategy. Some nations for which crime data are available have very small populations. For example, INTERPOL crime data for 1991–1992 are available for ten nations that have populations under 100,000, with three under 50,000. Even when crime rates are high in these nations, they account for very little of the crime in the world. Yet when included in analysis, they have as much influence on results as larger nations.

A very small change in the number of crimes in these nations can result in a very large change in the rate of crime. This can unduly influence both cross-sectional and trend analyses. Many analysts use multiyear averages in order to adjust for anomalous very low or high rates, but this only partially addresses the problem. The dynamics of causation may also be different in very small nations as compared to larger ones. For these reasons, analysts should consider dropping very small nations from models or doing analyses with and without them and comparing results.

As discussed in Chapter 2, direct inspection of crime data can reveal nations for which the data are of highly questionable accuracy and/or comparability. In these cases, such nations should not be included in analysis simply to increase sample size or representativeness.

Another issue is the availability of data for both the independent and control variables of interest. There are some nations for which crime data are available, but data are unavailable for almost all other variables of interest. Depending on the research question, methodological approach, and variables of interest, some nations should probably be excluded from analysis due to lack of data.

It may also be best—at least for some research questions—to focus on specific categories of nations. As noted in preceding chapters, much past research has focused exclusively on the most developed nations (e.g., Gartner, 1990; Gurr, 1977). Some research has analyzed only developing nations (e.g., Neapolitan, 1995), and some has analyzed developed and developing nations separately (e.g., Fiala & LaFree, 1988).

As noted in Chapters 2 and 3, both official and victimization crime data are likely to be more accurate and more comparable across space and time if only highly developed nations are included in analysis. Also, more and better data for independent variables are available, particularly if long-term trend or time-series analysis is undertaken. Thus, we can have greater confidence in research which includes only developed nations. Variables may have different effects on crime in developed and developing countries. For example, Arthur and Marenin (1995) note that female labor force participation may be positively associated to thefts in developed but not developing nations. In the former, a female working may result in an unguarded home, but in the latter other family members may remain at home. Of course, the generalizability of results and types of hypotheses which can be examined are quite limited if only highly developed nations are analyzed.

Fiala and LaFree (1988) also suggest that separate analysis of developed and developing nations may be necessary because social disorganization may apply more to developing nations, and the greater resources of developed nations might make state welfare intervention more important there. As noted in Chapter 4, developing nations are doing so in different historical and situational contexts than already developed nations, which might influence the associations of all manner of variables to crime. Also, as discussed in Chapter 2, there might be systematic differences in the reporting and recording of crimes between nations at different levels of development.

If separate analysis of developed and developing nations is desired, some criteria for distinguishing among nations must be established. Fiala and LaFree (1988) designated nations as less developed if they were classified as developing nations in the *United Nations Demographic Yearbook* (U.N., 1969–). Neapolitan (1995) used this criterion but added nations classified as third world nations in the *Encyclopedia of the Third World* (Kurian, 1992) for nations not covered in the UNDY. The *Human Development Report* uses several classification schemes, including least developed nations, all developing nations, and industrial nations (UNDP, 1995).

Bennett (1991) used GDP per capita, with $4,100 (1984) being the dividing point.[1] It has been noted that modernization involves much more than simply economic development (e.g., Heiland & Shelley, 1992; Zvekic, 1990), and thus use of such arbitrary divisions is questionable. For example, Kuwait is classified as developed and Greece as developing, if GDP per person is the sole criterion guiding classification. A newer measure of development—the human development index (HDI)—includes longevity, knowledge, and standard of living (UNDP, 1995). In addressing more aspects of modernization, the HDI provides better criteria for dividing nations in future research. The dividing point, of course, would still be arbitrary. The HDI is discussed further in the next chapter.

Nations in transition of the former U.S.S.R. and Eastern-Central Europe present particular problems in terms of inclusion in samples used. Their radical change and upheaval in recent years have resulted in great increases in crimes of all types (Lotspeich, 1995; Savelsberg, 1995). Their inclusion in analysis with other nations that are not undergoing similar social change might confound associations of independent variables to crime rates. Crime in these nations is an interesting area of research but should probably be studied separately from research on other nations.

Some investigators have focused on samples of nations from one geographic region, for example, African nations (Arthur, 1991), Nordic nations (Joutsen, 1992), and Latin American nations (Carranza, 1990). This strategy allows research to focus on what is associated to variation in crimes among nations with similar histories, cultural configurations, and climates.

There is a growing body of opinion that cross-national research should shift away from the inclusion of all nations in analysis to focus on strategically selected, smaller samples (Gartner, 1995; Hartrais, 1996; Kohn, 1987). Nations can be chosen to provide maximium leverage for theory testing by maximizing their similarities, differences, or both. Smaller samples allow for choosing nations in whose crime and other data we have the greatest confidence, controlling for some types of variables, and more dramatically indicating what is and what is not associated with low or high rates of crime. Smaller samples also allow for combining quantitative and qualitative data and a more interpretive type of analysis. This is further addressed later in the chapter.

MULTIVARIATE REGRESSION ANALYSIS

The majority of research on cross-national variation in crimes has used multivariate regression analysis of official crime rates. While this type of analysis has not yet been undertaken with IVS or ISRD data, the methodological problems would be similar. The numerous problems with cross-national crime data have already been discussed in Chapters 2 and 3, where I stressed the importance of careful inspection of data for anomalies and inexplicably deviant cases. I also addressed the use of multiyear averages and the need to adjust homicide rates for attempts. Independent variables should be similarly inspected and, when necessary, dropped or adjusted.

Cross-nationally, crime risk and offending both vary by age and sex. Therefore, consideration should be given to analyzing age-/sex-specific rates or age-/sex-adjusted rates. Deane (1987) suggests a good method of standardization of rates for age and sex, when age-/sex-specific rates are not available.

Almost all linear analysis of cross-national crime rates has used multivariate least-squares regression. Such analysis should begin with inspection of univariate distributions and bivariate plots of all independent variables and crime rates under consideration. This inspection should look for highly skewed distributions, extreme nonlinearity, heteroskedasticity, and extreme outlier rates (Fox, 1991). Direct inspection should be followed by testing for various problems and making adjustments when necessary.

Heteroskedasticity—a nonrandom pattern in the residual error term—can bias hypothesis testing in regression analysis and negatively influence the accuracy of prediction (McClendon, 1994). Several tests are available for detecting this problem. The problem can be addressed by weighted least squares or transforming the dependent variable for variance stabilization (Weisberg, 1985). Most cross-national research on crime has used log natural transformation, which contracts the scale on which crime rates are measured (e.g., Conklin & Simpson, 1985; Krahn, Hartnagel, & Gartrell, 1986; Messner, 1989; Rahav, 1990). Natural log transformations have also been performed on independent variables when high skewness is observed in univariate distributions (e.g., Krahn, Hartnagel, & Gartrell 1986; Messner, 1989; Neapolitan, 1994, 1995). For some variables, a value of one may have to be added to all scores to avoid nonzero values for log transformations.

Examination of bivariate plots might also reveal curvilinear associations between crime rates and independent variables. The most common way to test for a curvilinear association is to use the quadratic term by squaring the independent variable exhibiting the curvilinear association. Higher power polynomials test for more bends in the curve where the number of bends is equal to the power minus one (McClendon, 1994). The signs of the independent variables and their quadratic transformation indicate the form of the curve. Several investigators have used quadratic terms to explore curvilinear associations to cross-national crime rates (e.g., Bennett, 1991; Simpson & Conklin, 1992).

Examination of univariate and bivariate plots can also indicate the possibility that there are outlier cases which can unduly influence the fit of regression models. Some analysts have confused univariate and regression outliers, dropping nations from models simply because their crime rates were unusually high (e.g., Kick & LaFree, 1985). A nation should be considered a problem only if it constitutes a regression outlier, that is, the crime rate is unusual given the value of some independent variable or variables (Fox, 1991).

There are tests to indicate whether an outlier nation might severely bias results, with Cook's D being the one most often used in cross-national crime research. Weisberg (1985) suggests a Cook's D of 1.0 or greater as a criterion for outlier cases. If an outlier nation or nations are identified, analyses should be carried out with and without it/them and results compared. Several past studies of cross-national crime have identified and adjusted for outlier nations (e.g., Avison & Loring, 1986; Messner, 1989). Outliers should not solely be viewed as problems but also as interesting in their own right. Finding and explaining outliers might be an important part of cross-national crime research.

Multicollinearity is a persistent problem in macrolevel linear research. This is particularly the case with cross-national research, as so many variables tend to be highly intercorrelated, such as, urbanization, age structure, and GDP. High intercorrelations among independent variables can create large standard errors for regression coefficients and unstable parameter estimates (McClendon, 1994). Better than simply checking for high correlations among independent variables is checking the variance inflation factor, which is based on the multiple correlation of a particular independent variable on the others (Fox, 1991; McClendon, 1994). A variance inflation factor greater than four is generally considered large enough to indicate a multicollinearity problem sufficient to warrant concern (Fisher & Mason, 1981; Fox, 1991).

There are several ways to go if severe multicollinearity problems are indicated. One can experiment with models with different variables excluded and check for large fluctuations in coefficients and variance explained (Hanushek & Jackson, 1977; McClendon, 1994). If significant changes in the influence of important independent variables are detected, we can have little confidence in the parameter estimates. If a number of variables are highly intercorrelated, one can be chosen to represent the underlying concept they are measuring (Cohen & Land, 1984). Selecting the single variable that maximizes variance explained is a good criterion (Fox, 1991).

Probably the preferred way of handling multicollinearity is construction of an index from the intercorrelated variables (e.g., LaFree & Kick, 1986; Messner, 1989; Savage & Vila, 1995). This can be accomplished by doing a factor analysis of the intercorrelated variables and creating an index variable using z-score transformations. Polarities must be reversed when required to make sure all positive values indicate the same direction for the concept. Examples of various methods for handling multicollinearity can be found in studies by Gartner (1991), Kick and LaFree (1985), Messner (1989), Neapolitan (1995), and Savage and Vila (1995).

As further discussed in Chapter 8, data are not always available for all nations for independent variables of interest. If nations are dropped from analysis for which data are not available for one or more variables, sample size and representativeness can be severely affected. One strategy for handling this problem is to experiment with models using subsets of nations for which data are available for a particular set of variables, looking for variations in coefficients and variance explained. One of these models should include only nations for which all data are available for all variables.

Some investigators have used mean substitution for missing values (e.g., Neapolitan, 1994, 1995; Ortega, Corzine, Burnett, & Poyer, 1992). If this is done, there is the possibility that nations which are missing data on a variable systematically differ from those nations for which data are available. One way to check for this possibility is to include a dummy variable in analysis, which has value of zero for nations for which data are available and one for nations for which data are unavailable (Whitt, 1986). If this variable exhibits a significant association to crime rates in regression models, mean substitution should not be used in these models. Even when this variable does not exhibit a significant association in a model, models with and without mean substitution should probably be compared and contrasted.

As noted in previous chapters, sometimes the variables which explain cross-national variation in crimes may have interactive or moderating effects rather than strictly independent or additive effects. The usual method of testing for interactive associations in regression analysis is to enter the product of the two variables thought to have an interactive association into a model containing the two variables (Jaccard, Turrisi, & Wan, 1990). The model can than be examined to see if the interaction term has a significant coefficient and to what degree variance explained has been increased.

The nature of the interaction effect can be examined by entering representative values of one of the two variables into the regession model and then checking the slope of the regression of crime rates on the other variable (Cohen & Cohen, 1983; Jaccard, Turrisi, & Wan, 1990). Avison and Loring (1986) used this procedure in their research of the interactive effects of ethnic heterogeneity and income inequality on homicides. They used one standard deviation below the mean, the mean, and one standard deviation above the mean as low, medium, and high representative values of ethnic heterogeneity.

A problem with the use of interaction terms is that they usually have severe multicollinearity with either or both of the first order terms. One method for reducing multicollinearity is to center the variables around minimizing constants before forming the interaction term (Cronbach, 1987; Smith & Sasaki, 1979). This technique was used by Stack (1984) in his research on the interactive effects of income inequality and egalitarian culture on property crimes. Centering tends to reduce multicollinearity but does not guarantee it will be completely eliminated (Dunlap & Kemery, 1987).

Earlier I discussed the possibility that it may be appropriate to analyze subsamples of nations separately, such as, developed versus developing nations. There are two methods of examining whether the same variables affect crime differently in different samples. Intercept dummy variables can be created by giving a value of zero to one sample and a value of one to the other, and a slope dummy is then created by multiplying the value of each independent variable by the intercept dummy. The slope dummy indicates how the effect of an independent variable differs between samples (Hanushek & Jackson, 1977). This technique is used by Fiala and LaFree (1988) in their research on homicides of children.

An alternative is to examine regression models for both and each sample separately. The Chow test can be used to see if parameter values associated with crime rates in one sample differ significantly from those in the other (Kennedy, 1992). If one wants to examine the difference in the importance of individual variables in the two samples, squared semipartial correlations can be examined. This is the decrement in variance explained if a variable is removed from an equation and indicates the importance of the variable in the model (Darlington, 1990).

I have already alluded to dummy variables several times. A dummy variable is a dichotomous variable constructed from an originally categorical or qualitative variable, using binary—0,1—coding (Hardy, 1993). Dummy variables can be very valuable in cross-national models for examining the effects of such factors as different time periods, geographic regions, levels of development, political systems, and so forth. Examples of the use of dummy variables can be found in the work of Groves, McCleary, and Newman

(1985), Messner (1989), Neapolitan (1994), and Ortega, Corzine, Burnett, and Poyer (1992).

While the first models tested should include all possibly relevant variables, some analysts later trim models to eliminate the noise of variables which make small, nonsignificant contributions to variance explained. Several studies have used backward elimination to trim models. In this procedure, each variable is considered for removal on the basis of the corresponding F-value probability, with coefficients reestimated as each variable is removed. This continues until all variables with a probability of F greater than the criterion—generally .10—have been removed. Messner (1989) and Savage and Vila (1995) have used this procedure.

Hirschi and Selvin (1996) argue that stepwise regression analysis is best for studying associations to crime, as it best indicates the direct and indirect contributions of each independent variable. In this method the multiple correlation coefficient is recalculated as each new variable is entered or removed, thus indicating the contribution of the entered or removed variable. Variables are removed and entered according to tolerance tests generally set at .05 or .10. In actual practice, backward elimination and stepwise regression generally yield the same or very similar final models.

When the number of cases is small—as it is in much cross-national crime research—the multiple correlation coefficient can be a biased estimate of variance explained (Howell, 1992). Thus, cross-national crime research should also report the adjusted correlation coefficient, which is usually smaller but relatively unbiased. This reporting of adjusted correlation coefficients has been done in only a minority of studies (e.g., Conklin & Simpson, 1985; Neapolitan, 1995, 1997b).

A major problem with most of the research using multivariate regression analysis is that it has been cross-sectional, examining variation in crime across nations but not over time. Pooled time-series analysis—which combines cross-sectional analysis with analysis of variation over time—has been used in several studies (e.g., Bennett, 1991; Gartner, 1990; Ortega, Corzine, Burnett, & Poyer, 1992). An additional advantage of pooled time-series analysis is the greatly increased number of cases in the models.

Pooled time-series analysis treats the crime rate each year for each nation as a separate case. There are several pooled time-series models which differ both in the assumptions necessary and in the statistical power (Sayrs, 1989). Autocorrelation—where residual error terms from different observations are correlated—is a particular problem in pooled time-series analysis, as observations adjacent to each other in time generally have similar values for the independent and dependent variables.

There are also several methods for testing and adjusting for autocorrelation (Sayrs, 1989; Schroeder, Sjoquist, & Stephan, 1986). Applications of different methods can be found in the work of Bennett (1991), Gartner (1990), and Ortega, Corzine, Burnett, and Poyer (1992). A more thorough discussion of the statistical issues, methods, and problems involved in pooled time-series analysis is beyond the scope of this book.

There are, however, some general problems with pooled time-series analysis which should be noted. The most fundamental of these is that this type of analysis ignores the reality that each nation is a distinct entity. At a minimum, this means there is no way of distinguishing between what contributes to variation between nations and what contributes to change within nations. Also, there is no distinguishing among nations with increasing, decreasing, and stable crime rates. Random yearly fluctuations become just more individual cases, and the cultural and historical contexts of nations are completely lost. Some of these problems exist in all multivariate regression analysis, but as Sayrs (1989) notes, pooled time-series is a combination of the problems of time-series and cross-sectional analyses.

Isaac and Griffin (1989) argue that pooled time-series analysis renders research ahistorical, obscuring changing historical relations through time and discounting the importance of historical process. They suggest that the separation of theory from history inherent in time-series analysis masks historical reality, making the results of such research of questionable validity. They propose temporally moving covariance analysis as a way of moving closer to historical actuality and relations. Their article should be read for further details.

The data problems which plague all cross-national data are exacerbated in time-series analysis, particularly pooled time-series. Reliable consistent data are needed for a number of countries over a number of years for a number of variables. This means a great amount of effort, time, and care is necessary to create a good data set, and this assumes that data are available and of good quality. For both crime rates and independent variables, data quality, collection methods, definitions, and so on change over time and quite likely in different ways in different nations. Data for developing nations from many years back are of questionable quality. Also, for some key variables, such as income inequality, data for a number of adjacent years are simply not available.

The result is that the few pooled time-series studies of cross-national crime variation have covered few nations and/or few years or have used severely flawed data. Gartner (1990) and Gartner, Baker, and Pampel (1990) analyzed samples of only eighteen developed nations. Huang's (1995) research spanned only six years—not long enough to study change over time—and included only twenty-nine nations.

Bennett (1991), Bennett and Basiotis (1991), and Ortega, Corzine, Burnett, and Poyer (1992) used the previously discussed COC data set which covered fifty-three nations over twenty-five years. As noted, the creation of this data set was an impressive but severely flawed effort. The homicide rates are not adjusted for attempts and the theft rates do not properly account for the definitional changes which occurred in INTERPOL data in 1977. Thus, pooled time-series analysis of these data uses a highly sophisticated and complex method on data not of sufficient quality for such analysis.

As collection of all types of data improves in developing nations, the potential for doing quality pooled time-series analysis on more than only developed nations increases. However, someone has to go to the enormous effort of creating a good data set. Even then, given the problems inherent in pooled time-series analysis and cross-national crime data, this method may be more appropriately used as an exploratory technique rather than for confirming hypotheses.

LONGITUDINAL ANALYSIS

Longitudinal analysis focuses exclusively on change over time, without the confounding influence of variation among nations. This type of research requires much less data than pooled time-series, as measuring the same variables at at least two points in time is sufficient. Preferably, each point would cover several years, averaged for each variable to adjust for random yearly fluctuations and aberrant years. This is clearly more important for some types of variables than others, for example, homicide rates versus income inequality.

Longitudinal research has several advantages over cross-sectional research.[2] Data problems are reduced, as you need not assume definitions, recording, and so on are consistent across nations but only over time. For crimes such as rapes or drug offenses, which are likely to be inconsistently reported and defined across nations, longitudinal analysis may be the only type even somewhat defensible. Still, as I have noted, there have been changes in definitions used by INTERPOL, the U.N., and WHO which preclude longitudinal use of crime data from before the late 1970s.

Longitudinal designs allow for more directly getting at causal rather than associational relationships, as temporal precedence and covariation can be established (Menard, 1991). Both magnitude and direction of change can be identified, studied, and possibly explained. Another concern of longitudinal analysis can be the examination of changes in the relationships among variables over time. It might be instructive to find that different variables are important in explaining cross-national crime variation at two different points in time.

Of course, there are also disadvantages to longitudinal analysis of cross-national crime. Crime, and possibly other data, from years past are of more questionable quality than recent data. Also, definitions, recording practices, and so on do change over time, and they change differently in different nations and data sets. Other factors can also influence crime rates over time and confound the association of variables of interest, such as, the previously discussed likelihood that more victims survive assaults as medical care improves in a nation.

The number and representativeness of nations included in analysis will generally be smaller in longitudinal than cross-sectional analysis. For many nations, data will be available for one point in time but not the other, usually in the present but not the past. This is more true of developing than developed nations, particularly those in sub-Saharan Africa.

Furthermore, longitudinal analysis cannot address as great a degree of difference among nations as can cross-sectional analysis. For example, in examining modernization theory, cross-sectional analysis can include nations at vastly different levels of development, whereas longitudinal analysis is generally restricted to relatively brief periods of change. There are exceptions, such as Eisner's (1996) analysis of crime trends in Western Europe since 1800. These studies necessarily involve few nations and use data of very questionable quality.

An important issue in longitudinal research is how to measure the magnitude of change. The most direct method, of course, is simply to use raw or absolute change. However, it is misleading to suggest that a nation which experienced an increased homicide rate from 3.0 to 6.0 has changed to the same degree as one which has increased from 20.0 to 23.0. An alternative is to use percent or rate of change, but it is misleading to suggest a nation which experienced an increased homicide rate from 1.0 to 1.5 has changed to the same degree as one which increased from 10 to 15.

Another alternative suggested by Menard (1991) is to look at residual change. The value of a variable at time two is predicted by linear regression on its value at time one. The residual change is the difference between the predicted and actual values at time two. Given the questionable quality of cross-national crime data over time, it may be best to classify nations as having increased, decreased, or remained relatively stable. Discriminant or tabular analysis could be used to distinguish among these. Of course, what constitutes an increase or decrease would still need to be somewhat arbitrarily determined.

Some researchers have looked at patterns of change over time, rather than just magnitude and direction (e.g., Adler, 1977; Eisner, 1996; Gurr, 1977). This, of course, requires that data be obtained for a number of points in time rather than just two points. These studies indicate change over time is not always unidirectional and can be curvilinear or even erratic. Thus, examining change simply in direction or magnitude between two or three points can be misleading.

The analysis of UNCS crime data in the official U.N. reports looks at change in crime rates over time in terms of percents and patterns (U.N., 1992, 1993, 1995). They report worldwide trends, trends for developed versus developing nations, and trends for individual nations.

Some investigators have done quasilongitudinal research. For example, Savage and Vila (1995) did a lagged effects study using child welfare indicators from 1960 to explain 1980 crime rates. Other researchers have used the rate or degree of change in development variables in the recent past to explain current crime rates (e.g., Fiala & LaFree, 1988; Krahn, Hartnagel, & Gartrell, 1986; Neapolitan, 1995). Ortega, Corzine, Burnett, and Poyer (1992), using a pooled time-series data set and analysis, subtracted the mean for each nation on both the independent and dependent variables from the value of each variable in any given year. They argue this results in all variation occurring within nations and thus examines concurrent change over time.

The 1992 workshop Cross-National Longitudinal Research in Human Development and Criminal Behavior—which represented fifteen nations and forty-five universities—concluded that little has been accomplished in the area of comparative longitudinal crime research (Weitekamp & Kerner, 1993). Thus, this clearly is an area for future researchers to address more fully.

OTHER TYPES OF ANALYSIS

It may not be appropriate to use high-powered statistical analysis on data which is of highly questionable quality. Such analysis should at the very least not have the predominance it has had in cross-national crime research. Also, analysis at such a high level of abstraction—which treats nations as collections of isolated variables—does not consider the uniqueness of nations or differing historical and cultural contexts. Methods beyond the scope of this book are being developed which combine qualitative and quantitative research strategies and allow for multilevel analysis in cross-cultural research (Bryk & Raudenbush, 1992; Gartner, 1995; Ragin, 1991). These have not yet been used in cross-national crime research.

There have also been comparative case studies of crime variation between nations, but these involve one, two, or at most several nations, and thus the results cannot be generalized to other nations (e.g., Adeyemi, 1990; Dooley, 1995; Helal & Coston, 1991; McClintock & Wikström, 1990; Souryal, 1987). Also, most of these are generally narrow in focus, concentrating on a specific issue or policy, and do not address many of the issues of interest in broader cross-national crime research (Lynch, 1995). Arthur and Marenin (1995) argue that only case studies can produce valid explanations of crime in developing nations. In their view, statistical analyses of large samples of nations lack sufficient complexity and consideration of context to yield valid results. They suggest that only case studies consider context sufficiently and are complex enough to reflect both unique and common aspects of nations conducive to crime.

I conclude this chapter with some simple suggestions for research that avoids the pitfalls of macrolevel regression analysis but is truly cross-national in scope and applicability. Earlier I suggested that dividing nations into categories of increased, decreased, or stable crime rates might be more appropriate in longitudinal analysis than analysis of change indicated by continuous measures. Cross-sectional analysis might also be more appropriately accomplished by dividing nations into those low, medium, and high on a particular crime than using the rates as continuous ratio variables. The decision to place a nation in a low, medium, or high category can be based on both quantitative data and the more subjective evaluations discussed in Chapter 2. Definitional, reporting, and recording differences among nations might bias the relative order of nations substantially, but they will unlikely result in many nations being inaccurately classified as low, medium, or high. Also, using categories of crime levels rather than actual frequencies avoids the problem of skewed distributions.

Using categories would also allow for more effectively combining data from several sources, as it would not matter if rates in one source systematically differed from those in another. If a nation falls into the same category for two or more sources, we can be more certain it belongs in that category, even if the actual rates between sources vary substantially. If a nation falls in different categories in different data sets, we can have little confidence as to where it belongs and thus should probably not include it in analysis. Once nations have been classified, they can be studied using tabular or discriminant analysis, depending on the independent variables. Analysis of variance or covariance might also be considered.

The investigators actually involved in the collection of UNCS and IVS data opt for tabular and trend rather than multivariate linear analysis (Zvekic & Alvazzi del Frate, 1993; U.N., 1992, 1993, 1995). They look at crime rates and changes in crime rates in terms of individual nations and nations grouped by developmental level or geographic region. Perhaps this is because they do not have enough confidence in the data for other types of analysis, and thus perhaps neither should we; those who collect INTERPOL and WHO data do not do analysis.

In doing simple categorical analysis, there is the danger of finding spurious associations and reaching faulty conclusions. For example, in Rushton's (1990, 1995a, b) research on race and crime, he identifies nations as predominantly African, Asian, and Caucasian. Finding the mean homicide rate for African nations to be significantly higher than for Asian or Caucasian, he reaches the racist conclusion that this is because Africans have evolved to be less intelligent and more aggressive than other races. There is no consideration of the structural, developmental, demographic, or cultural/historical factors that contribute to national variations in violence. When these factors are considered in multivariate regression analysis, the association of race to homicide disappears (Neapolitan, 1997a).

The opinion that macrolevel analysis cannot adequately explain cross-national crime variation is becoming increasingly prevalent (e.g., Adler, 1996; Gartner, 1995; Hartrais, 1996; Lynch, 1995). These critics argue that this methodology fails to treat nations as coherent entities, does not sufficiently consider sociocultural context, and frequently tests social-psychological theories with national-level data. They argue research must shift away from universalist, macrolevel analysis and become multilevel, multidisciplinary, and multimethodological.

One possible strategy for avoiding the problems of macrolevel research using data of questionable quality is to study smaller, strategically selected samples. For example, Adler (1983) studied ten very low crime-rate nations and what they had in common. Kersten (1993) compared and contrasted low, medium, and high crime-rate nations as to violent sex offenses. Nations could be grouped to maximize similarities and/or differences on crime rates and/or cultural or structural variables, such as religious ecology or developmental level. For example, Souryal (1987, 1990) focused his research on Islamic nations, contrasting them according to application of Shariah (divine) law.

Use of smaller samples makes it easier to do analysis at multiple levels and with differing methods. One approach is to compare correlates of crime within and across nations (LaFree & Birkbeck, 1991). Correlates of crime could also be compared within and across geographic regions. Another approach is to combine quantitative and qualitative data and analysis (Adler, 1983). Lynch (1995) has noted that much cross-national crime research uses macrolevel data to test social-psychological theories. And Hartrais (1996) has argued that the quantitative approach used in most research does not take sufficient account of varying sociocultural settings.

Future investigators should consider a multidisciplinary approach combining ethnographic and historical analyses, with secondary analysis of quantitative national-level data (Gartner, 1995; Hartrais, 1996). Lynch and Groves (1995) argue that theory and research attempting to explain crime in all milieus without reference to culture and history cannot be adequate or complete. This strategy would retain the reality of nations as coherent entities and shift research away from descriptive, universalistic approaches and toward giving more consideration to contextualization and historical/cultural variation. Rather than testing preconceived hypotheses, more emphasis would be given to discovering commonalities and differences that relate to variations in crime. Such research should also take variations in criminal justice systems into account in more than a simplistic, categorical manner.

Of course, research which uses smaller samples of nations that do not represent the total population of the nations in the world is also problematic. We cannot be sure about the generalizability of findings or whether some particular theory or hypothesis has been properly tested. What is gained in the depth and complexity of analysis is lost in the lack of full diversity of nations and general understanding of causes of cross-national variation in crimes.

NOTES

1. Bennett (1991) not only divides nations into less- and more-developed categories but also into low and high growth rates. The result is a four-way classification: high development and high growth, high development and low growth, low development and high growth, and low development and low growth.

2. See Archer and Gartner (1984) for an excellent discussion on the advantages of longitudinal analysis in cross-national research.

REFERENCES

Adeyemi, A. A. (1990). Crime and development in Africa: A Case study on Nigeria. In U. Zvekic (Ed.), *Essays on crime and development* (pp. 135–194). Rome, Italy: UNICRI.

Adler, F. (1977). The interaction between women's emancipation and female criminality: A cross-cultural perspective. *International Journal of Criminology and Penology*, 5, 101–112.

Adler, F. (1983). *Nations not obsessed with crime, Vol. 50*. Littleton, CO: Fred B. Rothman.

Adler, F. (1996). Our American society of criminology, the world, and the state of the art. *Criminology*, 34 (1), 1–10.

Archer, D. & Gartner, R. (1984). *Violence and crime in cross-national perspective*. New Haven, CT: Yale University Press.

Arthur, J. (1991). Development and crime in Africa: A test of modernization theory. *Journal of Criminal Justice*, 19, 499–513.

Arthur, J. & Marenin, O. (1995). Explaining crime in developing countries: The need for a case study approach. *Crime, Law, and Social Change*, 23 (3), 191–214.

Avison, W. & Loring, P. (1986). Population diversity and cross-national homicide: The effects of inequality and heterogeneity. *Criminology*, 24, 733–750.

Bennett, R. (1991). Development and crime: A cross-national, time-series analysis of competing models. *The Sociological Quarterly*, 32, 343–363.

Bennett, R. & Basiotis, P. (1991). Structural correlates of juvenile property crime: A cross-national time-series analysis. *Journal of Research in Crime and Delinquency*, 28, 262–287.

Bryk, A. & Raudenbush, S. (1992). *Hierarchical linear models*. Newbury Park, CA: Sage.

Carranza, E. (1990). Development, crime, and prevention: Reflections on Latin America. In U. Zvekic (Ed.), *Essays on crime and development* (pp. 207–227). Rome, Italy: UNICRI.

Cohen, J. & Cohen, P. (1983). *Applied multiple regression for the behavioral sciences*. 2nd ed. Hillsdale, NJ: Lawrence Erlbaum.

Cohen, L. & Land, K. (1984). Discrepancies between crime reports and crime surveys: Urban and structural determinants. *Criminology*, 22, 499–530.

Conklin, G.H. & Simpson, M. E. (1985). A demographic approach to the cross-national study of homicide. *Comparative Social Research*, 8, 171–186.

Cronbach, L. J. (1987). Statistical tests for moderator variables: Flaws in analyses recently proposed. *Psychological Bulletin*, 102 (3), 414–417.

Darlington, R. (1990). *Regression and linear models*. New York: McGraw Hill.

Deane, G. (1987). Cross-national comparison of homicide: Age-/sex-adjusted rates using the 1980 U. S. homicide experiences as a standard. *Journal of Quantitative Criminology*, 3 (3), 215–227.

Dooley, E. (1995). *Homicide in Ireland, 1972–1991*. Dublin, Ireland: Ireland Department of Justice.

Dunlap, W. & Kemery, E. (1987). Failure to detect moderating effects: Is multicollinearity the problem? *Psychological Bulletin*, 102 (3), 418–420.

Eisner, M. (1996). *Modeling the effects of economic fluctuations on homicide rates in Europe, 1830–1993*. Paper presented at the European Social Science History Conference, May 9–11, Leeuwenhort, Netherlands.

Fiala, R. & LaFree, G. (1988). Cross-national determinants of child homicide. *American Sociological Review*, 53, 432–445.

Fisher, J. E. & Mason, R. L. (1981). The analysis of multicollinear data in criminology. In J. Fox (Ed.), *Methods in quantitative criminology* (pp. 99–125). New York: Academic Press.

Fox, J. (1991). *Regression diagnostics*. Newbury Park, CA: Sage.

Gartner, R. (1990). The victims of homicide: A temporal and cross-national comparison. *American Sociological Review*, 55, 92–106.

Gartner, R. (1991). Family structure, welfare spending, and child homicide in developed democracies. *Journal of Marriage and the Family*, 53 (1), 231–240.

Gartner, R. (1995). Methodological issues in cross-cultural large-survey research. In B. Ruback & N. Weiner (Eds.), *Interpersonal violent behaviors: Social and cultural aspects* (pp. 7–24). New York: Springer-Verlag.

Gartner, R., Baker, K., & Pampel, F. (1990). Gender stratification and the gender gap in homicide victimization. *Social Problems*, 37, 593–612.

Groves, W. B., McCleary, R. & Newman, G. (1985). Religion, modernization, and world crime. *Comparative Social Research*, 8, 59–78.

Gurr, T. (1977). Crime trends in modern democracies since 1945. *International Annals of Criminology*, 16, 41–85.

Hanushek, E. & Jackson, J. (1977). *Statistical methods for social scientists*. New York: Academic Press.

Hardy, M. A. (1993). *Regression with dummy variables*. Newbury Park, CA: Sage.

Hartrais, L. (1996). Comparative research methods. *Social Research Update* 13, online. Available: http://www.soc.surrey.ac.uk/sru/sru.htmlo or sociology@soc.surrey.ac.uk.

Heiland, H. & Shelley, L. (1992). Civilization, modernization, and the development of crime and control. In H. Heiland, L. Shelley, & H. Katoh (Eds.), *Crime and control in comparative perspectives*. (pp. 1–20). New York: Walter de Gruyter.

Helal, A. & Coston, C. (1991). Low crime rates in Bahrain: Islamic social control— Testing the theory of synnomie. *International Journal of Comparative and Applied Criminal Justice*, 15 (1), 125–144.

Hirschi, T. & Selvin, H. (1996). *Delinquency research: An appraisal of analytic methods*. New Brunswick, Canada: Transaction.

Howell, D. (1992). *Statistical methods for psychology*. Boston: PWS-Kent.

Huang, W. S. (1995). A cross-national analysis on the effect of moral individualism on murder rates. *International Journal of Offender Therapy and Comparative Criminology*, 39 (1), 63–75.

Isaac, L. & Griffin, L. (1989). Ahistoricism in time-series analyses of historical process: Critique, redirection, and illustrations from U.S. labor history. *American Sociological Review*, 54, 873–890.

Jaccard, J., Turrisi, R., & Wan, C. (1990). *Interaction effects in multiple regression*. Newbury Park, CA: Sage.

Joutsen, M. (1992). Developments in delinquency and criminal justice: A Nordic perspective. In H. Heiland, L. Shelley, & H. Katoh (Eds.), *Crime and control in comparative perspectives* (pp. 23–44). New York: Walter de Gruyter.

Kennedy, P. (1992). *A guide to econometrics*. Cambridge, MA: MIT Press.

Kersten, J. (1993). Crime and masculinities in Australia, Germany, and Japan. *International Sociology*, 8 (4), 461–478.

Kick, E. & LaFree, G. (1985). Development and the social context of murder and theft. *Comparative Social Research*, 8, 37–57.

Kohn, M. L. (1987). Cross-national research as an analytic strategy. *American Sociological Review*, 52, 713–731.

Krahn, H., Hartnagel, T., & Gartrell, J. (1986). Income inequality and homicide rates: Cross-national data and criminological theories. *Criminology*, 24, 269–295.

Kurian, G. (1992). *Encyclopedia of the third world*. New York: Facts on File.

LaFree, G. & Birkbeck, C. (1991). The neglected situation: A cross-national study of the situational characteristics of crime. *Criminology*, 29 (1), 73–98.

LaFree, G. & Kick, E. (1986). Cross-national effects of developmental, distributional, and demographic variables on crime: A review and analysis. *International Annals of Criminology*, 24, 213–235.

Lotspeich, R. (1995). Crime in the transition economies. *Europe-Asia Studies*, 47 (4), 555–589.

Lynch, J. (1995). Crime in international perspective. In J. Wilson & J. Petersilia (Eds.), *Crime* (pp. 11–37). San Francisco, CA: ICS Press.

Lynch, M. & Groves, W. (1995). In defense of comparative criminology: A critique of general theory and the rational man. In F. Adler & W. Laufer (Eds.), *The legacy of anomie theory* (pp. 367–394). London: Transaction.

McClendon, M. J. (1994). *Multiple regression and causal analysis*. Itasca, IL: F. E. Peacock.

McClintock, F. H. & Wikström, P-O. (1990). Violent crime in Scotland and Sweden. *British Journal of Criminology*, 30 (2), 207–228.

Menard, S. (1991). *Longitudinal research*. Newbury Park, CA: Sage.

Messner, S. F. (1989). Economic discrimination and societal homicide rates: Further evidence on the cost of inequality. *American Sociological Review*, 54, 597–611.

Neapolitan, J. L. (1994). Cross-national variation in homicide rates: The case of Latin America. *International Criminal Justice Review*, 4, 4–22.

Neapolitan, J. L. (1995). Differing theoretical perspectives and cross-national variation in thefts in less-developed nations. *International Criminal Justice Review*, 5, 17–31.

Neapolitan, J. L. (1997a). Cross-national variation in homicides: Is race a factor? *Criminology*, forthcoming.

Neapolitan, J. L. (1997b). Homicides in developing nations: Results of research using a large, representative sample. *International Journal of Offender Therapy and Comparative Criminology*, forthcoming.

Neuman, L. & Berger, R. (1988). Competing perspectives on cross-national crime: An evaluation of theory and evidence. *The Sociological Quarterly*, 29, 281–313.

Ortega, S., Corzine, J., Burnett, C., & Poyer, T. (1992). Modernization, age structure, and regional context: A cross-national study of crime. *Sociological Spectrum*, 12, 257–277.

Ragin, C. C. (Ed.). (1991). *Issues and alternatives in comparative social research.* New York: E. J. Brill.

Rahav, G. (1990). Cross-national variations in violence. *Aggressive Behavior*, 16, 69–76.

Rushton, J. P. (1990). Race and crime: A reply to Roberts and Gabor. *Canadian Journal of Criminology*, 32, 315–334.

Rushton, J. P. (1995a). Race and crime: An international dilemma. *Society*, 32 (2), 37–42.

Rushton, J. P. (1995b). Race and crime: International data for 1989–1990. *Psychological Reports*, 76, 307–312.

Savage, J. & Vila, B. (1995). *Lagged effects of nurturance on crime: A cross-national comparison.* Paper presented at American Society of Criminology meeting, Nov. 15–18, Boston.

Savelsberg, J. (1995). Crime, inequality, and justice in Eastern Europe: Anomie, domination, and revolutionary change. In J. Hagan & R. Peterson (Eds.), *Crime and inequality* (pp. 206–225). Stanford, CA: Stanford University Press.

Sayrs, L. W. (1989). *Pooled time-series analysis.* Newbury Park, CA: Sage.

Schroeder, L., Sjoquist, D., & Stephan, P. (1986). *Understanding regression analysis.* Newbury Park, CA: Sage.

Simpson, M. E. & Conklin, G. H. (1992). *Homicide, inequality, political systems, and transnational corporations: A cross-national study.* Paper presented at American Sociology Association meeting, Aug. 24–27, Pittsburgh, PA.

Smith, K. & Sasaki, M. (1979). Decreasing multicollinearity: A method for models with multiplicative functions. *Sociological Methods and Research*, 8 (1), 35–56.

Souryal, S. (1987). The religionization of a society: The continuing application of Shariah law in Saudi Arabia. *Journal for the Scientific Study of Religion*, 26 (4), 429–449.

Souryal, S. (1990). Religious training as a method of social control: The effective role of Sharia law in Saudi Arabia. In U. Zvekic (Ed.), *Essays on crime and development* (pp. 261–298). Rome, Italy: UNICRI.

Stack, S. (1984). Income inequality and property crime. *Criminology*, 22, 229–258.

U.N. (1969–). *Demographic yearbook.* New York: Author.

U.N. (1992). *Trends in crime and criminal justice, 1970–1985, in the context of socio-economic change.* New York: Author.

U.N. (1993). *Crime trends and criminal justice operations at the regional and interregional levels.* Vienna, Austria: Author.

U.N. (1995). *Ninth United Nations Congress on the prevention of crime and the treatment of offenders.* Cairo, Egypt: Author.

UNDP. (1995). *Human development report 1995.* New York: Oxford University Press.

Weisberg, S. (1985). *Applied linear regression.* 2nd ed. New York: John Wiley & Sons.

Weitekamp, E. & Kerner, H-J. (Eds.). (1993). *Cross-national longitudinal research on human development and criminal behavior.* Dordrecht, Netherlands: Kluwer.

Whitt, H. P. (1986). The sheaf co-efficient: A simplified and expanded approach. *Social Science Research*, 15, 174–189.

Zvekic, U. (1990). Development and crime in Yugoslavia: Results of the preliminary analysis. In U. Zvekic (Ed.), *Essays on crime and development* (pp. 299–342). Rome, Italy: UNICRI.

Zvekic, U. & Alvazzi del Frate, A. (1993). Criminal victimization in the developing world: An overview preliminary findings from the 1992 International Victim Survey. In A. Alvazzi del Frate, U. Zvekic, & J. van Dijk (Eds.), *Understanding crime: Experiences of crime and crime control* (pp. 51–86). Rome, Italy: UNICRI.

8

Sources and Types of Explanatory Data

Valid and reliable indicators of explanatory concepts are necessary for quality cross-national crime research. Unfortunately, these indicators are subject to the same problems and inconsistencies across nations and over time as the crime indicators themselves. Unlike crime indicators, however, there is not a body of research investigating whether there are systematic biases by level of development, cultural variation, or political differences for most of these indicators.

Fortunately, as with crime data, the data on economic, social, political, and cultural aspects of nations have recently improved in quality and quantity and should continue to do so. The number and variety of indicators with which to compare nations are increasing, as is the number of nations for which data are available. The quality of cross-national crime research should improve as the quality of explanatory variables improves. The probability that older data are not of good quality further casts doubt on the validity of older cross-national crime research. Most data more than twenty years old from developing nations in particular are of very questionable quality and should probably not be used.

Many of the concepts which might explain variation in crimes across space and/or time—such as, anomie, modernization, and violent norms and values—are vague, ambiguous, and not easily operationalized. As noted in Chapter 5, the same variables have been used to indicate not only different but even opposite concepts. This chapter identifies indicators used in past research and new indicators not yet used. Exactly what they indicate and how they relate to crime are for investigators to determine, explain, and defend.

This chapter cannot cover all available types or sources of data which might explain cross-national crime variation. I try to cover the most important indicators, as well as the best and most comprehensive sources. As just noted, indicators and sources of data are increasing in number and changing rapidly, especially considering what is becoming available on the Internet. By the time this book is in print, the situation will have changed from what is described here. However, these sources should continue to be the best for the foreseeable future and should serve as a gateway to new sources. A major part of the research process is developing new explanatory concepts and then finding good ways to indicate them.

Indicators and sources are organized by theoretical perspectives or substantive areas. Some indicators could fall into more than one area but are covered only once. Some classifications are by necessity arbitrary. As noted earlier, it is the job of future investigators to determine both how to use indicators and what they indicate.

Some indicators are available annually—with variable retroactivity—and thus can be used in time-series analysis. Some are available for several points in time, while others are available for only one point in time. I note for each indicator whether it is available annually, intermittently, or for just one time period. The number of nations for which indicators are available also varies greatly, and general differences in coverage are noted.

Space does not allow listing each source in which data for an indicator are available. The best sources are listed in Appendices B and C, with a brief description of the types of data each provides and at times discussion as to what is unique or special about the source. If data for an indicator are available only from one or two sources, these are noted.

Addresses, telephone numbers, e-mail addresses, and World Wide Web (WWW) sites of organizations and data sources are given in Appendices B and C. Some of these may have changed by the time this book is in print, especially WWW addresses. What is given, however, should make it easier to locate current sites and information.

DEVELOPMENT AND MODERNIZATION INDICATORS

The level of development of nations has most frequently been measured by gross national product (GNP) or gross domestic product (GDP) per person. Definitions of these and some of the other indicators included in this chapter can be found in Appendix D. These are good measures not only in that they are similarly defined across nations but also in that they are available annually for virtually all nations and territories for well back into the past and from many sources. Thus, they are easy to obtain and can be used in cross-sectional and time-series analyses.

A more recent and improved measure of economic development is the GDP converted at purchasing power parity (PPP), which is the number of units of a nation's currency required to buy the same amounts of goods and services in the domestic market as one dollar would buy in the United States (UNDP, 1990–). Called the "real GDP," this measure equalizes dollar prices across nations, making comparisons more valid. This "real GDP" is not available for as many nations as the GNP, although coverage is fairly good, and is available annually only for recent years. The "real GDP" is available from several World Bank and United Nations publications.

As modernization involves more than just economic development, other indicators of development might also be considered. Some of these are the percent of the labor force involved in agriculture, industry, or services and the percent of the GDP determined by each of these. Some research has also used energy consumption per capita to indicate development. These and other indicators that accompany development tend to be highly correlated with each other, and thus it might be best to create a modernization index using a number of indicators. Most of these and similar variables are available annually for most nations from a variety of World Bank and United Nations sources.

As modernization theory tends to see urbanization as an important aspect of development vis-à-vis crime, it is probably important to indicate the degree of urbanization of nations in cross-national crime research. The most frequently used measure of urbanization has been the percent of the population living in urban areas. Data on urbanization are available annually for most nations from a number of sources. A major problem with this indicator is that different nations use different definitions of what constitutes an urban area.

Thus, better measures are those which indicate the percent of population in cities of more than 750,000 or urban agglomerations of more than one million. However, these are not available for as many nations or as far back in time as percent of the population in urban areas. They are now available annually from several World Bank and United Nations publications, and coverage of nations is increasing. *World Resources*, published biennially since 1986, divides urban areas into six categories by size, giving the percent of the population in each category (World Resources Institute, 1986/87–1996/97).

Some investigators have also considered indicators of cultural and social change which accompany development, such as, percent literate, percentage of different age groups enrolled in education, newspapers per 100,000, and physicians per 100,000. Data on these are available from a variety of sources for most nations, usually on an annual basis.

POVERTY AND DEPRIVATION INDICATORS

Absolute Poverty Indicators

GNP, GDP, and PPP are sometimes seen as indicating the relative poverty among nations, as they generally indicate the standard of living of the people. However, these measures tell us nothing about the distribution of wealth and/or income, how much actual deprivation there is, and how many people are severely deprived. Morris D. Morris has provided excellent critiques of the use of GNP to indicate deprivation across nations (Morris, 1979, 1996).

Morris developed the Physical Quality of Life Index (PQLI) which combines infant mortality, life expectancy, and literacy into a measure of general welfare of the people in a nation. It is available for most nations on an intermittent basis from the Overseas Development Council (ODC, periodic) and is also reported in various publications from Facts on File (Kurian, 1990, 1991a, b, 1992).

Ruth Sivard developed the Economic and Social Rank from eleven different variables representing GNP, education, and health to indicate and compare the general quality of life in nations. It is reported in her *World Military and Social Expenditures* (Sivard, 1974–), which was issued annually from 1974 to 1983 and since 1983 every few years, most recently 1996. Thus, the progress of a nation can be measured over more than thirty years.

Richard Estes created the Index of Social Progress, using forty-four different indicators. It was first issued in 1984 in the *The Social Progress of Nations* and is supposed to be intermittently updated, although I have been unable to locate any recent data (Estes, 1984, 1988). The Population Crisis Committee has twice issued the International Human Suffering Index, which is based on ten different indicators (Population Crisis Committee, 1987, 1992). It is likely to be updated in the future. These indicators are available for many nations, if not for as many as GNP or GDP.

Probably the best indicator of its type is the Human Development Index (HDI), which is a composite measure based equally on life expectancy, educational attainment, and income. It is superior to the other measures because it has been reported annually in the Human Development Report (HDR) and values for 1960, 1970, and 1980 are provided (UNDP, 1990–). Also, it is available for more nations than any other quality of life index. In 1994 the Gender-related Development Index (GDI) was added to the HDR. The HDI can be used in cross-sectional and time-series analyses and is available for a large number of nations. Consideration is being given to reporting disaggregated HDIs by gender, race, geographic region, income disparity, and so forth, within nations.

A problem with all quality of life indicators is that they report an average quality of life in nations, rather than the proportion of the population living in poverty or suffering. There are several different indicators of the proportion of people in developing nations who live in poverty or absolute poverty. For all of these, data are unavailable for a good number of nations, with coverage ranging from around thirty to around eighty-five nations. So, representation from even a moderate number of nations requires using data from a number of different years in a time period spanning at least ten years. This is because in any one year, data are available for only a small number of nations. As the period for which data are available varies among nations, time-series analysis using poverty indicators is not currently possible. It is possible with some of the indicators to get data for two different points in time—for example, circa the late 1970s and early 1990s—and thus do longitudinal analysis.

Several indicators show the percent in poverty in a nation as a whole, while the HDR reports separate proportions for rural and urban areas (UNDP, 1990–). Several report only one poverty level, while the priority poverty indicator given in the *Social Indicators of Development* uses lower and upper poverty lines (World Bank, 1987–). Inspection of different rates from different sources indicates large differences in the proportion of people in poverty for the same nations for the same time period and some differences in the relative order of nations, depending on the source and indicator used.

It is generally acknowledged by sources providing poverty data that they are patchy, inconsistent, and may not be highly accurate (Overseas Development Council, periodic; UNDP, 1990–; World Bank, 1989–). The *Social Indicators of Development* specifically states that poverty measures are "country specific and not comparable across countries" (World Bank, 1994:388).

The newly-developed absolute poverty indicator based on the PPP (DeGeyndt, 1996) and the capability poverty measure reported for the first time in the 1996 HDR (UNDP, 1990–) have been more carefully developed and measured than older ones. Thus, for the first time we may have useful measures for cross-national comparisons. Definitions of poverty indicators and some of the sources of different indicators are given in Appendix D.

The proportion of income going to the poorest 20 percent in nations is available from several sources. This, along with GNP, GDP, or PPP, could be used to create a poverty measure by multiplying one of the three by this percent. This measure would indicate how absolutely poor the poorest segment of a nation is as compared to the poorest in other nations. As data on income distribution are not available for a number of nations, this measure would not result in substantially larger samples than some of the poverty measures. Also, as in the case of poverty, data are available for different years for different nations, making time-series analysis impossible. However, data for two general time periods can be compared.

In investigating the possible influence of poverty on crime, consideration should be given to the amount of help the poor receive from the government. There are no direct indicators of this available for cross-national comparisons. However, several annual sources provide social security benefits expenditure as a percent of the GDP. This percentage covers compensation for loss of income for persons ill or temporarily disabled; payments to the elderly, persons with permanent disability, and the unemployed; family, maternity, and child allowances; and the cost of welfare services. Including this variable in analysis that examines the association of poverty to crime may help clarify the association of deprivation to crime.

In addition to continuous developmental and quality of life indicators, nations can also be categorized by developmental or quality of life level. Such categorizations can be used to divide nations for separate analysis or as dummy variables in analysis of all nations. The *United Nations Demographic Yearbook* divides nations into developed and developing, this being the most commonly used categorization (U.N., 1969–). The HDR distinguishes among the least developed, developing, and industrial nations (UNDP, 1990–). The HDR also divides nations by low, medium, and high HDI and low, medium, and high GNP per capita.

The HDR classifications include the nations of Eastern-Central Europe along with other nations. Kurian (1990, 1991a, 1992) places these nations in a separate grouping, dividing nations in his encyclopedia into first, second, and third world classifications. Because of their recent political and economic volatility, the nations of Eastern-Central Europe should probably be kept separate from developing and developed nations, whatever classification scheme is used.

The World Development Report (WDR) adds the dimension of debt to its classification, dividing nations into low, middle, and high income and low, middle, and high indebtedness and then combining the two for low and middle income nations (World Bank, 1978–). Bennett (1991) used GDP and change in GDP over time to create a fourfold classification of low and high development and rate of growth. Other classifications are also available, or new ones can be created from various continuous variables.

Inequality Indicators

Much of the theorizing on crime proposes that relative inequality is as, or more, important than absolute deprivation in explaining crime. Thus, in order to study variation in crime across nations, indicators of relative inequality within nations are needed. Most frequently used in past research has been the Gini coefficient of household, or individual, income concentration, which ranges from 0—for perfectly equal distribution—to 1.0. It is available from a number of sources, including Jain (1975), Paukert (1973), Roberti (1974), and Weatherby, Nam, and Isaac (1983). However, even if numerous sources are used, data are unavailable for many nations. As all of these data are from the mid-1960s to the early 1970s, they are of limited value in explaining crime in the present. So they probably should not be used in research on recent crime data. The structure of inequality in most nations is probably fairly stable over short time periods, but over thirty years there are likely to be substantial changes in at least some nations. Deininger and Squire (1996) have created a new data set on the inequality of distribution of income, including new Gini coefficients.

The WDR shows the proportion of income going to each quintile in nations, and this data can be used to calculate Gini coefficients (Kakwani,

1980; Savage & Vila, 1995). More commonly, income inequality is now indicated by the ratio of the proportion going to the highest 10 or 20 percent to the proportion going to the lowest 20 percent. These data are available from several of the sources listed in Appendix C. The data on income distribution reported in any single year—in publications such as the HDR or WDR—can come from years spanning a fifteen-year period, depending on the nation. Thus, for some nations data may not be comparable. Also, in many nations data are not systematically collected or organized, and for some nations they are based on per capita household income and for others on total household income. A more detailed description of the problems with income distribution data can be found in the technical notes of the WDR (World Bank, 1978–).

Messner (1989) argues economic discrimination is more important than inequality in explaining crime across nations. There are two indicators of economic discrimination in *The World Handbook of Political and Social Indicators* (Taylor & Jodice, 1983). The first represents the scope of discrimination and the second the intensity, with each indicated on a 0-to-4 ordinal scale. Unfortunately, these indicators are unavailable for many nations and are based on data from the early to mid-1970s. Apparently, there are no current plans to update. Gurr and Scarritt (1989) have developed an economic discrimination index based on expert judgments as to the extent to which groups experience objective economic disadvantages that are attributable to deliberate discrimination.

Unemployment can and has been used to indicate inequality within a nation. It is available for more nations than income distribution data and is available on an annual basis for time-series analysis. Probably the best source for cross-national unemployment data is the *Yearbook of Labour Statistics* (International Labour Office, 1935/36–). However, it is probably not a very good indicator of actual deprivation or the degree of inequality. The United States, for example, tends to have lower unemployment but much more poverty and inequality than most Western European nations. Controlling for social security benefits expenditure would make unemployment a more meaningful indicator.

If the focus of research is exclusively on developed nations, incidence of long-term unemployment is available in the HDR, and this probably better indicates severe deprivation than the overall unemployment rate. The HDR also reports unemployment rates which include discouraged workers for many industrial nations. For cross-checking, another measure of inequality for developed nations in the HDR is the ratio of earnings of the upper half of the labor force to the lower half.

Bennett (1991) argues educational inequality is superior to income inequality for cross-national comparisons. He uses data for primary, secondary, and college enrollments to create Ray and Singer's index of concentration. This measure normalizes variation and has an upper limit of unity. Educational data are available for more nations than income inequality data, and they are almost certainly of better quality. They are also available on an annual basis for time-series analysis. I do not believe educational inequality is intrinsically as good a measure of inequality as income, and it has not been as consistently found to be associated to cross-national variation in crime.

Conklin and Simpson (1985) and Simpson and Conklin (1992) have used infant mortality to indicate the degree of inequality in nations. Infant mortality rates—as well as such related indicators as percent of malnourished children—are available from a number of sources on an annual basis for most nations. Inflation has been used as an indicator of economic distress and is available from a number of sources on an annual basis for most nations.

DEPENDENCY THEORY INDICATORS

Dependency theory has primarily been examined using inequality and poverty indicators. These only indirectly address the dependency theory perspective, however, as it is based more on the economic position of nations vis-à-vis each other than on the economic situation within nations. Some indicators which measure the relative dependency of nations on each other have been developed but are now quite dated. The most recent is the measure of penetration by transnational corporations (Bornschier & Chase-Dunn, 1985) which is based on 1977 data. Other older indicators are the measures of commodity concentration and foreign investment extraction (Ballmer-Cao, Scheiddegger, Bornschier, & Heintz, 1979), and Bollen's (1980) index of the position of nations in the world economic system.

Krahn, Hartnagel, and Gartrell (1986) used capital formation as a percentage of GDP to indicate the development of capital relations of production. This indicator is available on an annual basis in the *United Nations Statistical Yearbook* (U.N., 1948–). Many other dependency-related variables are available on an annual basis from a number of sources, such as external debt as percent of GNP, import-export ratio, long-term debt ratios, and balance of payments. Data for most of these variables are unavailable for many nations. An important task for future investigators is to discover and/or develop good indicators of the relative dependency of nations and their place in the economic world order.

OPPORTUNITY AND DEMOGRAPHY INDICATORS

Some demographic variables can generally indicate the potential pool of offenders in nations as well as circumstances that might provide opportunities for, or encourage, crime. Most conventional crime is committed by young males. Therefore, it is probably important to include age structure and gender distribution variables in cross-national crime research. The proportion of the population under fifteen is available on an annual basis from many sources, with other age categories also available annually but from fewer sources. *Britannica World Data* is a good source for annual age structure data (Daume, 1985–). Similarly, the percent of the population which is male is available annually from several sources. Both age and gender are available for most nations.

The proportion of women in the labor force—available annually from several sources—might indicate both lack of protection of homes and exposure of women to crime. Mean household size—similarly available— might also generally indicate the likelihood both of households being unprotected and of intimates clashing and becoming violent with each other. Data on the female labor force are not available for a number of nations, while data on household size are available for almost all nations. Population size and density are available for all nations annually from many sources. It is generally considered important to include these in research as control variables. Size and density might relate to critical masses of offenders or alter the association of other variables.

ANOMIE AND SOCIAL INTEGRATION INDICATORS

The degree of anomie or lack of social integration in nations is very difficult to quantify, yet it may be one of the most important concepts explaining variation in crimes among nations.[1] Generally, anomie is not directly measured but is implied to be higher or lower depending on the degree to which factors thought to foster anomie are present. The level and speed of development and social change are thought to contribute to anomie, and I have already discussed developmental variables, such as GDP and urban population.

As noted in Chapter 5, the degree of education in nations has been used to indicate the opposite concepts of anomie and social integration. Data on primary, secondary, and higher education school enrollment are available annually from several sources for most nations. Annual literacy data are available for almost all nations. Probably the most comprehensive source for educational data is the UNESCO *Statistical Yearbook* annual (UNESCO, 1963–).

Heterogeneity is thought to contribute to a lack of social integration and has usually been indicated by the Ethnic and Linquistic Homogeneity Index originally published in *Atlas Narodov Mira* (Academy of Sciences, 1964) and available in a number of sources. This measure has been created only once and is based on data from the 1960s. It thus cannot be used in time-series or longitudinal analysis, and it may not reflect the current heterogeneity in nations.

Sullivan (1991) proposes the proportion of people in the most populous ethnic group as a measure of ethnic homogeneity in a nation. These data are available annually from several sources, including the annual *World Factbook* (CIA, 1981–) and annual *Britannica World Data* (Daume, 1985–). These sources provide data on the percent of people in each ethnic and religious category in nations, and thus they can be used to develop more comprehensive measures of heterogeneity. For example, one could create the measure of ethnic heterogeneity developed by Blau (1977), wherein heterogeneity is equal to one minus the squared fractions of the population in each category. Some information on linguistic heterogeneity is also provided in these sources. Comprehensive information on the languages and dialects used in 228 nations is available in the Ethnologue database (Grimes, 1996; see Appendix C).

The amount of immigration into nations and the proportion of the population that is foreign born might also contribute to anomie in nations. Probably the best source for annual data of this type is *World Resources* (World Resources Institute, 1986/87–1996/97). These data are not available for a number of nations.

Religion has been used to indicate anomie in terms not only of heterogeneity but also of the type of religion predominant in a nation. Protestantism is suggested to contribute to individualism and anomie, for example, whereas Islamic religion is suggested to contribute to social integration. As noted earlier, information on the religious makeup of nations is available annually from several sources, including the *World Factbook* (CIA, 1981–) and *Britannica World Data* (Daume, 1985–).

It has been suggested that divorce promotes social disintegration, and marriage social integration. Annual data on divorce and marriage rates are available from a number of sources. Data are not available for a number of nations.

Adler (1983) used qualitative data to discover the degree of social integration and informal social control in nations, as well as how they relate to crime. Neapolitan (1997) has suggested that historical analysis—especially analysis of the colonial past of nations—can help in understanding the social integration of nations. Of course, qualitative and historical information can be acquired in many ways from numerous sources. Some of these are listed on page 162.

POLITICAL AND HUMAN RIGHTS INDICATORS

The simplest measures of human rights are the political and civil rights indices published annually by Freedom House since 1978 (Gastil, 1978–). Each index is based on a 1-to-7 (most-to-least freedom) scale and then combined to create three categories of nations: free, partly free, and not free. These indicators allow for cross-sectional and time-series analyses and are available for most nations. Also reported in each edition of *Freedom in the*

World is a brief discussion of human rights problems and changes in each nation as well as a list of human rights organizations.

A more complete and complex guide to the human rights situation in nations can be found in the *World Human Rights Guide* (Humana, 1992), published intermittently. This book gives each nation an overall human rights rating from 0 to 100, based on forty different freedoms or rights including legal, political, speech, and women's rights. Each individual right is rated on a four-point ordinal scale: unqualified freedom, qualified freedom, frequent violations, and a constant pattern of violations. Brief descriptions are given of the reasons for the overall and individual ratings. Data are provided for fewer nations than in the Freedom House reports.

The U.S. Department of State issues annual, in-depth *Country Reports on Human Rights Practices*, qualitatively describing the human rights practices of the nations of the world (U.S. Department of State, annual; see Appendix C). Cingranelli and Wright (1986), using these reports, categorized nations in an eight-cell classification scheme based on implementation of law as consistent or inconsistent and then cross-referenced with due process protection as not provided, moderate, extensive, or very extensive. This categorization was based on 1980 data and may not be accurate for all nations today.

Amnesty International issues the annual *Amnesty International Report* which qualitatively describes the human rights situation in many nations of the world (Amnesty International, 1976–). The general political system of nations can be found in numerous sources, including the *World Factbook* (CIA, 1981–) and Kurian's encyclopedia (1990, 1991a, 1992).

CULTURAL VALUES INDICATORS

There is a growing consensus that the task of measuring cultural values and examining their role in explaining variation in cross-national crimes is one of the most important and difficult for future investigators (Gartner, 1995; Neapolitan, 1997; Vincentnathan, 1995). This is particularly true for violent crime, as it has more often been associated to cultural variation within nations (e.g., Huff-Corzine, Corzine, & Moore, 1986; Wolfgang & Ferracuti, 1983).

Krahn, Hartnagel, and Gartrell (1986) note that cross-national data on the distribution of different values are simply not available. They argue this makes culture-of-violence hypotheses impossible to test. While direct indicators of values are not available, indicators can be used which imply the presence of violent values and norms.

Gartner (1990) suggests that the use of official violence indicates a cultural context of violence. Amnesty International issues periodic reports on use of the death penalty, dividing nations into abolitionist, abolitionist de facto, and retentionist (Amnesty International, 1995–). Wiechman, Kendall, and Bae (1990) surveyed 163 nations on their use of the death penalty from 1980 to 1985. They provide data not only on whether nations use the death penalty but also on how many executions were actually performed each year. Of course, these data are becoming dated. Schumacher (1990) provides another statistical overview of international use of the death penalty.

Wars not only reflect official violence but may generally desensitize people to, and promote justification of, violence. Small and Singer (1981) report the number of wars and war deaths nations have experienced from 1816 to 1980. More recent data on wars can be found in the formerly annual and now intermittent publication, *World Military and Social Expenditures*, most recently published in 1996 (Sivard, 1974–). Data on wars are not available for a good number of nations.

Information on other types of government violence—including the illegal—can be found in most of the publications discussed in the human rights section. This is particularly true for the annual rights reports of the U.S. Department of State and Amnesty International as well as *Getting Away With Murder: Political Killings and Disappearances in the 1990s* (Amnesty International, 1993). Sullivan (1991), using several sources, reports data for many nations on government killings, torture, and political prisoners for the time period circa the late 1980s.

Probably the best, if most time consuming, way to indicate variation in cultural values of violence is to examine the history and general culture of each nation. Neapolitan (1994, 1997) proposes that an important factor in the high rates of violence in many developing nations can be traced to their histories of colonization, subjugation, and postcolonial violence. Many who have studied the culture of Latin American nations discuss the cultural value of machismo as conducive to violence, and they identify the roots of machismo in their histories of subjugation and rebellion (e.g., Lancaster, 1992; Rivera, 1978). The role of historical and cultural factors in explaining crime has too often been ignored in favor of ahistorical sociological, psychological, and economic irregularities.

Probably the best source of in-depth information on nations is provided by the *Library of Congress Country Studies* Internet site. Each study is written by a multidisciplinary team of social scientists and provides extensive information on the history of nations as well as their current political, economic, and social systems and institutions. Included is information on crime and the criminal justice and penal systems for seventy-one nations. Similar, but less comprehensive, are the *Background Country Notes* provided via the Internet for about 150 nations by the U.S. Department of State.

While not as valuable as a thorough historical and cultural analysis of nations, brief histories can be found in several sources. These include Dushkin's *Global Studies* annuals (*Global Studies*, 1989–), Kurian's encyclopedia (1990, 1991a, 1992), *The Guide to Places of the World* (Mountjoy, 1987), and *Britannica World Data* (Daume, 1985–).

Property crime might be related to materialistic norms and values. Like violent values, these cannot be directly indicated. Per capita consumption might indicate materialism and is available for many nations on an annual basis from several sources, including *Britannica World Data* (Daume, 1985–) and the *World Factbook* (CIA, 1981–). Perhaps a better measure of materialism or consumerism would be the ratio of per capita consumption to GDP per person. Television might be thought to indicate and promote materialistic values, and data on persons per television are available annually from several sources, including the UNESCO *Statistical Yearbook* (UNESCO, 1963–).

THE PARTICIPATION AND EQUALITY OF WOMEN INDICATORS

Data on cross-national variation in the participation and equality of women can be used to study crime by women, women as crime victims, and crime rates in general. The most commonly used indicator of female public role participation has been the proportion of females in the labor force. It is available annually from a number of sources. The fertility rate has been used to indicate the opposite of this, female domestic role participation. This also is available annually from numerous sources.

Female inequality can be indicated by female school enrollment in relation to male enrollment. Data on relative female enrollment are available annually for primary, secondary, and university schools as well as for literacy. With the exception of literacy, data on education are unavailable for a number of nations. The WDR and the UNESCO *Statistical Yearbook* are good sources of these data (World Bank, 1978–; UNESCO, 1963–).

There are four main sources of data for a large number of variables on the status and roles of women cross-nationally. Data on proportionate occupational and political participation, share of income, life expectancy, and other variables are available. Past research has most often used the *Handbook of International Data on Women*, but this has now become dated (Boulding, Nuss, Carson, & Greenstein, 1976).

The World's Women: Trends and Statistics publication includes data on the economic, political, and social differences that separate men from women for various time periods (U.N., 1991, 1995). The 1995 HDR focused on women's issues and the relative position of women in nations, including data on proportionate female involvement in education, occupations, politics, and so on (UNDP, 1990–). The most comprehensive source of cross-national data on women—and the one from which *The World's Women* and the HDR culled their data—is the Women's Indicators and Statistics database (WISTAT) on CD-ROM, which is issued intermittently (U.N., 1988, 1992, 1996). This database includes 1,667 statistical series, grouped into seventy-two topics in nine subject areas for over two hundred nations and areas. Data for many variables are available from 1970 through 1994.

While many of the variables on proportionate female involvement and participation can be used individually to indicate cross-national variation in inequality of the sexes and roles of women, composite measures may be more valuable. Steffensmeier, Allan, and Streifel (1989) created an occupational segregation measure to represent female economic disadvantage. It represents the proportion of women who would have to change jobs in order for men and women to be equally distributed across occupations.

As noted earlier, recent editions of the HDR report an HDI adjusted for inequality in achievement between men and women called the Gender-related Development Index (GDI) (UNDP, 1990–). A relative indicator of gender inequality can then be created by taking the percentage reduction of the GDI from the HDI, that is, (HDI-GDI)/HDI.

The 1995 HDR and WISTAT also report the Gender Empowerment Measure (GEM), which is based on the relative participation of women in political and economic activity (U.N., 1995; UNDP, 1990–). The GDI focuses on achievement in basic capabilities, while GEM focuses on the ability to use capabilities and participate in economic and political spheres. Data in 1995 were available for GDI for 130 nations and for GEM for 116 nations. These numbers should increase in the future.

CHILDREN'S WELFARE INDICATORS

Children's welfare indicators can be used to study crimes by young people, children as victims, or overall crime rates. In contrast to other indicators—which are best if they represent the same time period as the crime data—child welfare indicators should probably be from ten to twenty years earlier if they are used to explain youth or overall crime. This is because the effects of these variables should be lagged, that is, deprivation at age five should contribute to crime at ages fifteen to twenty-five.

Nations with high infant mortality rates probably also have many children with problem births and early-life deprivation. As noted earlier, infant mortality data are available annually from many sources for almost all nations. Several sources, including the HDR and WDR, also report the prevalence of malnutrition under age five, under-five mortality, and low-birthweight babies (UNDP, 1990–; World Bank, 1978–). With the exception of under-five mortality, these indicators are available for fewer nations than infant mortality. Data on proportion of children enrolled in school at primary and secondary levels, as well as public expenditures on education, are also available for most nations annually from several sources.

Broken homes and single-parent homes might also negatively impact on children and help explain crime variation across nations. As noted earlier, annual data on divorce rates are available for many nations from several sources. Data on the percent of female-headed households in nations is collected by the UNDP and is available directly from them or in the WISTAT

CD-ROM (U.N., 1995) and the HDR (UNDP, 1990–). These data are not available annually but for several time periods, and they are not available for a large number of nations. Currently, data are available for 1980, 1990, and 1994. A problem with this indicator is that it includes female-headed households with, and without, children. This is a particular problem in developed nations where there are numerous elderly females heading households.

The 1994 HDR reports the percent of single-parent households and births outside of marriage but only for Western industrialized nations. Each year the HDR reports the unemployment rate for persons aged fifteen to twenty-four for Western industrialized nations and those of Eastern Europe. This may better explain crime than the overall unemployment rate, as teens and young adults are more crime prone than other age groups.

CRIMINAL JUSTICE SYSTEM INDICATORS

Earlier in this chapter, I discussed availability of data on the legal rights in nations and on the legality and use of the death penalty. For data on other aspects of the criminal justice systems of nations, the five UNCS surveys are probably the best overall source. These were already discussed in Chapter 1, where it was noted data are collected in many areas of criminal justice, including criminal justice personnel, arrests, convictions, sentences, and prison rates. The number of nations for which data are available varies greatly, depending on the area of interest, but is not great for most. Similar—and likely more accurate—data are provided for many Western European nations in the *European Sourcebook of Crime and Criminal Justice Statistics* (Council of Europe, 1995). INTERPOL's *International Crime Statistics* reports the percent of crimes solved by police for each crime category (INTERPOL, 1986–1990).

Data on population per police officer are available for most nations in *Britannica World Data* (Daume, 1985–). While this is an annual publication, the police data are not updated annually, and data reported are not for the same year for each nation. Population per police officer, circa 1985, is also reported in *The World Encyclopedia of Police Forces and Penal Systems* (Kurian, 1989) and for 1975, 1980, and 1986 in *The Compendium of Social Statistics and Indicators* (U.N., 1988–). Figures from the various sources are identical or very close for most nations, but for a few nations they differ greatly. For example, for the time period circa the mid-1980s, the figures for Gambia and Jamaica are 812 and 660, respectively, in *The World Encyclopedia of Police Forces and Penal Systems* and 3,310 and 450, respectively, in *Britannica World Data*.

In addition to the UNCS data, prison population data for various nations are available in *The Compendium of Social Statistics and Indicators* (U.N., 1988–), *Americans Behind Bars: The International Use of Incarceration*

(Sentencing Project, periodic), the bimonthly publication *The Overcrowded Times* (Tonry, bimonthly), and the Penal Lexicon WWW site.[2] From all sources, data are available for a limited number of nations. The Council of Europe provides prison data on Western European nations in the *Prison Information Bulletin* (Council of Europe, 1983–1992).

Information on the number of people in prison in different nations and prison conditions can also be found in the United Nations report, *United Nations Standards and Norms in the Field of Crime Prevention and Criminal Justice* (U.N., 1996). It is based on a questionnaire sent to member nations with replies received from seventy-eight nations.

General information on penal systems, criminal justice systems, police forces, and so forth can be found in several places. Some of the better sources are *The World Encyclopedia of Police Forces and Penal Systems* (Kurian, 1989), Kurian's encyclopedia (1990, 1991a, 1992) and *The Overcrowded Times* (Tonry, bimonthly). There are, of course, some good books on comparative criminal justice systems, although they generally cover fewer than ten nations (e.g., Beirne, 1991; Ebbe, 1996; Fairchild, 1993; Terrill, 1997). There are also comparative books available on such topics as juvenile justice (e.g., Shoemaker, 1996), alternatives to imprisonment (e.g., Zvekic, 1994), and systems of law and control (e.g., Fields & Moore, 1996).

The Bureau of Justice Statistics (BJS) International Statistics Program encourages universities and research centers to supply data on crime, criminal justice, and criminal justice studies to the National Archive of Criminal Justice Data (NACJD) at the University of Michigan. Annual statistical reports on crime and justice from statistical agencies in other nations are maintained and disseminated through the National Criminal Justice Reference Service (NCJRS). Information on contacting and obtaining information from BJS, NACJD, and NCJRS can be found in Appendix B. All these agencies can be located on the WWW and reached via telephone, mail, or e-mail.

The Office of International Criminal Justice (see Appendix B) publishes three bimonthly criminal justice newsletters: *CJ International*, *CJ Europe*, and *CJ The Americas*. The World Criminal Justice Library Network has been established at Rutgers University for the sharing and dissemination of criminal justice information on a worldwide scale. The International Centre for Criminal Law Reform and Criminal Justice Policy was established in 1991 at the University of British Columbia and can be contacted for various types of criminal justice information on nations. The *World Directory of Criminological Institutes* (Santoro, 1995) is published periodically, covering over four hundred institutes in over seventy nations. These can be contacted individually for various types of criminal justice information on different nations.

The most exciting and promising way of obtaining crime and criminal justice information on nations is via the Internet. The United Nations

Criminal Justice Information Network (UNCJIN) is probably the single best site but there are many others, some of which are given in Appendix B. An excellent way to discover how to obtain data or information is to send out a request on an electronic discussion or news group. Again, at writing, the best of these for international crime and criminal justice issues is probably the UNCJIN discussion group. The American Society of Criminology has recently established a Division of International Criminology which has an electronic discussion group as well as a newsletter.

The WWW *World Factbook of Criminal Justice Systems* (see Appendix B) is currently in the state of development under a BJS grant. It provides descriptions and data on crime and criminal justice systems of nations in extensive detail. Everything from the political system of a nation to its prison conditions is covered. At this writing, forty-two nations are in the *Factbook*, but the goal is to add more on a regular basis. It is not clear whether there will be print and/or computer disk versions of the *Factbook*. The previously mentioned *Library of Congress Country Studies* provide information on the criminal and penal systems of nations, as do the State Department's *Country Reports on Human Rights Practices*.

CONCLUSION

We are in the midst of an explosion of sources, types, and amount of data on the nations of the world. There are also numerous efforts underway to provide for the sharing of information and ideas on a worldwide basis. The Internet, through discussion lists and WWW sites, will make ever more data instantly accessible and provide for more cooperation and cross-fertilization among investigators. Several World Bank databases and the CIA's *World Factbook* are already accessible via the WWW, and there are several international criminal justice electronic discussion groups. Cross-national research on crime should benefit greatly by easier access to more and better data with which to explain variation in crimes within and across nations.

NOTES

1. Anomie is used in the general meaning of the concept to indicate a lack of normative consensus and social integration rather than the specific meaning of a gap between desired goals and legitimate means.

2. Ken Pease (1994) provides an excellent critique of international comparisons of imprisonment per level of population and makes some suggestions for use of more detailed indices.

168 Data and Analysis

REFERENCES

Academy of Sciences. (1964). *Atlas narodov mira*. Moscow: Author.

Adler, F. (1983). *Nations not obsessed with crime, Vol. 50*. Littleton, CO: Fred B. Rothman.

Amnesty International. (1976–). *Amnesty International reports*. London: Author.

Amnesty International. (1993). *Getting away with murder: Political killings and disappearances in the 1990s*. New York: Author.

Amnesty International. (1995–, periodic). *The death penalty: A list of abolitionist and retentionist countries*. London: Author.

Ballmer-Cao, T., Scheiddegger, J., Bornschier, V., & Heintz, P. (1979). *Compendium of data for world-system analyses*. Zurich, Switzerland: Soziologisches Institut der Universität Zurich.

Beirne, P. (1991). *Comparative criminology: An annotated bibliography*. New York: Greenwood Press.

Bennett, R. (1991). Development and crime: A cross-national, time-series analysis of competing models. *The Sociological Quarterly, 32*, 343–363.

Blau, P. (1977). *Inequality and heterogeneity*. New York: Free Press.

Bollen, K. A. (1980). Issues in the comparative measurement of political democracy. *American Sociological Review, 45*, 370–390.

Bornschier, V. & Chase-Dunn, C. (1985). *Transnational corporations and under-development*. New York: Praeger.

Boulding, E., Nuss, S. A., Carson, D. L., & Greenstein, M. A. (1976). *Handbook of international data on women*. New York: Sage.

CIA. (1981–). *The world factbook*. Washington, D.C.: Author.

Cingranelli, D. L. & Wright, K. N. (1986). Measurement of cross-national variations in the extensiveness and consistency of due process. *Policy Studies, 15*, 106.

Conklin, G. H. & Simpson, M. E. (1985). A demographic approach to the cross-national study of homicide. *Comparative Social Research, 8*, 171–186.

Council of Europe. (1983–1992, irregular). *Prison information bulletin*. Strasbourg, France: Author.

Council of Europe. (1995). *European sourcebook of crime and criminal justice statistics: Draft model*. Strasbourg, France: Author.

Daume, D. (Ed.). (1985–, annual). *Britannica world data:Britannica book of the year*. Chicago: Encyclopaedia Britannica.

DeGeyndt, W. (1996). *Social development and absolute poverty in Asia and Latin America: Technical Paper No. 328*. Washington, D.C.: World Bank.

Deininger, K. & Squire, L. (1996). A new data set measuring income inequality. *The World Bank Economic Review, 10* (3), 565-591.

Ebbe, O. (Ed.). (1996). *Comparative and international criminal justice systems: Policing, judiciary, and corrections*. Boston, MA: Butterworth-Heinemann.

Estes, R. J. (1984). *The social progress of nations*. New York: Praeger.

Estes, R. J. (1988). *Trends in world social development: The social progress of nations, 1970–1987*. New York: Praeger.

Fairchild, E. (1993). *Comparative criminal justice systems*. Belmont, CA: Wadsworth.

Fields, C. B. & Moore, R. H. (1996). *Comparative criminal justice:Traditional and nontraditional systems of law and control*. Prospect Heights, IL: Waveland.

Gartner, R. (1990). The victims of homicide: A temporal and cross-national comparison. *American Sociological Review*, 55, 92–106.

Gartner, R. (1995). Methodological issues in cross-cultural large-survey research. In B. Ruback & N. Weiner (Eds.), *Interpersonal violent behaviors: Social and cultural aspects* (pp. 7–24). New York: Springer-Verlag.

Gastil, R. (1978–, annual). *Freedom in the world*. New York: Freedom House.

Global Studies: Africa, China, India and South Asia, Japan and Pacific Rim, Latin America, Middle East, Russia and Central Europe, Western Europe. (1989–, annual). Guilford, CT: Dushkin.

Grimes, B. (Ed.). (1996). *Ethnologue: Languages of the world*. 13th ed. Dallas, TX: Summer Institute of Linguistics.

Gurr, T. R. & Scarritt, J. R. (1989). Minorities at risk: A global study. *Human Rights Quarterly*, 11, 375–405.

Huff-Corzine, L., Corzine, J., & Moore, D. (1986). Southern exposure: Reciphering the south's influence on homicide rates. *Social Forces*, 64, 906–924.

Humana, C. (1992). *World human rights guide*. 3rd ed. New York: Oxford University Press.

International Labour Office. (1935/36–). *Yearbook of labour statistics*. Geneva, Switzerland: Author.

INTERPOL. (1986–1990). *International crime statistics*. Paris: Author.

Jain, S. (1975). *Size distribution of income: A compilation of data*. Washington, D.C.: World Bank.

Kakwani, N. (1980). *Income inequality and poverty: Methods of estimation and policy applications*. New York: World Bank, Oxford University Press.

Krahn, H., Hartnagel, T. & Gartrell, J. (1986). Income inequality and homicide rates: Cross-national data and criminological theories. *Criminology*, 24, 269–295.

Kurian, G. (1989). *World encyclopedia of police forces and penal systems*. New York: Facts on File.

Kurian, G. (1990). *Encyclopedia of the first world*. New York: Facts on File.

Kurian, G. (1991a). *Encyclopedia of the second world*. New York: Facts on File.

Kurian, G. (1991b). *The new book of world rankings*. 3rd ed. New York: Facts on File.

Kurian, G. (1992). *Encyclopedia of the third world*. New York: Facts on File.

Lancaster, R. (1992). *Life is hard: Machismo, danger, and the intimacy of power in Nicaragua*. Berkeley, CA: University of California Press.

Messner, S. F. (1989). Economic discrimination and societal homicide rates: Further evidence on the cost of inequality. *American Sociological Review*, 54, 597–611.

Morris, M. D. (1979). *Measuring the condition of the world's poor: The physical quality of life index*. New York: OCD, Pergamon Press.

Morris, M. D. (1996). *The changing condition of the world's poor, 1960–1990: Some development policy implications*. Unpublished manuscript, Brown University.

Mountjoy, A. (1987). *Guide to places of the world*. New York: Reader's Digest.

Neapolitan, J. L. (1994). Cross-national variation in homicide rates: The case of Latin America. *International Criminal Justice Review*, 4, 4–22.

Neapolitan, J. L. (1997). Homicides in developing nations: Results of research using a large, representative sample. *International Journal of Offender Therapy and Comparative Criminology*, forthcoming.

ODC. (periodic). *Physical quality of life index*. Washington, D.C.: Author.

Paukert, F. (1973). Income distribution at different levels of development: A survey of evidence. *International Labor Review*, 108, 97–125.

Pease, K. (1994). Cross-national imprisonment rates: Limitations of method and possible conclusions. *British Journal of Criminology*, 34, 116–130.

Population Crisis Committee. (1987, 1992). *The international human suffering index*. Washington, D.C.: Author.

Rivera, J. (1978). *Latin America: A sociocultural interpretation*. New York: Irvington.

Roberti, P. (1974). Income distribution: A time-series and a cross-sectional study. *Economic Journal*, 335, 629–638.

Santoro, C. (Ed.). (1995). *A world directory of criminological institutes*. 6th ed. Rome, Italy: UNICRI.

Savage, J. & Vila, B. (1995). *Lagged effects of nurturance on crime: A cross-national comparison*. Paper presented at American Society of Criminology meeting, Nov. 15–18, Boston, MA.

Schumacher, J. (1990). An international look at the death penalty. *International Journal of Comparative and Applied Criminal Justice*, 14 (1–2), 307–315.

Sentencing Project. (periodic). *Americans behind bars: The international use of incarceration*. Washington, D.C.: Author.

Shoemaker, D. J. (Ed.). (1996). *International handbook on juvenile justice*. Westport, CT: Greenwood Press.

Simpson, M. E. & Conklin, G. H. (1992). *Homicide, inequality, political systems, and transnational corporations: A cross-national study*. Paper presented at American Sociology Association meeting, Aug. 24–27, Pittsburgh, PA.

Sivard, R. (1974–, periodic). *World military and social expenditures*. Leesburg, VA: World Priorities.

Small, M. & Singer, J. (1981). *Resort to arms: International and civil war, 1816–1980*. Beverly Hills, CA: Sage.

Steffensmeier, D., Allan, E., & Streifel, C. (1989). Development and female crime: A cross-national test of alternative explanations. *Social Forces*, 68, 262–283.

Sullivan, M. (1991). *Measuring global values: The ranking of 162 countries*. New York: Greenwood Press.

Taylor, C. & Jodice, D. (1983). *World handbook of political and social indicators*. 3rd ed. New Haven, CT: Yale University Press.

Terrill, R. (1997). *World criminal justice systems: A survey*. 3rd ed. Cincinnati, OH: Anderson.

Tonry, M. (Ed.). (bimonthly). *The overcrowded times*. Castine, ME.

U.N. (1948–). *Statistical yearbook*. New York: Author.

U.N. (1969–). *Demographic yearbook*. New York: Author.

U.N. (1988–, irregular). *Compendium of social statistics and indicators*. New York: Author.

U.N. (1988, 1992, 1996). *United Nations women's indicators and statistics database (CD-ROM)*. New York: Author.

U.N. (1991). *The world's women, 1970–1990: Trends and statistics*. New York: Author.

U.N. (1995). *The world's women, 1995: Trends and statistics*. New York: Author.

U.N. (1996). *United Nations standards and norms in the field of crime prevention and criminal justice*. Vienna, Austria: Author.

UNDP. (1990–). *Human development report*. New York: Oxford University Press.

UNESCO. (1963–). *Statistical yearbook*. Paris: Author.

U.S. Department of State. (annual). *Country reports on human rights practices*. Washington, D.C.: U.S. Government Printing Office.

Vincentnathan, S. (1995). Social reaction and secondary deviance in culture and society: The United States and Japan. In F. Adler and W. Lauter (Eds.), *The legacy of anomie theory* (pp.329–348). London: Transaction.

Weatherby, N., Nam, C., & Isaac, L. (1983). Development, inequality, health care, and mortality at older ages: A cross-national analysis. *Demography*, 20, 27–43.

Wiechman, D., Kendall, J., & Bae, R. (1990). International use of the death penalty. *International Journal of Comparative and Applied Criminal Justice*, 14 (2), 239–260.

Wolfgang, M. E. & Ferracuti, F. (Eds.). (1983). *Criminological diagnosis: An international perspective*. Lexington, MA: Lexington Books.

World Bank. (1978–). *World development report*. New York: Oxford University Press.

World Bank. (1987–). *Social indicators of development*. Washington, D.C.: Author.

World Bank. (1989–). *Trends in developing economies*. Washington, D.C.: Author.

World Bank. (1994). *Social indicators of development*. Washington, D.C.: Author.

World Resources Institute. (1986/87–1996/97). *World resources*. New York: Oxford University Press.

Zvekic, U. (Ed.). (1994). *Alternatives to imprisonment in comparative perspective*. Chicago, IL: Nelson-Hall.

Conclusion

As stated in the introduction, I believe cross-national crime research to be of great importance in discovering the underlying causes of crime and in formulating informed public policy to combat crime. Unfortunately, the cross-national crime research to date has not contributed much toward either of these goals. Results have been contradictory, unclear, and often at a level of abstraction to be of little practical value. The biggest problem has been with the quality of the data by which crime and explanatory variables have been indicated. And the dearth of reliable data from developing nations means any research including these is particularly suspect.

The hard work and pioneering efforts of such reseachers as Bennett (1990) and Archer and Gartner (1984) to develop quality data bases for cross-national crime research are to be commended, they were necessary to promote interest in the area. It is not the fault of these and other analysts, including myself, that the data available have simply not been of sufficient quality to do meaningful research. As data have improved greatly in quality, quantity, and variety in recent years, I believe we are on the verge of a great leap forward in the quality and quantity of cross-national crime research.

1997 saw the release of the fifth and most complete UNCS, the third IVS covering many more nations than the past two surveys, the 1993 and 1994 INTERPOL ICSs, and plans are underway for a second ISRD and future issues of the *European Sourcebook of Crime and Criminal Justice Statistics*. The United Nations has predicted that the criminal justice statistical systems of member states will continue to improve (U.N., 1993a). And it has released two publications—the *Guide to Computerization of Information Systems in Criminal Justice* (U.N., 1993b) and the *Manual for the Development of Criminal Justice Statistics* (U.N., 1993c)—to assist nations in continued improvement in the collection of crime data. WHO is currently working to increase the representation of developing nations in their annuals and is also improving the methodology used to collect and report data (WHO, 1995; O. Frank, e-mail message, December 23, 1996).

In terms of explanatory variables, the new indicators and measures which have been, and are being, developed for World Bank and United Nations publications are increasingly sophisticated and accurate. Just as developing nations are improving in the collection of crime data, they are also becoming more accurate and comprehensive in the collection of economic and social data. The increasing availability of quality descriptive information on nations via the World Wide Web—for example, the U.S. Department of State *Human Rights Country* Reports (see Appendix C), *The Library of Congress Country Studies* (see Appendices A and C) and the *World Factbook of Criminal Justice Systems* (see Appendices A and B)—will also contribute greatly to quality cross-national crime research.

Methodological approaches to data are increasingly more sophisticated and varied. In the future, we should see not only more sophisticated statistical methods but also the blending of multiple methodologies and approaches to data.

Perhaps as important as the improved quality and quantity of data and methods are the prospects for greater cooperation and cross-fertilization among researchers worldwide. The ninth United Nations Commission on Crime Prevention and Criminal Justice focused on fostering international cooperation among member nations. The United Nations Crime Prevention and Criminal Justice Programme Network has begun holding annual meetings to review and promote cooperative activities among agencies and nations. The twelth annual International Congress on Criminology, sponsored by the International Society of Criminology and to be held in Seoul, Korea in August 1998, will focus on fostering international cooperation in research and information sharing. The formation of the WCJLN at Rutgers and the International Document Exchange Program sponsored by the National Institute of Justice NCJRS should also help the international sharing of data and ideas. A current project of WCJLN is to disseminate through online data bases and other means national and international crime statistics and criminal justice profiles.

Through WWW locations and electronic discussion groups, the Internet will likely serve as the greatest impetus to the international sharing of information, cooperative endeavors, and cross-fertilization of ideas. A recent issue of the UNCJIN *Crime and Justice Newsletter* was devoted to the potential of the Internet to assist researchers and practictioners worldwide in sharing information and ideas (U.N., 1995). Discussed in this issue are the importance of expanding Internet access to developing nations and its potential for greater democratization of cross-national perspectives on crime.

While we should use the insights and research results of past investigators for their heuristic value, we must essentially start anew in our approach to explaining cross-national variation in crimes. With the larger samples of nations for which data are available and the improved quality of these data, those hypotheses which have and have not been supported by past research must be reexamined. The inconsistencies and contradictions in past research results might be used to formulate hypotheses and theoretical perspectives.

Of course, as often noted in this book, substantial problems remain in cross-national crime data. Some of these must be resolved before great strides forward can be made. For example, official police data indicate that the developed nations have by far the highest rates of property crime, while IVS data indicate developing nations have higher rates. No conclusions regarding cross-national variation in property crimes can be reached until this contradiction is resolved.

It is important that while building on and reexamining past research, we also develop new concepts, perspectives, and methodologies. As often alluded to in this book, the cultural dimension of nations has been largely neglected in past research. Culture quite likely directly influences variation in crimes and certainly moderates the effects of other factors. Operationalizing cultural values and integrating cultural variation among nations into cross-national crime research is among the most important tasks facing future investigators.

Closely linked to culture is the history of nations, as history shapes culture. History, other than modernization, has been largely ignored in past cross-national crime research. Historical analysis can not only give us insights into the culture of nations but also assist us in examining the sequence of events that result in low or high crime rates. Integrating historical, structural, and cultural factors into analysis is key to genuine understanding of variation in crimes among nations.

As noted earlier, we must also blend micro- and macro-perspectives and analyses, explaining variation in crimes among and within nations and how these are linked. Variation among nations in who commits crimes and why is a much understudied area. Qualitative and quantitative approaches should both be used, and the two should complement and inform each other. I believe the best approach for the near future is neither case studies nor all-inclusive samples but rather analysis of strategically selected subsamples.

There are several newly emerging areas of interest which have not yet been systematically addressed. As the nations in transition of the former U.S.S.R. and Eastern-Central Europe experiment with various political and economic systems, most have also experienced increased crime. Variations in crime among these nations and between these nations and other nations represent new areas of inquiry.

The increased concern with transnational crime has prompted the United Nations to collect data on this phenomenon for the purpose of analysis and understanding. Related to this is the increased migration of people across national borders and how this influences crime rates, perceptions, and reactions to crime. In terms of shaping national policies, no area of cross-national crime research may be more important than the role of immigrants in crime. The 1995 United Nations Congress on Crime Prevention focused on the increased internationalization of crime as well as the effect of immigrants and ethnic conflict on crime. Better data are needed on crime by and against immigrants as well as the handling of immigrants in criminal justice systems.

Cross-national crime research is an extremely important area of inquiry, which as yet has yielded little in the way of concrete findings. As a result, it has had little influence on public perceptions of crime or on public policy. This has largely been due to the lack of quality data and research being conducted by isolated specialists. Data quality is rapidly improving, as are avenues and opportunities for increased cooperation among investigators from different nations and disciplines. We should see a great increase in the quality, quantity, and variety of cross-national research in the near future. I hope this book contributes to more and better cross-national crime research and makes the task of future investigators a little less daunting.

REFERENCES

Archer, D. & Gartner, R. (1984). *Violence and crime in cross-national perspective.* New Haven, CT: Yale University Press.

Bennett, R. (1990). *Correlates of crime: A study of 52 nations, 1960–1984.* Ann Arbor, MI: Interuniversity Consortium for Political and Social Research.

U.N. (1993a). *Crime trends and criminal justice operations at the regional and inter-regional levels.* Vienna, Austria: Author.

U.N. (1993b). *Guide to computerization of information systems in criminal justice.* New York: Author.

U.N. (1993c). *Manual for the development of criminal justice statistics.* New York: Author.

U.N. (1995). *UNCJIN crime and justice letter 2,* (4). Vienna: U.N. Office.

WHO. (1995). *The world health statistics annual: 1994.* Geneva, Switzerland: Author.

APPENDIX A

Cross-National Crime Data Sources

World Wide Web sites and e-mail addresses change frequently. So, those reported here may not be accurate. Most home pages related to international crime and criminal justice can be reached through the UNCJIN WWW site. Also, search engines can be used to locate current site addresses.

1. United Nations Crime Surveys (UNCS) are available on computer diskettes from:

Chief, Crime Prevention and Criminal Justice Branch
United Nations Office
P.O. Box 500, A-1400
Vienna, Austria
Fax: 0043–1–209–2599
E-mail: evetere@unov.un.or.at

The surveys are also available through the UNCJIN World Wide Web site.

Linkname: The World Crime Survey
Filename: http://www.ifs.univie.ac.at/~uncjin/wcs.html

The first two surveys—and possibly more when this book is in print—are also available from the National Archive of Criminal Justice Data (NACJD) on diskette, tape, or via their World Wide Web (WWW) site. See Appendix B for more information on NACJD.

2. INTERPOL International Crime Statistics (ICS)
These data are only available in print format and must be ordered from the INTERPOL office in Washington, D.C.

Arthur Ross
U.S. Department of Justice
INTERPOL USNCB
600 E Street N.W.
Washington, D.C. 20530

Older volumes can be found in many university libraries. The University of Michigan has all volumes dating back to 1973–1974. Data for only crime rates, with no information on attempts, gender, and so on, are included on the World Atlas CD-ROM. See Appendix C for more information on the World Atlas CD-ROM.

3. *Correlates of Crime: A Study of 52 Nations 1960–1984*, Richard Bennett (COC)

This data set, including INTERPOL crime information, is available from the NACJD on tape, diskette, or online via its WWW site. Information on murder attempts, however, is not included.

4. *World Health Statistics Annual*

These data are available in print format directly from WHO and can be found in the libraries of most large universities. They can also be ordered directly from:

Dr. Odile Frank
Health Situation Analysis and Projection Unit
World Health Organization
20 Avenue Appia
CH-1211 Geneva 27
Switzerland
Phone: +41–22–791–33–84
Fax: +41–22–791–41–94
E-mail: franko@who.ch

These data have recently become available via File Transfer Protocol (FTP), although at writing of this book they were still fine-tuning the system. To copy mortality data from WHO's Mortality Data Base on server ISMSVO2.WHO.CH, use anonymous file transfer. At FTP user prompt, give "anonymous" as user name and your e-mail address as password. After connection, change directory to '/FTP/MORTALIT', and you will find five files:

1. DOCUMENT.ZIP has a READ.ME with instructions, file structures, code reference tables, and country-year availability
2. ICD7.ZIP = data for country-years coded with ICD7
3. ICD8.ZIP = data for country-years coded with ICD8
4. ICD9.ZIP = data for country-years coded with ICD9
5. POPULAT.ZIP = reference populations and live-births

UNZIP files as required with PKUNZIP software.

5. *United Nations Demographic Yearbook* (UNDY)

These yearbooks are available in print form through the United Nations (see Appendix C) or are in most libraries of large universities.

6. International Victimization Data

These data are available on tape or diskette from:

John van Kesteren
Institute of Criminology
Faculty of Law
University of Leiden
Garenmarkt la
2311 PG Leiden
Netherlands
Phone: 0171–273–2339
Fax: 0171–222–0211
E-Mail: Gonzalez@ROL.ORG

Crime Prevention Directoratea
Ministry of Justice
Postbus 20301
2500 EH The Hague
Netherlands
Phone: 31–70–370–6558
Fax: 31–70–370–7905

The first two surveys are available through the UNCJIN WWW site. The first survey is also available through NACJD.

7. International Self-Report Delinquency (ISRD) Data
    At writing of this book, these data were not yet being made available to analysts. Gert-Jan Terlouw can be contacted on future availability:

Gert-Jan Terlouw
WODC Ministry of Justice
P.O. Box 20301 / 2500 EH
The Hague, Netherlands
Phone: +31–0–70–3–70–76–09
Fax: +31–0–70–3–70–79–48
E-mail: G.J.Terlouw@wodc.minjust.nl

8. *Crime in Western Societies 1945–1974*, Ted and Erika Gurr
    These data are available through NACJD on tape or diskette and online via the WWW.

9. *The Comparative Crime Data File*, Dane Archer and Rosemary Gartner
    These data are available through NACJD on tape or diskette and online via the WWW.

10. *European Sourcebook of Crime and Criminal Justice Statistics*
    The sourcebook can be obtained in print form by contacting:

Max Kommer
WODC Research and Documentation Centre of the Ministry of Justice
P.O. Box 20301, EH
The Hague, Netherlands
Phone: +31–0–70–370–73–25
Fax: +31–0–70–370–79–48
E-mail: MKOMMER@MINJUST.NL

11. The Foreign & Commonwealth Office's Consular Division Travel Advice of the British Government has crime information for many nations via its Internet site:

   http://www.fco.gov.uk/reference/travel_advice/countries.html

12. U.S. Department of State Consular Information Sheets provide information on the crime situations in many nations:

   http://travel.state.gov/travel_warnings.html

13. The World Factbook of Criminal Justice Systems is published by the Bureau of Justice Statistics in the U.S. Department of Justice:

   http://www.ojp.usdoj.gov/bjs/abstract/wfcj.htm

14. The Library of Congress Country Studies can be found at:

   http://www.lcweb2.loc.gov/frd/cs/cshome.html

15. Overseas Security Advisory Council Country Reports: General Crime Information from the U.S. Department of State can be found at:

   http://www.owens.com/tradescp/cr.html
   http://travel.state.gov/ds/text/gci/index.htm

16. Crime data can also be obtained directly from organizations in individual nations.

A good place to find contacts is *A World Directory of Criminological Institutes*, published annually since 1990 by the United Nations. See Appendix C for information on the United Nations Bookstore.

APPENDIX B

International Criminal Justice Organizations and Contacts

World Wide Web sites and e-mail addresses change frequently. So, those reported here may not be accurate. Most home pages related to international crime and criminal justice can be reached through the UNCJIN WWW site. Also, search engines can be used to locate current site addresses.

1. United Nations Crime and Justice Information Network (UNCJIN)

Crime Prevention and Criminal Justice Branch
United Nations Office
P.O. Box 500, A-1400
Vienna, Austria
Phone: 43–1–21131–4272/4278
E-mail: evetere@cpcjb.unvienna.or.at
        evetere@cpejb.un.or.at
WWW: http://www.ifs.univie.ac.at/~uncjin/uncjin.html

Adam Bouloukos, UNCJIN systems operator:
        aboulouk@unov.un.or.at
        aboulouk@unvienna.iaea.or.at

Graeme Newman, UNCJIN coordinator
School of Criminal Justice
SUNY
135 Western Avenue
Albany, NY 12222

2. National Criminal Justice Reference Service: International

NCJRS International
P.O. Box 6000
Rockville, MD 20849-6000
Phone: 301–251–5500
Fax: 301–251–5212
E-mail: askncjrs@ncjrs.org
WWW: http://amcom.aspensys.com/ncjrs/

3. National Archive of Criminal Justice Data

ICPSR
P.O. Box 1248
Ann Arbor, MI 48106
Phone: 800–999–0960 / 313–763–5011
E-mail: nacjd@icpsr.umich.edu
WWW:http://www.icpsr.umich.edu/nacjd/index.html

4. Bureau of Justice Statistics: International

Carol B. Kalish, International Program
Bureau of Justice Statistics
U.S. Department of Justice
633 Indiana Avenue N.W.
Washington, D.C. 20531
Phone: 202–307–0235
E-mail: kalish@ojp.usdej.gov
WWW: http://www.ojp.uspoj.gov/bjs/

5. World Criminal Justice Library Network (WCJLN)

Phyllis Schultze
Rutgers University NCCD Collection
Newhouse Center for Law and Justice
15 Washington Street
Newark, NJ 07102
Phone: 201–648–5522
Fax: 201–648–1275
WWW: http://info.rutgers.edu/newark/WCJLEN.html

6. International Centre for Criminal Law Reform and Criminal Justice Policy

Ms. Hanne Jensen, Executive Director
ICCLRCJP
555 West Hastings Street, #2060
Vancouver, British Columbia
Canada V6B 4N5
Phone: 604–822–9875
Fax: 604–822–9317
WWW: http://www.law.ubc.ca/centres/crimjust.html

7. United Nations International Crime and Justice Research Institute (UNICRI)

UNICRI
Via Giulia
52,00186
Rome, Italy
Phone: 39–6–687–7437
Fax: 39–6–689–2638
E-mail: unicri.org@agora.stm.it
WWW: http://193.205.57.21

8. International Criminal Police Organization (INTERPOL)

Mr. Raymond Kendell, Secretary General
INTERPOL
50 Quai Achille Lignon
F-69006
Lyon, France
WWW: http://193.123.144.14/interpol–pr/contents.html

9. Helsinki Institute for Crime Prevention and Control (HEUNI)

HEUNI
P.O. Box 161
FIN-00131
Helsinki, Finland
Phone: +358–9–1825–7880
Fax: +358–9–1825–7890
E-mail: heuni@joutsen.pp.fi
WWW: http://heuni.unojust.org/

10. United Nations Online Justice Information (UNOJUST)

National Institute of Justice
633 Indiana Avenue N.W., #1386
Washington, D.C.
E-mail: chapkey@rol.org
WWW: http://www.ncjrs.org/unojust/maptext.htm

11. Office of International Criminal Justice

University of Illinois-Chicago
1033 West Van Buren
Chicago, IL 60607
Phone: 312–996–9636
E-mail: oijc@uic.edu
WWW: http://www.acsp.uic.edu/index.htm

12. United Nations Asia and Far East Institute (UNAFEI) for the Prevention of Crime and the Treatment of Offenders

UNAFEI Secretariat
26-1, Harumi-chi, Fuchu
Tokyo 183, Japan
WWW: http://www.ncjrs.org/unojust/unafei.htm

13. United Nations African Institute (UNAFRI) for the Prevention of Crime and the Treatment of Offenders

UNAFRI Secretariat
P.O. Box 10590
Kampala, Uganda
Phone: 256–41–242–656/234–463/285–236
Fax: 256–41–232–974
WWW: http://unafri.or.ug/

14. Australia Institute of Criminology (AIC)

AIC Office
2 Marcus Clarke Street
Canberra AJC
ACT 2601, Australia
Phone: +61–6–260–9256
Fax: +61–6–260–9260
E-mail: aicpress@aic.gov.au
WWW: http://www.aic.gov.au/

15. United Nations Latin American Institute (ILANUD) for the Prevention of Crime and the Treatment of Offenders

ILANUD Secretariat
Apartado 10.071 / P.O. Box 10071-1000
San Jose, Costa Rica
Phone: 506–257–5826
Fax: 506–233–7175
WWW: http://200.9.61.226/

16. International Criminal Justice

WWW: http://www.mcs.com/~jra/police/pages/international.html

17. The World Factbook of Criminal Justice Systems

WWW: http://www.ojp.usdoj.gov/bjs/abstract/wfcj.htm

18. International Prison Populations

WWW: http://www.penlex.org.uk/sttabint.html

19. United Nations International Drug Control Programme

   WWW: http://www.undcp.org/index.html

20. American Society of Criminology (ASC) Division of International Criminology (DIC)

   To subscribe to this discussion list, send an e-mail message with your e-mail address and this line in the body of the message—"subscribe dis-asc"—to majordomo@s–cwis.unomaha.edu.

APPENDIX C

Locating Explanatory Data

World Wide Web sites and e-mail addresses change frequently. So, those reported here may not be accurate. Search engines can be used to locate current site addresses. The frequently-mentioned CIESIN site address is: http://www.ciesin.org.

SOURCES FOR EXPLANATORY DATA AND INFORMATION

Most of these sources provide many more types of information than are indicated in my brief descriptions. I give only a general idea of the type of data provided and any special features. The number of nations for which data are available from a source varies from year to year. Also, some sources provide data only for nations, while others include other types of territories or economies. Therefore the N = figures are approximate.

Annuals

1. *Human Development Report*

    United Nations Development Project
    Oxford University Press
    New York, NY
1990–
N = 174
Print
Economic, social, and demographic data
Special or unique: HDI, GDI, GEM, and inequality and poverty data

2. *World Resources*

    United Nations Development Project
    Oxford University Press
    New York, NY
1986–

$N = 145$
Print and diskette. Diskette has time-series data for up to twenty years.
Economic and demographic data
Special or unique: Good data on urban populations

3. *World Development Report*

    World Bank
    Oxford University Press
    New York, NY
1978–
$N = 132$
Print, diskette, CD-ROM, and probably CIESIN. CD-ROM has time-series data back to 1978.
Economic, social, and demographic data
Special or unique: Income distribution for all five quintiles; good technical notes on variables; poverty data.

4. *Social Indicators of Development* (SID)

    World Bank
    John Hopkins University Press
1987–
$N = 191$
Print, diskette, and CIESIN. Diskette has time-series data back to 1970.
Economic and social data
Special or unique: Priority Poverty Indicator and supplementary poverty indicators

5. *Trends in Developing Economies*

    World Bank
1989–
$N = 119$
Print, diskette, CD-ROM, and CIESIN. Diskette and CD-ROM have time-series back to 1970.
Economic, debt, and trade data for developing nations
Special or unique: Substantial amount of data on the world economic position of nations

6. *World Tables*

    World Bank
1976–
$N = 159$
Print, diskette, and CIESIN. Diskette has time-series back to 1972.
Economic, social, and demographic data
Special or unique: The most complete economic data published by the World Bank

7. *World Debt Tables*

    World Bank
1977–

$N = 150$
Print, diskette, magnetic tape, and possibly CIESIN. Diskette has time-series data back to 1972.
Comprehensive debt data and debt rates for low- and middle-income nations

8. *World Bank Atlas*

World Bank
1967–
$N = 209$
Print
Limited amount of economic and social data
Special or unique: Inexpensive

9. *World Data*

World Bank
CD-ROM with time-series data back to 1960.
All the data from: Social Indicators of Development, World Tables, World Debt Tables, and Trends in Developing Economies (TIDES)

10. *Demographic Yearbook*

United Nations
1948–
$N = 250$
Print
Demographic and population data
Special or unique: Good source for marriage and divorce data. It also has death by cause, including homicides and suicides.

11. *Statistical Yearbook*

United Nations
1955–
$N = 245$
Print and CD-ROM. Latter has time-series data back to 1980.
Economic and social data
Special or unique: Unemployment and employment by industry data. Television, radio, newspaper, and telephones data.

12. *International Trade Statistics Yearbook*

United Nations
1983–
$N = 182$
Print
External import and export data

13. *World Statistics Pocketbook*

United Nations
1988–
$N = 205$
Print
Economic, social, and demographic data in compact form
Special or unique: Inexpensive

The United Nations also publishes *UNSTAT's Guide to International Computerized Statistical Databases* on diskette. It provides information on the organization, content, producing agency, and means of access for a number of international social and economic databases.

14. *Yearbook of Labour Statistics*

International Labour Office
Geneva, Switzerland
1942–
$N = 200$
Print
The best source for employment, unemployment, hours worked, and so on, data.

15. *UNESCO Statistical Yearbook*

UNESCO
Paris, France
1963–
$N = 200$
Print
Probably the most complete source for educational and communications data (televisions, radios, books, etc.)

16. *World Factbook*

CIA: National Technical Information Service
Springfield, VA
1985–
$N = 191$
Print, diskette, CD-ROM, and WWW.
The *World Factbook* can be found at many sites, including:
    http://pacbell.yahoo.com/pb/regional/cia_world_factbook/
    http://homer.louisville.edu/groups/library-www/ekstrom/govpubs/
All types of data—numerical and text
Special or unique: Religion, ethnicity, and political system data

17. *The World Atlas*

Mindscapes
Novato, CA
1991–
$N = 218$

Diskettes or CD-ROM
All types of data gathered from numerous sources, such as, WHO, CIA, INTERPOL, World
Bank, and so forth.
Special or unique: Data which would otherwise have to be gathered from numerous sources
in one source

18. *Penn World Tables*

> NBER Publications
> Cambridge, MA

1950–1992
N = 152
Diskette and WWW (http:www.auckland.ac.nz/lbr/pennwt.htm)
Economic data

19. *International Data Base*

> International Programs Center
> U.S. Bureau of the Census
> Washington, D.C.

1950–
N = 248 (all nations of the world)
Diskette and
WWW (http://www.census.gov/ftp/pub/ipc/www/idbnew.html)
Demographic and socioeconomic data
Special or unique: Very good for ethnicity, language, and religion information

20. *Britannica World Data*

> Britannica Book of the Year
> Encyclopaedia Britannica
> Chicago, IL

1985–
N = 217
Print
Economic, social, and demographic data, limited political information
Special or unique: Data on religion, ethnicity, and language distribution; age structure by six
categories; household size and household source of income data; communications data, such
as televisions, newspapers, and so on.

21. *Global Studies: Africa, China, India and South Asia, Latin America, The Middle East,
Russia, the Eurasian Republics, and Central/Eastern Europe, Western Europe*

> Dushkin Publishing Group
> Guilford, CT

1989–
N = 190
Print
Limited social and economic data; text on current world situation.

22. *Country Background Notes*

    U.S. State Department
    Washington, D.C.
1977–
N = 153
Print and WWW (http://www.state.gov/)
Special or unique: Very good source of all types of data from historical and social to economic

    The DOSBACK list: *Background Notes* is updated periodically and includes information on U.S. bilateral relations with foreign countries and on their governments, political conditions, and foreign relations. You can expect the DOSBACK list to generate 3–4 e-mail messages per month. Via DOSBACK you will receive the full-text version of newly released *Background Notes*. Items distributed on the DOSBACK list may also be found at the U.S. Department of State Foreign Affairs Network (above WWW site). To subscribe to DOSBACK, send e-mail to "listserv@listserv.uic.edu" and type in the message: Subscribe DOSBACK YourName.

23. *Human Rights Country Reports*

    U.S. State Department
    Washington, D.C.
1977–
N = 194
Print
WWW: http://www.state.gov/www/issues/human_rights/index.html
Descriptions of the current human rights situations in nations and recent changes in these

24. *Freedom in the World*

    Freedom House
    London, England
1978–
N = 218
Print
Political and civil rights

25. *Amnesty International Report*

    Amnesty International
    New York, NY
1976–
N = 133
Print
Text human rights reports

26. *Compendium of Statistics on Illiteracy*

    UNESCO
1988
N = 143

Print
Literacy estimates and projections, 1980 to 2010.

27. *The Ethnologue Database*

Summer Institute of Linguistics
Dallas, TX
1996
$N = 228$
Data on the languages and dialects used in the nations of the world
WWW: http://www.sil.org/ethnologue/

28. The U.S. Department of State Country Background Notes

Brief description of the history of nations and their current economic, political, and social situations, including both quantitative and qualitative data.
WWW: http://www.state.gov/www/background_notes/index.html

Periodic or Intermittent Publications

1. *World Resources*

The World Resources Institute
Oxford University Press
New York, NY
1986 (biennial)
$N = 145$
Print
Data on economic development, debt, urbaness, children, and resources
Special or unique: WRI has recently published *World Resources Data Base* on diskette including twenty years of data.

2. *Compendium of Human Settlements Statistics*

United Nations
1980 (quinquennial)
$N = 243$ nations or areas, 338 cities
Print
Population, demographic, and so forth, data
Special or unique: Data for cities

3. *World Military and Social Expenditures*

Ruth Sivard
World Priorities
Washington, D.C.
1974 annual until 1983, most recent 1995, 16th edition
$N = 140$
Print
Military, social, and economic data
Special or unique: War deaths

4. *Encyclopedia of the Third World: 1978, 1981, 1987, 1992*
   Encyclopedia of the Second World: 1991
   Encyclopedia of the First World: 1990

   George Kurian
   Facts on File, Inc.
   New York, NY
N = 160 (Total for all three)
Print
Very extensive data and text covering all aspects of nations
Special or unique: Text on history and world situation of nations

5. *The New Book of World Rankings*

   George Kurian
   Facts on File, Inc.
   New York, NY
1979, 1984, 1991
N = 206
Print
Over 200 tables of data of all types taken from many sources
Special or unique: Probably as much—and more different types of—data there are in one source.

6. *The World in Figures*

   The Economist
   London, England
1973, 1984, 1988
N = 200
Print
Social, economic, and demographic data

7. *Women: A World Survey*

   Ruth Sivard
   World Priorities
   Washington, D.C.
1985, 1995
N = 139
Print
Social, economic, and political data on the relative situation of women in nations in 1960 and 1995

8. *The World's Women: Trends and Statistics*

   United Nations
1991, 1995
N = 220
Print

Extensive social, economic, and demographic data on the relative situation of women in nations for 1970, 1990, and 1994

9. *Women's Indicators and Statistics Database (WISTAT)*

United Nations
1990, 1992, 1994
N = 220
CD-ROM
The most extensive collection of data on the situation of women in nations ever assembled
Special or unique: Time-series data

10. *World Human Rights Guide*

Charles Humana
Oxford University Press
New York, NY
1983, 1986, 1992
N = 125
Print
The most extensive and complete data on human rights in different nations

11. The Library of Congress Country Studies

N = 71
Extensive qualitative and quantitative data on all aspects of nations
WWW: http://www.lcweb2.loc.gov/frd/cs/cshome.html

One-time Publications

1. *Measuring Global Values: The Ranking of 162 Nations*

Michael Sullivan
Greenwood Press
Westport, CT
1991
N = 162
Print
Data taken directly from other sources and culled by Sullivan through his own research; wider variety of data than in any other single source, some of it unique.
Special or unique: Sullivan organizes data categories around various value concepts, giving more meaning to the data.

2. *The Economist Book of Vital World Statistics*

Introduction by Robert Samuelson
Random House
New York, NY
1990
N = 150
Print

Social, economic, and demographic data taken from many sources
Special or unique: Projections for some variables to 2010

3. *Compendium of Social Statistics and Indicators*

United Nations
1988
$N = 180$
Print
Extensive social, economic, and demographic data
Special or unique: Data on female-headed households and other housing information; crime, drug, police, and prison data

4. *Statistical Charts and Indicators on the Situation of Youth*

United Nations
1992
$N = 177$
Print
Economic and social data on children from 1970 to 1990, including household, education, and health data

The following do not contain numerical data but can be very helpful in finding, evaluating, and giving context to data.

5. *Human Rights on CD-ROM*

United Nations
1996
Over 14,000 bibliographic references from 1980 to 1994

6. *The Encyclopedia of Religion*

Mircea Eliade, Editor-in-chief
Macmillan
New York, NY
1987

7. *Poverty: A Global Review: Handbook on International Poverty Research*

Else Oyen, S. M. Miller, and Syed Samad, Editors
Scandinavian University Press / UNESCO Publishing
1996

8. Elections and Electoral Systems by Country

WWW: http://www.keele.ac.uk/depts/po/election.htm

WHERE TO PURCHASE AND GET INFORMATION ON DATA SOURCES

1. The World Bank
   1818 H Street N.W.
   Washington, D.C. 20433
   Phone: 800–590–1906 or 202–473–7824
   Fax: 202–522–1498
   E-mail: info@worldbank.org
   WWW: http://www.worldbank.org

2. United Nations Publications
   Room DC2-853, Dept. D002
   New York, NY 10017
   Phone: 212–963–8302 or 800–253–9646
   Fax: 212–963–3489
   E-mail: publications@un.org
   WWW: http://www.un.org
   United Nations Publications
   Sales Office and Bookshop
   Palais des Nations CH-1211
   Geneva 10, Switzerland
   Phone: 41–22–917–2614
   Fax: 41–22–917–0084

3. UNESCO Division of Statistics
   7 Place de Fontenoy
   75352 Paris 07 SP, France
   Fax: 33–1–45–66–48–44
   E-mail: statistics@unesco.org
   WWW: http://www.unesco.org/

4. United Nations Development Programme
   Division of Information, Room DC1-1927
   1 United Nations Plaza
   New York, NY 10017
   Phone: 212–906–5000
   Fax: 212–906–5364
   WWW: http://iisd1.iisd.ca/ic/sb/direct/sdun.htm#UNDP
   United Nations Development Programme
   Human Development Report Office
   336 East 45 Street / Uganda House 6th floor
   New York, NY 10017
   Phone: 212–906–3667
   Fax: 212–906–3679

5. Overseas Development Council
    1875 Connecticut Avenue N.W., #1012
    Washington, D.C. 20009
    Phone: 202–234–8701
    Fax: 202–745–0067
    WWW: http://www.odc.org

6. Amnesty International
    AI Secretariat
    1 Easton Street
    London WC1X 8DJ, England
    Phone: +44–71–413–5500
    WWW: http://www.io.org/amnesty/

7. Central Intelligence Agency
    Office of Public and Agency Information
    Washington, D.C. 20505
    Phone: 703–351–2053
    WWW: http://www.odci.gov/cia/publications/pubs.html

The CIA *World Factbook* can also be purchased in printed, photocopy, microfiche, magnetic tape, or computer diskette from either of the following:

    National Technical Information Service
    5285 Port Royal Road
    Springfield, VA 22161
    Phone: 703–487–4650

    Superintendent of Documents
    P.O. Box 371954
    Pittsburgh, PA 15250-7954

8. Facts on File, Inc.
    11 Penn Plaza, 15th floor
    New York, NY 10001
    Phone: 212–967–8800
    E-mail: custserv@factsonfile.com
    WWW: http://www.factsonfile.com

9. International Data Base
    c/o Peter Johnson
    International Programs Center
    U.S. Bureau of the Census
    Washington, D.C. 20233-8860
    Phone: 301–457–1403
    Fax: 301–457–1539
    E-mail: peterj@census.gov

10. Penn World Tables
    NBER Publications
    1050 Massachusetts Avenue
    Cambridge, MA 02138
    Phone: 617–868–3900
    Fax: 617–868–2742
    E-mail: orders@nber.harvard.edu

11. U.S. State Department
    2201 C Street N.W.
    Washington, D.C. 20520
    Phone: 202–647–4000

APPENDIX D

Definitions of
Selected Independent Variables

Except where noted, these are taken from the *Human Development Report*, 1995.

Absolute poverty. Absolute poverty is measured using the comparative yardstick of per capita income of less than one US dollar per day expressed in equivalent 1985 purchasing power levels or PPP, as used in The Social Development and Absolute Poverty in Asia and Latin America.

Gender Empowerment Measure (*GEM*). The GEM examines whether women and men are able to participate actively in economic and political life and take part in decision-making. The GEM focuses on three variables that reflect women's participation in political decision-making, access to professional opportunities, and earning power.

Gender-related Development Index (*GDI*). The GDI measures achievement in the same basic capabilities as the HDI, but it takes note of inequality in achievement between men and women.*Gross Domestic Product* (*GDP*). The total output of goods and services for final use produced by an economy, by both residents and nonresidents, regardless of the allocation to domestic and foreign claims. It does not include deductions for depreciation of physical capital or depletion and degradation of natural resources.

Gross National Product (*GNP*). GNP comprises GDP plus net factor income from abroad, which is the income residents receive from abroad for factor services (labour and capital), less similar payments made to nonresidents who contribute to the domestic economy.

Gross National Product per Capita Growth Rates. Annual GNP per capita is expressed in current US dollars, and GNP per capita growth rates are annual average growth rates computed by fitting trend lines to the logarithmic values of GNP per capita at constant market prices for each year in the period.

Human Development Index (*HDI*). The HDI is a composite measure of human development containing indicators representing three equally weighted dimensions of human development—longevity (life expectancy at birth), knowledge (adult literacy and mean years of schooling), and income (PPP$ per capita).

Income share. The distribution of income share or expenditure (or share of expenditure) accruing to percentile groups of households ranked by total household income, by per capita income, or by expenditure.

Physical Quality of Life Index (PQLI). The PQLI consists of three components— infant mortality, life expectancy at age one, and basic literacy—which are summarized on a 0-to-100 scale. The virtues and limitations of the PQLI are described in the 1979 book, *Measuring the Condition of the World's Poor: The Physical Quality of Life Index* (Morris D. Morris, Pergamon).

Poverty line. Based on the concept of an "absolute" poverty line, the poverty line is expressed in monetary terms: the income or expenditure level below which a minimum, nutritionally adequate diet plus essential nonfood requirements are not affordable. The capability poverty measure considers the lack of three basic capabilities. The first is the lack of being well nourished and healthy, represented by the proportion of children under five years of age who are underweight. The second is the lack of capability for healthy reproduction, shown by the proportion of births unattended by trained health personnel. The third is the lack of capability to be educated and knowledgeable, represented by female illiteracy. A higher ranking indicates a higher level of capabilities, as used in the 1996 *Human Development Report*.

Priority Poverty Indicators (PPIs). Levels of poverty can be assessed by monitoring changes in a number of key areas, or PPIs. Two thresholds (upper and lower poverty lines) have been established to convey more precisely what is meant by poverty in each country. These are presented along with headcount indexes that report what percentage of the country's population is below each threshold. In general, as countries develop, poverty lines change, as used in *The Social Indicators of Development* (World Bank).

Purchasing Power Parity (PPP$). The PPP$ represents the purchasing power of a country's currency, that is, the number of units of that currency required to purchase the same (or similar) representative basket of goods and services that a US dollar (the reference currency) would buy in the United States. Purchasing power parity could also be expressed in other national currencies or in Special Drawing Rights (SDRs).

Real GDP per capita (PPP$). The GDP per capita of a country converted into US dollars on the basis of the purchasing power parity of the country's currency. The system of purchasing power parities has been developed by the United Nations International Comparison Programme (ICP) to make more accurate international comparisons of GDP and its components than those based on official exchange rates, which can be subject to considerable fluctuation.

Special Drawing Rights (SDRs). A type of international money created by the International Monetary Fund (IMF) and allocated to its member nations. SDRs are an international reserve asset, although they are only accounting entries (not actual coin or paper, and not backed by precious metal). Subject to certain conditions of the IMF, a nation that has a balance of payments deficit can use SDRs to settle debts to another nation or to the IMF.

Index

About the Author

JEROME L. NEAPOLITAN is Professor of Sociology at Tennessee Technological University. In the last five years his research has focused on the quality of cross-national crime data and variation in crime across nations.

ISBN 0-313-29914-5

90000>

EAN

9 780313 299148

HARDCOVER BAR CODE